Integrated Heritage Management

Integrated
Heritage
Management

Principles and Practice

C Michael Hall and Simon McArthur

London: The Stationery Office

© The Stationery Office 1998

ISBN 0 11 290571 4

British Library Cataloguing in Publication Data.
A CIP catalogue record for this book is available from the British
Library.

Printed in the United Kingdom for The Stationery Office
by Hobbs the Printers, Southampton

J53723 C10 8/98

Contents

Plates

Figures

Tables

Case Studies

Preface

Heritage management is recognised as an increasingly complex and controversial domain. Practitioners and students of heritage management are coming under a diverse range of pressures and interests in determining not just the most appropriate methods of conservation and management but even the very question of what actually constitutes heritage – the things we want to keep – in the first place.

This book represents a further evolution in our thinking and writing in heritage management, particularly with respect to the development and applications of principles and techniques beyond Australia and New Zealand (see Hall and McArthur 1993, 1996a). There are a number of elements to the structure of this book which are designed to help the reader comprehend the complexity of heritage management. First, the order of chapters loosely fits the management sequence of considering values, principles and practice of heritage management. Second, several chapters identify and discuss a number of tools and techniques which may be utilised in a variety of heritage management contexts. Third, we include a number of short case studies from a variety of settings and environments to demonstrate key issues and organisational and individual responses. Finally, we try to identify and encourage the development of appropriate innovative strategies and techniques which meet the varied values which heritage managers have to meet.

There is a wide range of acknowledgements for putting together a book such as this, particularly because of its international context. Of great importance have been the various stakeholders in the heritage sites we have been fortunate to visit in recent years. However, just as important have been the many people who have helped us get there through assisting us with travel, providing us with food and drink, or just their sheer good company. In interpretive terms we also acknowledge the ideas and insights which have come from outside some of the traditional bounds of heritage management, but whose works have transformed our own understanding of how we might potentially best convey appropriate information to target audiences, especially through the development of multimedia. In particular we would like to note the contributions of Anthony Aardman, Gerry Anderson, David Attenborough, Gavin Bryars, Geoff Buckley, Keith Carmichael, Chris Carter, Nick Cave, Bruce Cockburn, Dave Crag, Neil and Tim Finn, Dave Graney, Rob Grant, Matt Groenig, Richard Leakey, Sarah McLaughin, Doug Naylor, Lloyd Rees, Gene Roddenberry, Gough Whitlam, and Chris Wilson. The support of Angela Elvey, Joanne Lynch, David Press, Isabel Sebastian, Kirsten Short and Meredith Walker has also been vital to the completion of this work.

We wish to thank the following publishers for permission to quote/adapt material: Ashgate Publishing (Glasson *et al.*. 1995),

Australasian Evaluation Society Inc. (Cauley 1993), Butterworth-Heinemann (Middleton 1994; Uzzell 1994), Colonial Williamsburg USDA (MacFarlane (1994), Faber and Faber Ltd (McLoughlin 1969), Forestry Tasmania (Forestry Tasmania 1994a; quoted in ACIL Economics and Policy 1993), General Secretariat of the Organization of World Heritage Cities (OWHC 1996a; OWHC 1996b), George Washington University (GWU 1996), Heldref Publications (Mullins 1985), KwaZululu-Natal Nature Conservation Service (formerly the Natal Parks Board and Department of Nature Conservation) (Natal Parks Board, undated), Mackinac State Historic Parks (Mackinac State Historic Parks, Mackinac Island State Park Commission 1995), Museum of London (Selwood *et al.*. 1996), Museums Australia Inc (Museums Australia 1997), National Park Service (NPS 1994; Paskowski 1991), Parks Canada (Canadian Parks Service 1988; Parks Canada 1996), Royal Australian Institute of Parks and Recreation (McArthur 1994), Simon & Schuster (Kotler & Andreasen 1987), State University of New York Press (Norkunas 1993), Steve Selin (Selin and Lewis 1991), U.S. Bureau of Land Management (BLM 1997), UNESCO (World Heritage Centre) (UNESCO 1993), University of North Carolina Press (Tilden 1977), Venture Publishing Inc. (Knudson et al. 1996) and Wiley Europe (Tunbridge & Ashworth 1996). We have also sought permission from the following publishers, but at the time of going to press no reply has as yet been received: American Association for State and Local History (Alderson and Low 1985), IUCN (Ceballos-Lacuarain 1996), John Wiley & Sons (Theobald 1979), Malpai Borderlands Group (MBG 1995), McGraw-Hill (Cravens and Lamb 1986; Primozic *et al.*. 1991), Oxford University Press (Hall and McArthur 1996b), Penguin (Ohmae 1983), Routledge (Hewison 1991) and Wiley Europe (Tunbridge & Ashworth 1996). Authors and publisher wish to thank the latter publishers and authors, and shall ensure that the correct acknowledgement appears in any future edition of the book.

Finally, we would like to thank our friends, families, and partners for their consistent support in whatever we do.

As some readers will note as they work through the book, we not only believe that the influences of what we do are varied but we also believe that our own interpretation should be fun. Heritage management is a process which needs to be integrated with the values and journeys of people's lives. This book is not an end point, it is merely a way station on our own discoveries and thoughts about heritage management. However, as we advocate in the book, it is vital that such evaluation and review go out to a wider audience in order to encourage discussion and the development of heritage management as a profession and as a field of study.

C Michael Hall
Simon McArthur

CHAPTER 1

Introduction: Towards Quality Heritage Management

One of the most important moments in our concern with heritage was a visit to Port Arthur, Tasmania, in January 1991. Port Arthur, one of the most significant sites of Australia's convict past and colonial history, is a major tourist attraction. On walking through the site we overheard a conversation between two English women who were wondering why the tour bus had stopped there. 'All it is,' said one of them, 'is a bunch of ruins.'

Clearly, the qualities of the site had not been effectively interpreted to these visitors. On listening in to their conversation we learnt that they had left the guided tour group because it was too big and they were at the back and could not hear the guide's voice in the breeze. But they had also found the interpretation to be 'boring', so had wandered off on their own and were trying to find their way back to the tea rooms.

This story is perhaps familiar to many readers. Where does the problem lie? With the tourist? The manager? The type of interpretation? Lack of government funding? Lack of staff? The wrong guide? To us, however, these questions were a part of a wider concern. What is the most appropriate system for managing heritage?

Heritage managers face an increasingly complex management environment. Barely a day passes without there being a report in the media about conservation or resident groups wanting to save a forest from being cut or an historic building from being demolished. National and state governments have lost office over their failure to protect wilderness (Hall 1992a). Throughout the world, regional and local governments have come under pressure from conservation groups. Municipal representatives have been elected on the basis of their desire to stop 'inappropriate developments'. Alternatively, many have also been elected for their desire to encourage development and create employment opportunities, often through heritage tourism developments.

Museums and art galleries now face the prospect of returning display pieces to their 'rightful' owners. Whether it be the return of antiquities to Greece and Egypt, the return of artifacts and human remains to indigenous peoples or the return of art treasures that were removed as the prizes of war, the 'ownership' of heritage is frequently shrouded in controversy.

In a desire to cut government spending, many traditionally 'public' assets, such as national parks, historical monuments and sites, museums, art galleries and zoos, are also having to adopt a more commercial orientation, if not outright corporatisation or privatisation. To attract the tourist's money becomes a new management goal, but one that does not come without a cost. Cathedrals, historic townships, national parks, rock art and archaeological sites around the world show the unwanted effects of visitation in the form of physical damage, overcrowding and insensitivity to the local community. For example, in the United Kingdom problems associated with visitation that have been identified by the English Tourist Board and the Department of Employment (1991) include: increased risk of fire, pilferage, graffiti, risk of car

Plate 1.1 'What you see from here'. Rocky Mountain National Park, Colorado, USA

Plate 1.2 A warning of things to come at heritage sites? Crater Lake National Park, Oregon, USA

Plate 1.3 Heavy pedestrian use on path to lookout. Rocky Mountain National Park, Colorado, USA

accidents, traffic congestion and parking (for both private cars and tour coaches), atmospheric pollution, impaired ambience, destruction of architectural and archae-ological integrity, and crowding. Indeed, many concerns are being expressed not only about the quality of the visitor experience but also about the quality of heritage itself (e.g., Tabata, Yamashiro and Cherem 1992; Boniface 1995) (Plates 1.1, 1.2 and 1.3).

Heritage managers are therefore being faced with an increasingly complex set of problems, not the least of which is the traditional concern to minimise visitor impacts, and which include such questions as:

- Who 'owns' heritage?
- How should concerns over ownership and development be dealt with?
- What should be conserved and why?
- What are the needs of visitors and the community?
- Have management goals been identified?
- What is the best way of meeting the needs of both the visitor and the community?
- What is the most appropriate means of achieving our management goals?

This book is written to address this complex context. Gone is the relative cer-tainty of the past for the heritage manager, the time (if it ever even really existed) when management 'problems' could be solved with purely technical solutions. In the face not just of growing visitor numbers but also of growing demands, heritage managers need to develop new skills, techniques and attitudes that will help them not only to cope in the short term but, hopefully, also to come to understand this new environment and adapt, change and turn it to their advantage.

Defining Heritage

Heritage does not just refer to old buildings. At its most basic, heritage represents the things we want to keep. For example, the notion of inheritance and the responsibilities that it entails are at the heart of the *World Heritage Convention*. Article 4 of the Convention states that each party to the Convention recognises 'the duty of ensuring the identification, protection, conservation, presentation and transmission to future generations of the world's cultural and natural heritage' (World Heritage Committee 1984). Therefore, heritage is the things of value that are inherited. If the value is personal we speak of family or personal heritage; if the value is communal or national we speak of 'our' heritage. The *World Heritage Convention* aims to conserve places that have universal values for the whole of humankind. More often than not, heritage is thought of in terms of acknowledged cultural values. For instance, a residence is not usually deemed as heritage unless it can be seen as part of the symbolic property of the wider culture or community, as an element of that culture's or community's identity. The linkage between heritage and identity is crucial to understanding not only the significance of heritage as something to be valued but also the difficulties managers face in identifying and conserving heritage. As the Wellington City Art Gallery (1991) stated with respect to an exhibition on heritage: 'References to heritage typically propose a common cultural heritage. Distinguished old buildings are spoken of as being part of "our" heritage. It is suggested that "we" metaphorically own them and that their preservation is important because they are part of our identity. But who is the we?'. Questions of identity, meaning, and values indicate the likelihood of there being conflicting notions of ownership attached to heritage and therefore conflicting sets of values and interests with which the manager has to contend. Indeed, the emergence of multiple perspectives on heritage has led to an expanded meaning of heritage beyond simply the things we want to keep.

Tunbridge and Ashworth (1996) have identified five different aspects of the expanded meaning of heritage:

- a synonym for any relict physical survival of the past;
- the idea of individual and collective memories in terms of non-physical aspects of the past when viewed from the present;
- all accumulated cultural and artistic productivity;
- the natural environment; and
- a major commercial activity, e.g., the 'heritage industry'.

Undoubtedly, there is significant overlap between these various conceptions of heritage. However, according to Tunbridge and Ashworth (1996), 'there are intrinsic dangers in the rapidly extending uses of the word and in the resulting stretching of the concept to cover so much. Inevitably precision is lost, but more important is that this, in turn, conceals issues and magnifies problems intrinsic to the creation and management of heritage.' Ironically, the uncertainty about what constitutes heritage is occurring at a time when heritage has assumed greater importance *because* of its relationship to identity in a constantly changing world. As Glasson *et al.* (1995) recognised, 'One reason why the heritage city is proving such a visitor attraction is that, in easily consumable form, it establishes assurance in a world which is changing rapidly.'

The formulation of what constitutes heritage is intimately related to wider political, social, economic and technological changes that appear to reflect 'postmodern' concerns over the end of certainty and the convergence between cultural forms that were once seen as separate aspects of everyday life – e.g., education and tourism or, in even more of a heritage context, marketing and conservation. Much discussion in heritage studies has focused on the recognition of multiple meanings of heritage, particularly with respect to the recognition of other voices in heritage, such as those of indigenous peoples. Yet, while the cultural construction and complexity of heritage is now readily acknowledged (e.g., Hudson 1987; Corner and Harvey 1991a; Hooper-Greenhill 1992; Tunbridge and Ashworth 1996), what has not been readily forthcoming is the translation of this understanding into practical approaches for heritage managers who are faced with the day-to-day reality of multiple demands on heritage and the quality of the heritage product.

The Heritage Management Problem

One of the most important aspects in determining management solutions is defining the problem. With respect to heritage management the problems have changed as society's relationship to heritage has changed. Until the late 1970s heritage management was focused on conserving the heritage resource itself – the problem was therefore the visitor. In the 1980s, as government funding for heritage began to fall, visitors became more important as they provided the financial resources for conserving heritage – the problem therefore shifted to finding an appropriate balance between visitors (number, type, behaviour, attitudes and characteristics) and the heritage resource. In the 1990s the management problem shifted again. The human dimension of heritage is now beginning to receive greater attention in the allocation of resources. This is not to discount the significance of physical conservation of resources; rather, attention to understanding the human dimension of heritage has led to the recognition that there are multiple meanings attached to heritage. As the present authors (1996b) recognised:

> The identification and management of heritage is dependent on our perceptions and values. Increasingly, heritage managers realise that it is not sufficient just to manage the physical heritage resource in isolation from the people who are the 'owners' of the heritage and those who come to experience it. Particularly at a time when, more and more, heritage managers are depending on visitors to provide economic, educational and social justifications for their activities.

There is not necessarily a given, concrete thing that is intrinsically heritage. Heritage resources are an expression of appraisal and represent an entirely subjective concept. 'Resources *are* not, they *become*; they are not static but expand and contract in response to human wants and human actions' (Zimmermann 1951 in Mitchell 1979). Heritage should be seen as a culturally constructed idea and set of values that are attached to a wide range of artifacts, environments and cultural forms. For example, the case of the regular rebuilding of temples and shrines in some Asian countries, such as the Ise shrine in Nara prefecture, Japan, indicates that the Western perception of the significance of the conservation of the original fabric of a building as being vital in terms of authenticity is culturally constructed and irrelevant in other cultures (Case Study 1.1). Heritage resources are therefore defined according to individual and collective attitudes, values and perceptions, wants, technology, economics, politics and institutional arrangements. What is a heritage resource in one culture may be 'neutral stuff' in another. Heritage resources are subjective, relative and functional (Mitchell 1979, 1989). As Tunbridge and Ashworth (1996) recognised, heritage is 'a product of the present, purposefully developed in response to current needs or demands for it, and shaped by those requirements' (Plate 1.4). This is not to say that heritage is unimportant; rather, it is to emphasise that the meaning and significance of heritage to various groups, interests and individuals are dependent on a range of different and changing sets of individual and collective values. The problem for heritage managers is therefore to be able to understand the way in which heritage and the demands placed upon it are shaped and how this knowledge can then be used to influence and satisfy the various interests in heritage.

Case Study 1.1
The Ise Shrine, Japan

Key point:

• Heritage managers need to recognise that different cultures attach different values to various aspects of heritage.

The Ise Shrine in southern central Honshu island is considered one of the oldest and most important shrines in Japan. Since the Middle Ages, organised groups of believers have visited the shrine in an annual pilgrimage that came to be called *O-Ise-mairi* (Worship at Ise). Such is the site's cultural significance that the area was designated a national park in 1946. The shrine and the national park continue to attract many domestic and foreign visitors throughout the year. However, the shrine demonstrates characteristics that are substantially different from those that are usually associated with the authenticity of built structures in the West.

The Naiku (Inner) and Gekku (Outer) complexes at Ise consist of a series of rectangular white gravel precincts surrounded by wooden fences that enclose groups of small shrine structures and treasure houses organised along a strong north–south axis. Adjacent to each shrine precinct is an empty site of equal dimensions; at Ise the entire shrine complex is ritually rebuilt every twenty years on this 'alternate' site. The practice of site alternation, which reflects patterns of crop rotation, is meant to guarantee the perpetual freshness and purity of the shrines.

The rebuilding of each shrine is a massive undertaking. The sixtieth rebuilding completed in 1973 was spread over eight years and took 122,535 hours of work. The wood used accounted for 13,671 hinoki trees, and 25,800 bundles of pampas-like susuki grass went into the roof thatching. Renewing the fences required 12,300 poles of bamboo; and 8,713 hours of metalworking used thirty-seven tonnes of copper and eleven kilograms of gold (Simpson 1975). While such concepts may seem alien to many in the West, where retention of the original built structure is often a component of heritage's authenticity, without the ritual cycle of destruction and construction the shrine would lose its much of its authentic value to those who follow the Shinto faith.

Transforming Heritage Management

Heritage management refers to the conscious process by which decisions concerning heritage policy and practice are made and the manner in which heritage resources are developed. The field of heritage management therefore encompasses analysis, management and development. Until recently, one of the great ironies in heritage management has been the lack of attention given to the contribution that business management ideas and theories can make to the management of heritage. Heritage management has for so long focused on conservation of the resource that only limited attention has been given to the human dimension, even though it is the

Plate 1.4 Student making 'Roman coins' for tourists at an award-winning heritage attraction, the 'White Cliffs Experience', Dover, England

human dimension that gives rise to heritage resources. However, given the increased demands that have been made on heritage and its managers by a wide range of groups and individuals, not least of which is the visitor, this situation has had to change. As V. Middleton (1994) recognised:

> Like it or not, around the world in the 1990s heritage and management are inevitably and inextricably linked. For many it is a very uneasy marriage of interests. Few people involved with heritage resources consider themselves part of an *industry* in which the management practices developed in business and commerce can be readily applied.

The realisation that heritage managers need to adopt appropriate approaches from the business world is leading to a transformation in heritage management strategies. For example, V. Middleton (1994) identifies three aspects of management strategy for heritage resources: managing the heritage resource; managing access; and managing organisations.

Managing the heritage resource, be it a collection, a historic house, a national park or a traditional event, is, not surprisingly, seen as the primary duty of management for heritage bodies (V. Middleton 1994). Yet, as Middleton has emphasised, there is clearly a need to expand the notion of what heritage management is about to enable managers to respond to the changing environment in which they are operating. Middleton, as with other authors (e.g., Hooper–Greenhill 1992; Hall and McArthur 1993, 1996a; Harrison 1994), have emphasised the need for managers to consider issues of access, quality, visitor demands, marketing and organisation, as well as traditional considerations of resource conservation. The present book seeks to take this evolution in heritage management thinking a stage further by considering the primacy of stakeholders in the heritage management system. Stakeholders are the individuals, groups and organisations with an interest in a common heritage management problem or issue, which are directly influenced or affected by the actions or non-actions taken by others to resolve the problem or issue (after Gray 1989). This book argues that the heritage manager is engaged in managing not so much a resource *per se,* but the multiple attitudes, values, perceptions, interests and wants of stakeholders with respect to heritage. This represents a fundamental shift in heritage management thinking. It does not deny the importance of physical conservation and restoration of heritage. Instead, it argues that such activities need to be seen not only in a cultural context but also in the context of the (at times conflicting) demands of the various stakeholders who determine that something *is* heritage and therefore requires the development of appropriate management strategies and practice.

Figure 1.1 provides a diagrammatic representation of the way in which heritage management and heritage itself are at the centre of a series of management environments that help to determine both what constitutes heritage and how it is managed. The micro-environment refers to the day-to-day practice and activities of heritage managers and the demands that are placed on them by various stakeholders. The meso-environment refers to broader factors, such as interests, values, access to power, and the structure of institutions that also influence the opportunities and abilities of stakeholders to influence heritage management. The final scale, the macro-environment, refers to the broader political, economic, social and technological trends which affect the definition and development of heritage and its consequent management.

Heritage managers and management organisations need to be able to understand, adapt and, where possible, influence their management environment if they are to meet stakeholders' demands and conserve the heritage that provides their *raison d'être* effectively. Strategic planning is the process by which an organisation adapts to its environments effectively over time (Hall and McArthur 1996c). Heritage

Figure 1.1 The heritage management environment

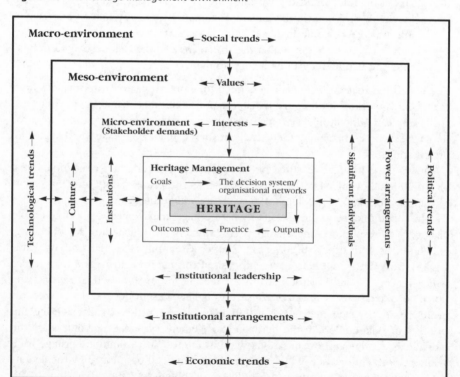

Source: after Hall (1994) and Hall and Jenkins (1995)

management is part of the growing area of service provision, not only in terms of visitor services but also the services that are provided to all the stakeholders who have interest in heritage. This book therefore advocates the adoption of a strategic approach to heritage management, which seeks to integrate the various dimensions of heritage management in a way that satisfies stakeholder demands. The various chapters outline the key elements for such an approach.

Quality and Heritage

Quality is now not only an integral part of business, management and services, but also an integral part of heritage management (e.g., Tabata, Yamashiro and Cherem 1992; Harrison 1994; Boniface 1995). Quality in its simplest form can be defined as conforming to standards – e.g., the accepted level of visitor impact on a heritage site or the level of visitor satisfaction following a heritage experience. Standards are set as part of the planning process and then operationalised and implemented as part of the control system so that deviations from these standards can be detected. Ideally, current performance is measured against the predetermined standards and deviations are then corrected (Pizam 1991; Tweed and Hall 1991).

At a more sophisticated level, quality management must take a causal approach to determine the underlying reason why deviations from standards occur; it is important to reduce the likelihood of recurrence of failure to reach standards (errors) due to the same basic cause. Here quality management is concerned with reducing the potential for error. In heritage management such an understanding is crucial, as failure to reduce errors may result in a loss in the value, quality and support for conservation of the heritage resource. The methodology for this approach is an examination of the heritage management system itself.

In heritage management the approach to managing quality and meeting management objectives is particularly important, as measurement of quality after the fact – e.g., after the service to visitors has been provided – is more difficult than for physical products. Fundamental shifts in the emphasis of measurement also occur when services are considered. For example, in manufacturing industries products can be sampled and measured against standards while still in the domain of the business, with relatively little or no input from stakeholders, such as consumers. In heritage management the quality of a service and of the resources itself is primarily measured by stakeholders at the point of contact – e.g., at the time of the visitor experience.

Quality in a Dynamic Environment

Operationalising quality as conforming to standards and removing the potential for error are relatively easy to conceptualise when the standards remain the same for long periods of time. In this situation the management system can be refined to the point where errors become extremely unlikely and standards are achieved consistently. However, the current operating environment for most heritage managers is in a state of flux because of:

- increasing competition from other attractions;
- the changing demands on heritage resources;
- conflicting notions of ownership; and
- the growth of social and environmental concerns surrounding the development of heritage for tourists.

Figure 1.2 The transformation of heritage management

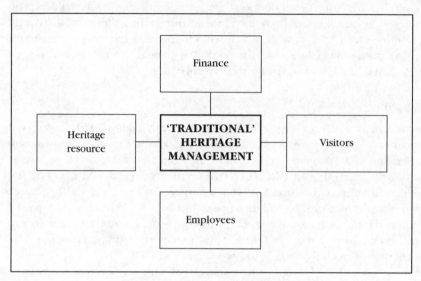

'Traditional' specialist areas

The strategic future?

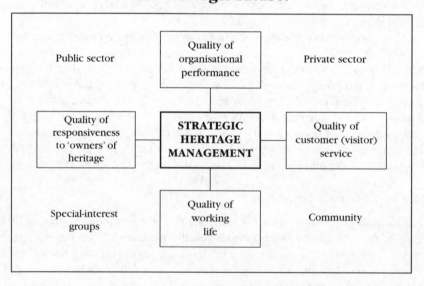

A dynamic environment poses far greater challenges for quality management than one that is relatively stable. Two management challenges arise from this situation. The first is that the standards by which quality is measured need constant reformulation, requiring regular input from stakeholders as to what the new standards should be. One of the implications of changing standards is that the heritage management system will need to be redesigned or refocused in order to achieve the new standards. System adaptation may require fundamental and massive change. This is quite different from the small incremental changes that are required in relatively stable environments to ensure that conformity to standards is achieved.

The second challenge arises from the impact of the changing environment on the system itself. Parts of the system that may have required no review previously can become vulnerable to problems due to changes in the environment. In other words, it could be argued that non-significant areas have become significant and that previously identified 'critical control points' in the heritage management system have become non-critical or are not functioning adequately as indicators of quality achievement. For example, issues of ownership and access to heritage by indigenous and other groups that may once have been ignored by authorities have now become substantial public concerns (e.g., Sullivan 1984; Mulvaney 1989; Birckhead *et al.* 1993).

The Dimensions of Quality

Quality has many dimensions depending on who it is for. Traditional thinking about heritage management is concerned with finance, visitors, employees and the heritage resource, with considerable emphasis on the latter (Figure 1.2). However, in the current environment heritage managers need to refocus their management approach in order to respond to the demands of key stakeholder groups, such as special interest groups (e.g., conservation groups); the private sector (e.g., tourism businesses); the public sector (e.g., heritage management agencies and elected officials); and the wider community. This therefore means that quality is also defined according to what each stakeholder group seeks (Tweed and Hall 1991).

An integrated model of heritage management that examines quality of service and views notions of quality from the perspective of stakeholders provides a better understanding of heritage and quality in all its dimensions and seeks to identify those with interests in heritage and how they may be best satisfied. Quality is a process that needs to be implemented at three levels of heritage management: macro, meso and micro scales (Figure 1.3). The framework offers a conceptual tool to understand the processes by which quality is determined. In its broadest sense the model identifies

Figure 1.3 Quality levels, dimensions and outcomes

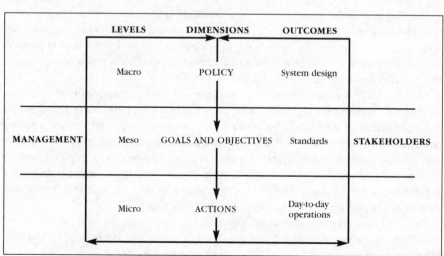

levels, processes and outcomes. The macro level examines the dynamic environment within which the heritage manager works and sets the overall framework within which the organisation operates. The meso level is concerned with the design and implementation, refinement and maintenance of the heritage management system through which goals and objectives will be achieved. Day-to-day actions and responses operate at the micro level and provide the mechanisms and tactics for meeting standards. The outcomes of the higher levels become the inputs for the lower levels so that system design is related to the selection of goals and objectives, and system design and goals and objectives are in turn related to the selection of the actions that will be undertaken. The effectiveness of these actions is then evaluated and the system and goals and objectives redefined according to the results of the monitoring and evaluation.

The model contains two feedback loops, one of which is provided by management and the other by the relevant stakeholder groups. However, it is the interaction between management and the various stakeholder groups that will in fact determine processes and outcomes at all levels of the organisation. The model recognises that quality of heritage cannot be defined in simple, rational, one-dimensional terms. Traditional concerns placed emphasis on the quality of the heritage resource, as defined by heritage experts, as the dominant factor in the determination of how heritage should be managed. The new model emphasises that heritage management and associated definitions of quality cannot be determined by one interest group at the expense of the others. This may be possible in the short term but will be detrimental to heritage in the longer term. Indeed, an appropriate heritage management strategy will be the outcome of a complex negotiation process participated in by different stakeholders that may have a mix of competing and complementary aims.

Integrated Heritage Management: The Importance of Learning

The adoption of strategic approaches to heritage management that emphasise the quality of the management process as well the quality of the heritage resource has a number of important benefits. In particular, it indicates the three main areas in which the managers and heritage management organisations need to improve their understanding or, as Garratt (1987) has described it, become responsive 'learning organisations'.

The first area is the learning that is required about the stakeholder groups – i.e., the 'who' of quality. According to this model, students of heritage management should learn about the owners, the visitors, the providers and the wider public – in particular, the demands that each group places on heritage managers in terms of quality and the management of heritage.

The second area concerns the level or plane at which management should focus its attention and focuses on the 'how' of quality. It becomes important to understand the formulation of goals and objectives – i.e., the standard setting process and the determinants of the standards that will be adopted. Strategy is the process by which appropriate heritage management systems will be designed and implemented to ensure that the standards are complied with. The day-to-day actions and responses are determined by the methods and techniques – e.g., education, interpretation and marketing – employed to ensure that objectives are met.

The third area concentrates on the outcomes of combining the first two areas and considers the 'what' of quality. It requires the evaluation and monitoring of systems, objectives, techniques and day-to-day actions, and that greater attention be given to the role of all stakeholders in heritage management and planning. In short, the focus on different aspects of learning in order to improve the quality of heritage management requires the adoption of an integrated and strategic approach to heritage which focuses on the values, principles and practices that heritage managers and organisations adopt.

This chapter has outlined some of the major problems facing heritage managers and notes that the management environment has changed dramatically in recent years, requiring the development of new management approaches, particularly with respect to understanding the central role of values in heritage management. It has also indicated some of the principles behind an appropriate framework for heritage management and has highlighted the need for strategic and integrated management that emphasise the role of quality, stakeholder involvement and organisational learning.

Chapter 2 discusses the role of strategic planning in managing change and provides the principles that underlie a strategic planning framework. It then considers the means by which strategic plans are created, the importance of setting objectives, the difference between goals, objectives and strategies, and the relationship between strategy and operations. The chapter concludes by noting the importance of matching resources, stakeholders and management tools.

Chapter 3 examines the integration of stakeholders into heritage management and the importance of understanding the various values placed by stakeholders on heritage management. It discusses why stakeholders are important, particularly with respect to the ownership of heritage, and the means by which they can be identified.

Chapter 4 discusses how to understand and work with communities and suggests that heritage is owned by the community, not the day-to-day managers. It emphasises that the community provides political, economic and tactical support and that it includes both actual and potential visitors, and notes that the members of the community are not always aware that they are stakeholders. The chapter also provides a series of tools for understanding the community that offer different levels of participation by the community in decision-making and planning in relation to heritage.

Chapters 5 and 6 focus on one of the most important stakeholders in heritage management – the visitor. Chapter 5 examines the why and the how of understanding the visitor–heritage relationship, while Chapter 6 applies this knowledge to the area of visitor management and argues that heritage managers must go beyond traditional reactive approaches such as site hardening and treating the symptoms rather than the cause of heritage management problems. The emphasis is therefore one of creating proactive rather than reactive approaches to visitor and heritage management, details of which are discussed in Chapter 7 (which looks at shaping expectations through marketing heritage) and Chapter 8 (which investigates heritage interpretation and education).

Chapter 9 examines one of the key aspects of a strategic approach to heritage management – the evaluation of heritage management policies and programmes. The chapter covers the consequences of not evaluating such policies and programmes, the benefits, principles and techniques of evaluation, and the relationship of evaluation to monitoring and research. The chapter concludes with a discussion of the political dimensions of evaluation.

The final chapter, Chapter 10, brings the reader back to the principles of an integrated strategic approach to heritage management and emphasises the importance of continually considering who are the stakeholders and why they are involved, as well as the need to create and adapt management solutions.

Heritage management, as heritage itself, does not occur in isolation. It is influenced by broader events in society and is continually being reassessed as to its significance and relevance. Heritage is clearly relevant to many peoples, communities and individuals. Heritage management needs to be able to respond and adapt to new pressures and demands. It is hoped that some of the ideas and tools within this book will help make heritage management not only more responsive but also more relevant to the various owners of the things we want to keep.

CHAPTER 2

Strategic Planning to Manage Change

Several years ago we met the head of a major heritage site that had recently been 'corporatised' and that, although still receiving some government funding, was expected to become increasingly self-reliant in terms of funds, especially as the site was regarded as a major international and domestic tourist attraction. The manager, however, had little idea how to adapt to these new circumstances, which offered both challenges and opportunities. We suggested that he should try and be more strategic in his thinking, especially with respect to developing relationships and partnerships with other visitor businesses and heritage organisations. He told us that he didn't want to be involved with any such management 'fads'. Several months later his job was advertised. One of the first things the successful applicant did on being appointed was to start to develop a strategic plan.

Introduction: The Importance of Strategic Planning

A 'strategy' is a means to achieve a desired end. Henderson (1989) defined strategy as 'a deliberate search for a plan of action that will develop a business's competitive edge and compound it'. Porter (1980), who focuses on the idea of thinking competitively, stated that 'essentially, developing a competitive strategy is developing a broad formula for how a business is going to compete, what its goals should be, and what policies will be needed to carry out those goals'. Strategic planning is the process by which an organisation effectively adapts to its management environment over time by integrating planning and management in a single process. The strategic plan is the document that is the output of a strategic planning process – the template by which progress is measured and which serves to guide future directions, activities, programmes and actions. The outcome of the strategic planning process is the impact that the process has on the organisation and its activities. Such impacts are then monitored and evaluated through the selection of appropriate indicators as part of the on-going revision and readjustment of the organisation to its environment. Strategic planning therefore emphasises the process of continuous improvement as a cornerstone of organisational activity (Figure 2.1), in which strategic planning is linked to

Figure 2.1 Principle of continuous improvement

management and operational decision-making. There are three key mechanisms to achieve this (Gluck *et al*. 1980; Reed 1992):

* a planning framework that extends beyond organisational boundaries and focuses on strategic decisions concerning stakeholders and resources;

* a planning process that stimulates entrepreneurial and innovative thinking; and

* a system of organisational values that reinforces managers and staff commitment to the organisational strategy.

Long a part of business and organisational planning, strategic planning has only recently begun to be adopted by heritage managers, one of the main reasons being that for much of the twentieth century many heritage management organisations have been part of the public sector and/or have not seen themselves as operating in a commercial, competitive environment. This has now changed. Although anathema for many heritage managers, competition for both corporate and government currency, as well as for visitors, is an unavoidable part of contemporary heritage management. For example, with regard to the museum sector in the United Kingdom, Uzzell (1994), observes that 'museums are increasingly subject to commercial competition from other tourism and leisure attractions.'

According to V. Middleton (1994), 'Successful organizations trading with the visiting public are outward looking, and constantly alert to opportunities and threats in the external environment.' One of the main values of strategic planning is its ability to respond to changes in the management environment, such as changing demographic trends or changes in attitudes towards how heritage is perceived. Much of conventional heritage planning has failed to address adequately the environment in which it operates because it has failed to understand the manner in which key stakeholders (e.g., visitors, community and government) and broader changes in the environment (see Chapter 1) place demands upon heritage managers. The changing environment has therefore led to changing needs for heritage managers in terms of the development of approaches that enable managers to respond to the pressures that are being placed upon them and the issues with which they are faced. Most fundamentally, heritage management must be able to be both reactive and proactive in relation to its environment.

V. Middleton (1994) identified a range of strategic management issues for British heritage managers in the 1990s that are also extremely relevant to their counterparts throughout the world, summarised as follows:

* recognising, through the formal adoption and operation of systematic strategic planning and monitoring procedures, that continuous change in the external environment affecting heritage is now a normal experience and not exceptional;

* recognising that, with or without revenue objectives based on admission charges, achieving measurable satisfaction of increasingly sophisticated and frequent visitors to heritage is an essential strategic objective for sustainable heritage organisations;

* accepting the need for setting measurable objectives and strategies, which reflect mission statements, response to identified change and visitor expectations, and aim to optimise the position for the heritage resource;

- committing managers and trustees to the necessary disciplines of continuous systematic performance monitoring needed to assess the achievement of objectives. In practice this also means setting up information collecting procedures which are a necessary requirement of monitoring and assessment, including the use of market research as necessary, for example to measure visitor satisfaction; and

- using, supporting and helping to create networks or consortia for heritage management purposes to contribute to the tasks above and share the expertise and costs.

These strategic heritage management issues have emerged for a number of reasons that are not confined to Britain alone. First, at a time of calls for 'smaller government' and a reduction in the size of bureaucracy, government is increasingly demanding that heritage 'pay its own way'. This has therefore meant the adoption of new financial strategies, such as the introduction, increase or expansion of visitor charges and/or the introduction of corporate sponsorship packages as part of a philosophy of 'user pays'. Second, there are increased demands from government, the private sector and the wider tax-paying public for accountability and responsibility for heritage funding. Third, there are greater demands for access to heritage both from the tourism industry, where it is a major attraction, and from the wider public. Fourth, there is increased concern over the conservation of heritage. Fifth, and related to the previous issues, there are widespread calls not only for heritage to be sustainable but also for it to be placed within a wider framework of sustainable communities and regions.

The shift in attitudes towards heritage requires a corresponding change in the way in which heritage management is undertaken and how it develops in the future. Consequently, approaches to heritage management need to shift from a predominantly one-dimensional outlook (one that is focused primarily on the resource) to one that is multi-dimensional and seeks to balance the concerns of stakeholders (including visitors and the community).

As noted in Chapter 1, one of the central themes of this book is improving the quality of heritage management by understanding the management environment, including the attitudes and values of stakeholder. Heritage values are human values. Many of the problems of heritage conservation and management lie not in the resource itself but within the interaction between the stakeholders and the resource and the role of the heritage manager as the mediator between the two. For example, fire is regarded by many as a 'threat' to natural ecosystems, even though it is often a part of the normal ecological process. In this case public perceptions of what is natural – developed over many years of advertising, education and promotion – may have such a strong influence that heritage managers are forced to satisfy these perceptions rather than ecological considerations in order to retain political support. Similarly, the demolition of parts of an historic site or the erection of barriers for 'safety reasons' to satisfy institutional regulations may not only decrease the quality of the visitor experience but may also give rise to complaints from heritage conservation groups that the heritage is being compromised. 'Solutions' in one area of heritage management may therefore give rise to problems in others. Mono-dimensional approaches that treat heritage as a static given can no longer be applied. Heritage management needs to develop strategic planning approaches for the methods, techniques and tools that are often the focus of managers. Nonetheless, methods, techniques and tools are important but are not ends in themselves. Rather, they must be integrated into a broader heritage management system, which treats them as means to an end (see Case Study 2.1) and which is itself developed through a systematic, strategic and integrated planning approach that seeks to answer the core basic heritage management questions:

- Where are we now? – Check (monitor and evaluate).
- Where do we want to get to? – Plan.
- How do we get there? – Do (action).

Case Study 2.1
Museum Accreditation in Victoria, Australia

Key point:
- The adoption of strategic planning principles is increasingly being used as an indicator of quality by heritage organisations.

Museums Australia (Victoria) manages a Museum Accreditation Program (MAP) in the State of Victoria, Australia. Instigated in 1993, the MAP is a two-tiered process in which museums first register for accreditation after demonstrating that they have developed or are developing the principles and practices of good museum collection management. Around sixty museums, or ten per cent of the museums in the State, have been accepted for registration towards accreditation. Accreditation is assessed after a maximum period of three years from the time of initial registration. According to Museums Australia (Victoria) (1997):

> Strategic planning is an integral part of the MAP registration process, and includes the development of a mission statement, collections, loans and de-accession policies, and short and long-term goals and objectives. Accreditation, as the next step, encompasses strategic planning for marketing and public relations, exhibitions and public programs, and education and community involvement, amongst other management policies and practices.

Strategic Heritage Planning

The adoption of a strategic approach to heritage planning arises from the need of managers to understand and interact with the environment within which they operate, particularly in terms of the difficulties of conserving heritage while still maintaining visitor access and meeting stakeholder demands. It is both a process, which leads to specific planning outputs, and a way of thinking about the management world. As Ohmae (1983) stated:

> The drafting of a strategy is simply the logical extension of one's usual thinking processes. It is a matter of long-term philosophy, not short-term expedient thinking. In a very real sense, it represents the expression of an attitude to life. But like every creative activity, the art of strategic thinking is practised most successfully when certain operating principles are kept in mind and certain pitfalls are consciously avoided.

Similarly, according to Primozic *et al.* (1991):

> Strategic thinking must be a continuous cycle. The cycle begins with formulating a strategic vision for the organization, proceeds through creating strategies that determine how the vision can be used to guide the organization's efforts,

continues with developing appropriate tactics to implement the strategic plans, and leads to the implementation and operational steps that all members of the organization must carry out in the day-to-day running of the enterprise.

Strategic planning is now increasingly recognised as an essential component of heritage management. Strategic planning processes 'enable managers and trustees to identify and devise creative responses to change while there is time to do so, without losing sight of the essential mission or vision' (V. Middleton 1994). As the Mackinac State Historic Parks, Mackinac Island State Park Commission (1995) stated, 'Long-term strategic planning is essential to respond to a changing workforce, facility deficiencies, and changing needs of park operations.' (See also Case Study 2.3.) A strategy is a means of achieving a desired end (Chaffee 1985) – e.g., the goals, objectives and actions identified for the management of heritage. A 'typical strategy' for heritage managers is the use of appropriate management practices to achieving three basic strategic goals: to ensure the conservation of heritage values; to enhance the experiences of the visitors who interact with heritage; and to satisfy stakeholder demands. Strategic heritage planning provides a process that can help to ensure that such management objectives are met.

The Strategic Heritage Planning Process

Figure 2.2 outlines a model of a strategic heritage planning process that identifies key components of the process, some of which will in turn correspond to the components of a formal planning document. The process is encompassed by the management environment identified in Figure 1.1. Therefore, the model recognises the importance of factors that affect the broad framework within which strategies are generated, such as institutional arrangements, institutional culture, and values and attitudes of stakeholders. These factors have been included because it is important to recognise that strategic plans will be in line with the legislative powers and organisational structures of the implementing organisation(s) and the political goals of government. However, it may also be the case that once the strategic planning process is under way, goals and objectives have been formulated and the process evaluated, the institutional arrangements may be recognised as inadequate for the successful achievement of certain goals and objectives. In addition, it must be recognised that in order to be effective, the strategic planning process needs to be integrated with the development of appropriate organisational structures and values. Indeed, with respect to the significance of values it may be noted that the strategic planning process is as important as its output – i.e., a plan. An inclusive planning process, by which those responsible for implementing the plan are also those who have helped to formulate it, will dramatically increase the likelihood of 'ownership' of the plan and, hence, its effective implementation (Heath and Wall 1992; Hall and McArthur 1996b).

A strategic planning process may be initiated for a number of reasons, including:

- *stakeholder demands:* demand for the undertaking of a strategic plan may come from the pressure of stakeholders – e.g., heritage conservation groups or government;

- *perceived need:* the lack of appropriate information by which to make decisions or an appropriate framework with which to implement legislative requirements may give rise to a perception that new management and planning approaches are required;

- *response to crisis:* the undertaking of strategic planning exercises are often the result of a crisis in the sense that the management and planning system has failed to adapt to certain aspects of the management environment – e.g., failure to conserve a heritage site or artifact;

- *best practice:* heritage managers can be proactive with respect to the adoption of new ideas and techniques. Therefore, a strategic planning process can become a way of doing things better; and

Figure 2.2 Elements of a strategic heritage planning process

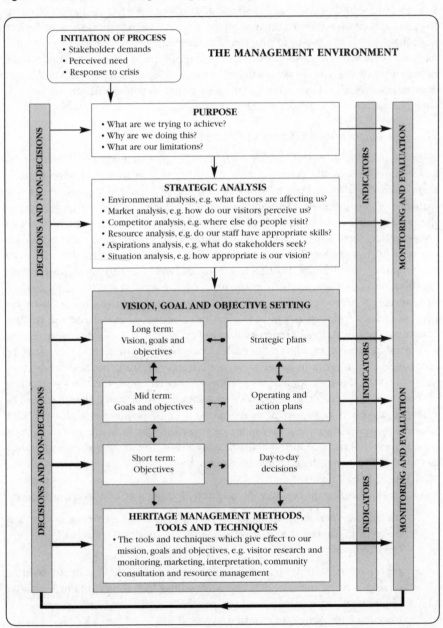

- *adaptation, innovation and the diffusion of ideas:* individuals within an organisation can encourage strategic planning processes as part of the diffusion of ideas within and between heritage management agencies.

Strategic planning is rarely initiated for a single reason, and often the real reasons are obscured from the public gaze. However, it is important to understand as well as possible why a particular planning process is being initiated, as this helps the participants understand the expectations that have been created with the commencement of the process. Once under way, strategic planning is designed to be iterative. In other words, planning systems are meant to be able to adapt and change; they *learn* how to be effective in terms of the most appropriate set of goals, objectives, actions, indicators, institutional arrangements and practices.

The strategic planning process is hierarchically structured from a vision or mission statement through to goals, objectives and action statements. Each level expands on the other in terms of detail, direction and attainability. Furthermore, for large heritage management organisations plans may be developed at three distinct organisational levels: the total organisational level (often referred to as the corporate level), the strategic business unit (SBU) – e.g., a division or a branch, and the product or market level within a SBU – e.g., a heritage site plan or a set of maintenance standards. This does not mean that decisions on each and every matter under the ambit of a heritage manager must await a planning statement. However, it emphasises that more detailed choices and the assessment of an organisation's effectiveness and efficiency will be facilitated by the existence of broader and more general statements that take account of inherent detailed implications. As McLoughlin (1969) stated with respect to physical planning in the urban environment:

> It follows from the hierarchical or tree-like nature of choices and alternatives that lower-level decisions tend to require higher-order choices to be clarified. For example, it is often found that a particular proposal such as the rebuilding of a row of older shops and houses cannot be resolved without consideration of the question of the future width and alignment of the street, which itself cannot be decided until the circulation and access system for that part of the city (and thus perhaps the whole city) is decided upon; this in turn forces attention onto the land use patterns which the transport system is to be designed to serve.

Purpose

It is important to identify the purposes for which a strategic planning process is being undertaken. As noted above, this is partly to recognise the expectations that may have been created with respect to what the process may provide. Indeed, one of the great difficulties often faced by managers is having to deal with false or unrealistic expectations as to the outcomes of planning. However, by clearly identifying the purposes of planning it becomes possible to state:

- what an organisation is trying to achieve;
- why an organisation is undertaking the planning process; and
- what the limitations of the process are.

It is ironic that many heritage managers will write a brief to state the purpose of a task for a consultant to undertake, but rarely take the time to sit down and write a statement of purpose for an exercise that they themselves must undertake. Once the purpose has been established, the heritage management organisation can move on to undertake a strategic analysis.

Strategic Analysis

Strategic analysis is concerned with understanding the strategic situation that an organisation faces (Richardson and Richardson 1989). It is, in effect, a form of pre-evaluation. Strategic analysis combines several different types of analysis:

- *environmental analysis*, which assists planners and managers to anticipate short- and long-term changes in the operational environment. It also includes *market* and *competitor analysis* as components of the management environment;

- *resource analysis*, which helps the heritage manager to understand the significance of the site's physical and human resource base to successful on-going environmental adaptation;

- *aspirations analysis*, which identifies the aspirations and interests of the major stakeholders in the heritage site and assists management to formulate its own strategic objectives in the light of the desires and interests of others; and

- *situation analysis*, which looks at existing structures, visions, goals, objectives, actions and practice, and the success of previous planning exercises and their associated outputs and outcomes.

The terms that are used to describe the elements of strategic analysis are often used interchangeably by different authors, in different countries and in different organisations (e.g., Johnson and Scholes 1988; Richardson and Richardson 1989; Kotler 1991; Lipscombe 1992; Reed 1992). However, it is the function itself rather than the terms used to describe it that is important. As Richardson and Richardson (1989) observed: 'If performed effectively, strategic analysis can generate tremendous insight (particularly for first time users) into the factors which underpin present success/failure levels and into the organisational changes which make greatest sense in the context of the anticipated future.' Indeed, strategic analysis is part of the process by which heritage management organisations can be turned into 'learning organisations' that can constantly adapt to the demands of their stakeholders and their environment (Garratt 1987).

One of the first steps in strategic planning is understanding the environment within which the organisation is operating. As noted in Chapter 1, change in the environment (e.g., in terms of social, economic, political and technological factors) has become the rule rather than the exception. Therefore, it is essential that organisations regularly examine the nature of their environment. Indeed, Kotler (1982) argued that if organisations are going to change and adapt they must understand what they are adapting to.

There are three main components of environmental analysis: macro-environmental analysis, market analysis and competitor analysis. Macro-environmental analysis examines the political, economic, social and technological factors that affect an organisation (see Figure 1.1). (It is also described as a PEST analysis.) A fifth factor – ecological trends or factors – can also be added to the analysis when examining the macro-environment of natural heritage management agencies (Hall and McArthur

1996b). Table 2.1 provides some examples of the trends that are affecting the environment within which heritage managers operate.

Table 2.1 Examples of macro-environmental trends that affect heritage management

Factor	Trends	Possible implications
Political	Minority and indigenous rights	Assertion of indigenous ownership over artifacts and possible removal from public display or scientific research
	Reduction in travel restrictions	Increased arrivals from Korea, Taiwan, and China and the countries of Eastern Europe and increased competition from heritage attractions in these areas
Economic	Economic rationalism	User-pays approach to visitation
	Corporatisation	Visitor services become more market-oriented
	Globalisation	Increased competition between places and use of heritage as means to differentiate the image of a place
	Tourism as a form of development	Increasing recognition is being given by government to the potential contribution of tourism to economic growth and employment generation. This may put more pressure on access and development of heritage sites
	Ecotourism	Greater recognition of the economic significance of nature-based tourist products and markets
	Quality	Greater emphasis on the provision of quality as a component of the value-for-money of visitor experiences and the conservation of heritage
Ecological	Global climate change	Potential impact on heritage sites, especially in coastal and alpine areas
	Biodiversity	Natural heritage sites may assume even greater importance in the maintenance of biodiversity as non-protected natural areas are altered or destroyed
	Resilience	Some environments are now at their resilience threshold
Socio-cultural	Ageing population	Demand to cater for physically impaired visitors
	Changing family structures	Increased numbers of single-parent families may lead to demands for specialised facilities
	Better-educated visitors	Particular segments of the visitor market are now looking for or expecting a higher quality of interpretation than that typically provided
	Convergence	The convergence of cultural forms previously perceived as separate, e.g. entertainment and museums, may lead to the loss of the 'uniqueness' of some heritage experiences
	Commodification	The need for some heritage organisations to attract more money in order to survive may lead to the commodification of heritage
Technological	Internet	Use of the Internet to gain information on heritage sites and to book visits
	Virtual reality	Potential use of computer simulation to recreate heritage experiences without endangering the resource

Source: after Hall and McArthur (1996a, 1996b)

Market analysis is also an important component of the environmental analysis. Although marketing is discussed in more detail in Chapter 7, it is important to note here that market analysis is vital in understanding who are – and who are not – our consumers (visitors). Kotler and Fox (1985) identified three major tasks in analysing the market environment, which may be summarised as:

- *market measurement and forecasting:* determining the current and potential future size of the market for a heritage product;

- *market segmentation:* determining the main groups that make up a market in order to choose the best target groups to be served; and

- *consumer analysis:* determining the characteristics of consumers and non-consumers – their attitudes, values, motivations, expectations and behaviour – in order to best match the product with the market.

Market analysis therefore includes pertinent market segmentation exercises, analysis of the present and potential competitive market structure, identification of the inherent attractiveness of the markets and identification of the openings that managers might exploit.

Many heritage managers may find it strange that competitor analysis is included as a component of environmental analysis. However, heritage sites and products are increasingly in competition not only with other heritage sites and products that may be visited but also with other leisure and entertainment activities. Like visitors, competitors must be monitored and evaluated on an on-going basis. Indeed, competition is one of the main drivers behind the adoption of a strategic planning approach in the business world. As Porter (1987) stated, 'The questions that good planning seeks to answer – the future direction of competition, the needs of the customer, the likely behaviour of competitors, how to gain a competitive edge – will never lose their relevance.' Therefore, heritage managers need to find out what other experiences can be substituted for those which are being offered at a particular heritage site in terms of such factors as price, accessibility, promotion and marketing, packaging, and, of course, the experience itself. Furthermore, collecting information on the mission, goals, objectives, strategies, performance, cost structures, strengths, weaknesses and possible future developments of the competitors may also provide a series of benchmarks by which to measure performance and therefore develop best-practice strategies for heritage management.

A resource analysis concerns the identification of the strengths and weaknesses of an organisation and, in the case of heritage management, of the heritage resource. It is primarily internally oriented. The resource analysis allows managers to know what is possible given the constraints of resource availability. Even in the case of a heritage resource, the resource analysis is more than just physical inventory: it is a mechanism by which the various values attached to heritage can be identified and then related to strategic objectives. When married to the objective setting process, resource analysis can help to indicate how resources could be redirected to improve the likelihood of meeting goals and objectives. There are several components to the resource analysis. The starting-point is the conduct of a resource audit, which tells us what resources we have. However, this is only the most basic information in terms of such items as physical resources, human resources, management systems (e.g., quality control measures) and intangibles, such as image and organisational morale. Such basic audits therefore have to be turned into strategic information by asking such questions as:

- How effective is the utilisation of our resources? (What is our productivity according to a range of measures? How many visitors can use a particular site without causing unwanted damage or loss of experience?)

- How flexible are our resources? (How easily can they be deployed from one section or site to another? How multi-skilled is our workforce? Can our interpreters assist with track maintenance and vice-versa?)

- How balanced are our resources? (Are we strong in natural resource management skills but weak in visitor management skills? Do we have too much emphasis on access and not enough on conservation and scholarship in order to achieve our mission?)

- How effective is our organisational 'fit'? (Are there sections of the organisation that do not support the organisation's mission and are therefore out of step with the organisation's strategic planning objectives? Do the conservation scientists support the visitor emphasis of our mission?)

- What is the extent and nature of any slack in the resources of our organisation? (Are any sections overstaffed in relation to the objectives they have to achieve? Do we need to downsize the maintenance division and hire more guides and interpreters?)

- What is the nature and extent of our strategic standing? (How are we perceived by our stakeholders and, in particular, by our major clients, our visitors?)

The last question leads in to the undertaking of an aspirations analysis. An aspirations analysis is used to determine who the important stakeholders are or will be, their aspirations, values and objectives with respect to heritage, their relative power in terms of ability to influence decision-making processes and their likely actions (Hall and McArthur 1996b). Although it is primarily focused on organisations and institutions, aspirations analysis may also include analysis of the aspirations of key individuals. Aspirations analysis is significant because it is used as an aid to understanding who is influencing or seeking to influence a heritage organisation or a specific management issue and why (Roberts and King 1989). Aspirations analysis ranges from the conduct of an audit of stakeholders, whereby we seek to identify and understand their interests and values, to the formal incorporation of those interests and values into the strategic planning process through public participation and community consultation techniques. The dimensions of stakeholder analysis are discussed in more detail in Chapters 3 and 4. Depending on their goals and objectives, heritage managers may utilise aspirations analysis at both ends of its spectrum, depending on whether they want to influence stakeholder perceptions or whether they merely want to include, or at least formally acknowledge, stakeholder perceptions and values.

The final form of strategic analysis is a situation analysis. Although all the above forms of analysis will serve to describe a heritage organisation's situation at a given time, the use of the term 'situation analysis' in this setting refers to the analysis of existing visions, goals, objectives and actions, and of previous outputs – e.g., earlier planning documents – and outcomes – e.g., the impact of previous planning processes on stakeholders, the heritage management organisation and the heritage resource itself. A situation analysis is particularly important when the strategic planning process is in full motion, as it helps to provide a 'reality check' on the success of previous planning exercises.

Mission, Goals and Objectives

All too often, heritage planning and management are focused on immediate issues. This is not to say that issue-based planning does not have a place in the tool-kit of the heritage manager, but an organisation does need to go beyond reactive issues-based planning to be able to place such issues within the bigger picture of what the organisation and its staff are trying to achieve. This is the realm of the organisation's vision, mission, goals and objectives.

Values and Visions

Alongside the conduct of a strategic analysis, the starting-point for an organisation's strategic plan should be its values. Understanding an organisation's values means understanding what it stands for. Underlying any vision for an organisation will be its core set of values and purpose, and its envisioned future (Collins and Porras 1996). The core values of an organisation are its essential and enduring tenets; and its core purpose is its reason for being – not a goal or a business strategy. In the private sector an organisation's purpose will often relate to a particular contribution to people's lives. However, in heritage organisations the purpose is often framed more descriptively and is often concentrated on the heritage resource rather than on the people who utilise or share in that resource. For many heritage organisations in the public sector the core values and purpose may be contained in legislation or may be revealed in the parliamentary debate that led up to the establishment of such legislation. For example, many national park organisations around the world have as core values and purposes conservation and provision for public access.

Collins and Porras (1996) describe the combination of purpose and values as constituting the core ideology of an organisation, which should be meaningful and, it is hoped, inspirational to those within the organisation. However, an ideology is not the same as an organisation's competencies. The latter describe what an organisation is good at, the former defines where it stands and why it exists. For example, a heritage tour company may have a competency of high-quality interpretation, while the ideology may relate to the conveying of knowledge through ensuring maximum customer satisfaction.

The core ideology, when combined with an envisioned future, provides a vision for an organisation. An envisioned future is a ten- to thirty-year goal that includes a description of what it would be like to achieve that goal. A good vision statement speaks of an ideal state that an organisation wishes to achieve. 'Visions, like definitions, must be plausible, generate confidence that they are attainable, and be important enough to be worth all the hard work necessary to obtain them. They are statements about the future and provide a focus for all activities' (Cortada 1993). For example, The George Washington University in Washington DC, USA, has adopted (1996) the following vision:

> We envision our GreenU as a harmonious organization carrying out its purposes and goals within the educational community, the natural environment, society, and the international arena. This is to be accomplished in a manner that optimizes the use of resources for the greatest good of all The George Washington University stakeholders.
>
> We envision that our GreenU: will incorporate into all our policies, programs, and practices the highest concern for our impact on the environment; will participate in research, development, and technology and

information transfer for the benefit of the environment; will contribute to the education of an environmentally-literate population; will become a major force in the education of the political, economic and scientific leadership of the next generation; and will work toward the creation of an international network of institutes of higher education committed to the goals of becoming 'greener' universities.

Such statements are designed to serve as a source of inspiration to members of the university community, as well as providing guidance as to future directions. Therefore, they also serve as the basis for the various aspects of an organisation's strategic plan. Nevertheless, it is important to note that many public heritage organisations often have a vision that has a wider ownership than that of private sector organisations because, by virtue of public ownership of the heritage resource, the community is treated as an internal stakeholder. For example, after taking into account information gained from a strategic planning process, the Bureau of Land Management (BLM) of the United States developed the following vision statement (1997) summarised as:

The Bureau of Land Management will:

- Provide for a wide variety of public land uses without compromising the long-term health and diversity of the land and without sacrificing significant natural, cultural, and historical values.

- Understand the arid, semi-arid, arctic and other ecosystems it manages and commit to using the best scientific and technical information to make resource management decisions.

- Resolve problems and implement solutions in collaboration with other agencies, states, tribal governments, and the public.

- Understand the needs of rural and urban publics and provide them with quality service.

- Maintain a skilled and highly professional work force.

- Clearly define and achieve objectives through the efficient management of financial, human, and information resources.

- Efficiently and effectively manage land records and other spatial data.

- Recover a fair return for the use of publicly-owned resources and reduce long-term liabilities for the American taxpayer.

The value of the BLM's vision statement is that it represents the values, beliefs and activities of the BLM to its various stakeholders and provides a basis on which goals, objectives and day-to-day operations can be built.

Missions

Mission, goal and objective formulation are critical components of strategic planning. An organisation's mission, goals and objectives are highly interdependent (Byars 1984). The formulation of mission statements and the development of goals and objectives need to be conducted hand-in-hand with the strategic analysis, identification of values (if these have not previously been recognised) and vision. As Heath and Wall (1992) noted, management strategies 'grow out of and reflect the environmental analysis, resource analysis and goal formulation steps. Unless ... goals have been set to be accomplished, there is no purpose in strategy formulation.'

   The mission statement describes what the organisation is trying to accomplish in the longer term. Whereas the 'vision' is primarily geared to the internal members of an organisation, the mission is a statement that is geared to all stakeholders. Goals generally emphasise the long-range intentions of the organisation and are not usually quantified. Objectives are measurable goals that have been made more specific with respect to magnitude, time and responsibility and that are judged to be attainable within a specific time (Heath and Wall 1992). The relationship between mission, goals and objectives is discussed in more detail below.

   The values and ambitions of a heritage management organisation can be imbued in a mission statement that provides the direction necessary to guide organisational and project goals, objectives, policies, strategies, implementation and evaluation. A clear set of aims or principles for heritage management is also extremely valuable in the context of both strategic planning and specific heritage site management plans and may also be included in a formal planning document. For example, the Wisconsin Department of Tourism (1996) in the United States has adopted the following set of principles, developed by the National Trust for Historic Preservation, with respect to its heritage tourism mission and programme:

- *Focus on authenticity and quality.* The true story of the area is the one worth telling. Authenticity adds real value and appeal. Each area is unique in its own way. Its special charm is what will draw visitors.

- *Preserve and protect resources.* By protecting the buildings or special places and qualities that attract visitors, we safeguard our future. The preservation and perpetuation of traditions is important in telling a story of the people who settled the land.

- *Make site come alive.* The human drama of history is what visitors want to discover, not just names and dates. Interpreting sites is important; so is making the message creative and exciting;

- *Find the fit between your community and tourism.* Local priorities and capabilities vary. For programs to succeed they must have widespread local acceptance and meet recognized local needs; and

- *Collaborate.* Building partnerships is essential. Success depends on the active participation of government, business leaders, tourism organizations, craftspeople and historical societies.

A further example of the use of sets of guiding principles in heritage planning is provided in Case Study 2.2 on the city of Bath in the United Kingdom.

   Mission statements should be realistic, motivating and distinctive, and are particularly important for the external audience. 'Since a mission statement must help communicate vision to stakeholders, formulating one is a crucial activity' (Cortada 1993). Ideally, the mission should outline both the philosophy (values and beliefs or vision) and purpose (activities undertaken) of the organisation. However, they may be split. For example, the mission for the Department of Canadian Heritage, of which Parks Canada is a part, is 'Building our future together – strengthening a shared sense of Canadian identity which respects the diversity of the land and people' (Parks Canada 1996). The purpose of Parks Canada, which they describe as a part of their policy context, is:

   To fulfill national and international responsibilities in mandated areas of heritage recognition and conservation; and to commemorate, protect and present, both directly and indirectly, places which are significant examples of Canada's cultural and natural heritage in ways that encourage public understanding, appreciation and enjoyment of this heritage, while ensuring long-term ecological and commemorative integrity (Parks Canada 1996).

The value of mission statements has been identified by Drucker (1974) in the business sphere: 'Defining the purpose and mission of the business is difficult, painful and risky. But it alone enables a business to set its objectives, to develop strategies, to concentrate on resources and go to work. It alone enables a business to be managed for performance.'

Case Study 2.2
A Manifesto for Retaining the Heritage Qualities of the City of Bath, United Kingdom

---

Key point:
- Guiding principles need to be integrated into the heritage planning process in order to achieve goals in keeping with the original vision.

Bath is one of the most significant urban heritage environments in the United Kingdom. It contains over 4,900 listed buildings, the majority of which date from the redevelopment of the city in the eighteenth century. Bath was added to the World Heritage List in December 1987 in recognition of its international architectural and landscape significance.

In the light of its World Heritage listing and also on-going issues of urban development and management, the city identified three main themes that underlay the need to review its city plan:
- the need for a philosophy of conservation which embraces landscape and activity as well as 'built fabric';
- the growing need to address the impact of new development and growth on traffic congestion; and
- the need to understand the limits on available land suitable for development manifesto (in Organization of World Heritage Cities 1996a).

As part of the review, the city developed a charter, or set of guiding principles, described as a 'manifesto' within the 1990 *City Plan Review*, with respect to its special heritage qualities and its needs as a living, commercial city. The manifesto (in Organization of World Heritage Cities 1996a), which was also published in order to elicit public response, included the following policy statements, which were then used as planning guidelines by the city when considering issues of development and change:
- When considering any development or management proposals, the City Council will have regard to the protection of the historic fabric. All new proposals for development should respect and enhance the fabric and landscape of Bath.
- The City Council will regard the status of the whole City of Bath as a World Heritage Site as a material consideration when considering applications for Planning Permission and Listed Building Consent.
- As far as it is able to anticipate change, the City Council will direct all pressure for change in such a way as to preserve and enhance the fabric and landscape of Bath.
- The Council will define and monitor the balance between preservation and adaptation of the City for the common good of all Bath's citizens.

- The Council will adopt policies which seek to preserve the fabric and landscape of the City, while retaining a balanced social, cultural and economic structure.

- The Manifesto will be reviewed and updated as necessary to respond to unforeseen and unpredictable pressures for change and the appropriate commitment by the City Council to the protection of the heritage of the whole city will be affirmed regularly.

Goal and Objective Setting

Objective setting is an important component in heritage management because it determines what we are attempting to achieve. Objectives are the yardsticks by which the organisation and its component parts will be judged. Therefore, heritage managers need to note the broad mission of their organisation, its purpose and the set of values it reflects. The majority of management plans and programmes prepared by heritage management organisations set generalised, long-term goals rather than obtainable, measurable objectives with a pre-determined time frame. The two terms are often confused. Nevertheless, by setting measurable objectives it is possible to indicate the effectiveness of any management programme. However, before discussing further the differences between goals and objectives it is worth noting the means by which they are actually set – a topic that is little discussed in the literature (Heath and Wall 1992), although its importance is well acknowledged.

Without goals and objectives strategic planning and management would take place in a vacuum. There are three major approaches in the establishment of goals and objectives. The first is a *top-down* approach, 'where goals at each level in the organisation are determined based on the goals at the next higher level' (Heath and Wall 1992). Such an approach is marked by internal decisions being made within an organisation, often with minimal discussion with stakeholders. The second is a *bottom-up* approach, where the strategic plans of individual units are aggregated to become the corporate plan. However, aggregation alone will often result in little coordination between units and the failure to create a sense of the whole. The final approach is an *interactive* approach, which requires participation and interaction between the various levels of an organisation and between the organisation and stakeholders. Although the planning framework shown in Figure 2.2 suggests that there is a progression from the purpose to the strategic analysis, and through to vision, goals and objectives, planning does not in reality follow this linear progression. As noted earlier in this chapter, strategic planning is iterative – in other words, we learn and adjust as work undertaken at one level is found to be incompatible with work undertaken at another and therefore requires adjustments and modifications to be made. For example, as Reed (1992) observes, 'work at the strategy determination stage may reveal that an objective previously set was unrealistic or unobtainable, and this may result in the objective being modified to meet the new circumstance.'

An interactive approach towards goal and objective setting is reflective of the responsive nature of strategic heritage planning. The emphasis is on planning *with* rather than *for* stakeholders. The approach reinforces the complex nature of the ownership of heritage by recognising that the opinions, perspectives and recommendations of external stakeholders are just as legitimate as those of the planner or the 'expert'. Such an approach may well be more time-consuming than a top-down approach, but the results of such a process will have a far greater likelihood of being implemented, because stakeholders will have a degree of ownership in the goals and objectives that are set. Furthermore, such a process may well establish greater cooperation between various stakeholders in supporting the goals and objectives of heritage management and also create a basis for responding more effectively to and for change (Hall and McArthur 1996b).

Goals and Objectives

Goals are statements of intended outcome expressed in broad terms. For example, the primary goal established by the Wet Tropics Management Authority is: 'To provide for the implementation of Australia's international duty for the *protection, conservation, presentation, rehabilitation and transmission to future generations* of the Wet Tropics of Queensland World Heritage Area, within the meaning of the World Heritage Convention' (Chester and Roberts 1992). In contrast, objectives are the ends towards which organisations or programmes are directed. They are the statements of conditions that an organisation or programme seeks to attain, expressed in such a manner that progress towards, or divergence away from them, can be measured (Lipscombe 1992). It follows that broad and general goals must be supplemented by fuller statements of the objectives that must be attained in order to move towards the goals (McLoughlin 1969). Therefore, long-term, mid-term and short-term objectives should:

- be specific;
- be able to be evaluated;
- be attainable;
- have specific time limits;
- be expressed in language that may be clearly understood by those responsible for its achievement;
- produce results which can be clearly and concisely communicated; and
- where appropriate, be integrated with the objectives of stakeholders which share a common interest with a heritage area and/or a visitor market. (Hall and McArthur 1996b)

Strategic objectives should have a currency of several years, although the priorities allocated to them are likely to change as unforeseen and unforeseeable events occur and enforce change (V. Middleton 1994). Even some of the most innovative strategies for heritage management have failed to indicate and differentiate clearly between the various levels of strategic planning and goal and objective setting. An example of the setting of objectives that are not clearly measurable is provided in the Memorandum of Understanding (MOU) between the Commonwealth of Australia, Australian Capital Territory, New South Wales and Victoria for the management and conservation of the Australian Alps. The MOU established formal mechanisms and processes for cross-border collaborative nature conservation and environmental and recreation management programmes for a number of protected areas. According to Mackay and Virtanen (1992), the 'key objectives' for the management of the Australian Alps were:

- protection of the landscape;
- protection of plants, animals and cultural values;
- provision of recreational opportunities to encourage the enjoyment and understanding of the alpine environment; and
- protection of mountain catchments.

Similarly, with respect to the renewal of the Hafnia quarter in the Medina of Tunis, Tunisia, following its declaration as a World Heritage site in 1979, the project had the following 'objectives':

- upgrade quality of health in the area;
- only demolish irrecoverable buildings;
- upgrade existing residential structures only after reducing the quarter's density to permit installation of appropriate hygienic features;
- rehouse in the quarter [as] great a proportion of those displaced by previous demolition as possible;
- permit a measured and controlled upgrading of rents;
- upgrade public infrastructure;
- stimulate appropriate commercial and artisanal activity;
- link the area's monuments to socio-cultural activity;
- maintain urban forms, spaces and patterns; and
- reinterpret traditional typologies and details.
  (Organization of World Heritage Cities 1996b)

In both of the above cases, the intentions of the planning statements are laudable, but they are goals, not objectives. How is it possible to measure just how successful the projects are, unless a time scale is provided and they can be clearly evaluated? Indeed, in the case of the Hafnia quarter it is interesting to note that although, 'on balance the project was very successful, particularly given its highly successful budget performance ... only 13% of relocated families returned to their original space' (Organization of World Heritage Cities 1996b). Examples of clear objectives might be:

- eliminate all cross-country skiing on non-designated trails in the Australian alpine national parks by the end of the current financial year;
- provide temporary accommodation for all persons who are displaced by demolition in the Hafnia quarter at least one month before such demolition begins;
- rehouse in the Hafnia quarter at least 75 per cent of those displaced by demolition by the end of the current financial year; and
- survey and assess the level of support for the demolition and rehabilitation of housing within the Hafnia World Heritage Site, within eighteen months of the completion of the second phase of the renewal plan.

(Please note, these objectives are fictitious!)

Many heritage organisations provide 'half-way objectives', which, although providing a relatively clear statement of intent, often ignore the evaluative and time components. For example, Parks Canada (1996), in reference to national historic sites, identified the following 'objectives':

- to foster knowledge and appreciation of Canada's past through a national program of historical commemoration;
- to ensure the commemorative integrity of national historical sites administered by Parks Canada by protecting and presenting them for the benefit, education and enjoyment of this and future generations, in a manner

that respects the significant and irreplaceable legacy provided by these places and their associated resources; and

- to encourage and support the protection and presentation by others of places of national historic significance that are not administered by Parks Canada.

The above objectives are important guiding principles, but they are not clear enough to provide a basis for a monitoring and evaluation programme that sets standards for success, effectiveness, efficiency and accountability. Clearly stated objectives improve heritage management by:

- providing guidance to appropriate organisational behaviour;
- reducing uncertainty and the lack of direction in the development of an event;
- motivating people to work toward specific ends;
- providing a measure with which to assess the success of management; and
- providing a focal point for coordination of the heritage management organisation.

A recent development from the objectives is the idea of 'desired outcome'. Desired outcomes are statements of a tangible future scenario resulting from the strategic planning process. However, it could be argued that the difference is semantic and that 'desired outcomes' provide a term that is easier for people to understand. Nevertheless, well-defined objectives by themselves are not sufficient for effective planning and management. Strategic planning documents must contain a statement of action which demonstrates how each objective will be achieved.

Actions, Operations and Strategies

Actions are even more specific than objectives. Actions identify directly *how* we will implement the objective; they state what must be done. They are related to the concept of a strategy that, as noted at the beginning of the chapter, refers to a statement of the mechanisms and process by which objectives will be achieved. An action refers to the means by which a strategy will be implemented in order to achieve an objective. As in the case of the setting of objectives, considerable problems emerge in concept definition. In the case of the draft Wet Tropics management plan, noted above, some of the actions were ill-defined and are probably closer to being objectives. For example, in the case of the conservation of vegetation communities the action was defined as to 'determine the level and types of disturbance of these rare rainforest communities and assess during 1992/1993 their need for conservation and/or rehabilitation' (Wet Tropics Management Authority 1992). In contrast, an example of a true action would be 'to allocate three staff members to measure the density of seedlings for known disturbed and undisturbed rare rainforest communities' (fictitious example, Hall and McArthur 1996c). Indeed, the action plan can become even more specific by indicating the priority and likely cost of such an action, thereby creating a useful basis for financial evaluation as well as programme evaluation.

Statements of action are usually left out of management plans. Why? One reason may be concern at being tied to an action regardless of changing circumstances in the internal and/or external environment. Many possible shifts can be identified: e.g., a rapid change in the visitor market, cuts in budget allocation from government, gaining a new sponsorship, discovery of new artifacts of heritage significance, title claim from indigenous peoples, or the appointment of a new government minister. Nevertheless, if the strategic planning process is formulated appropriately, the feedback mechanism will enable heritage managers to adapt and respond accordingly to such changes, as it will provide a basis of information upon which appropriate decisions and new strategies can be made. In some strategic planning exercises in the commercial world, strategic plans may even include planning scenarios in case such contingencies happen (Richardson and Richardson 1989). Indeed, in certain situations a thorough strategic analysis would alert managers to the possibilities of crises occurring (for example, if a heritage site were located in an area that was subject to natural disasters, such as a flood plain or a cyclone region). Similarly, a thorough analysis of the political environment may also alert managers to potential shifts in funding or legislation.

A more cynical observation on the lack of attention to action and operational planning would be that some heritage managers are fearful of setting performance standards that could be assessed by all stakeholders throughout the planning process. However, heritage managers must realise that it is those very same performance standards and clear definition of output that will both make the management process more effective and efficient and provide extra weight in the search for resourcing. It is the successful meeting of performance standards that will provide support for the goals of heritage management (Hall and McArthur 1996c).

Indicators, Monitoring and Evaluation

One of the essential elements in setting performance standards is the selection of appropriate performance indicators. In the context of strategic planning, indicators serve several important roles; they:

- help make complex systems understandable;
- provide a measure of how well objectives are being met;
- provide a basis for comparisons within and between organisations;
- help measure organisational performance over time; and
- help ensure that hidden agendas, unanticipated consequences and inadequate sensitivity and responsiveness to stakeholder concerns are revealed and can be addressed.

An effective indicator or set of indicators therefore helps an organisation determine where it is, where it is going, and how far it is from chosen goals, objectives and strategies. The performance of an indicator provides a check to ensure that actions are moving in desired directions and also helps to ensure that individuals and organisations are held accountable for the choices they make.

Indicators can be classified either by their role or by their methodological base. For example, Bonoma and Clark (1988) describe two classes of indicators: one that measures effectiveness and the other that measures efficiency. Effectiveness indicators relate outputs and outcomes to the goals or objectives of the heritage organisation as stated in the strategic plan. Efficiency indicators are essentially productivity ratios of results over costs. According to Drucker (1974 in Bonoma and Clark 1988), 'effectiveness is the foundation of success – efficiency is the minimum condition for survival after success has been achieved. Efficiency is concerned with doing things right. Effectiveness is doing the right things.'

A variety of indicators are required that specifically meet the multi-faceted need of heritage managers. For example, V. Middleton (1994), while noting the importance of financial data (Table 2.2), stresses the need to obtain qualitative and quantitative measures of performance. Many heritage operations count the number of visitors they receive. Museums may do this in order to demonstrate the value and worth of their collections and the activities that they undertake (Prince and Higgins-McLoughlin 1987). Nevertheless, the number of visitors alone is a very poor indicator. Such indicators as levels of visitor satisfaction, frequency of visit, preparedness to recommend the experience, receptiveness to interpretive messages and willingness to pay may provide a far richer and more useful set of data. Furthermore, it is also important for heritage managers to ensure, wherever possible, that their selection of indicators fits into wider regional, national or international indicators that may have been established. This will facilitate information exchange and comparative evalu-ations and will improve partnerships for the achievement of common goals such as maintenance of biodiversity and cultural diversity. Indicators therefore need to be carefully chosen to provide the right answers and insights.

Table 2.2 Strengths and weaknesses of financial and budgetary indicators

Strengths

- Clarify the aims and policies of business
- Help translate policies into programmes
- Clarify the priorities of the manager and increase awareness of responsibility
- Improve financial control by comparing actual performance with planned (budgeted) performance
- Help development of corporate strategy by focusing the attention of management on specific areas of operation
- Help improve efficiency by showing which resources are used in which areas of the operation and assess how efficiently they are being used

Weaknesses

- Information may be too old and too late to be acted upon
- Information may be too technical to be easily understood by non-accounting managers
- Cost allocations may not be reflective of true costs
- Costs may be inadequately categorised and do not give sufficient information about the underlying factors that cause costs to occur or how they might be controlled
- Reports do not focus on critical success factors, such as improved quality and stakeholder service
- Reports are usually cost-centre or departmentally based and do not provide for costing business activity that spans interrelated departments
- Reports fail to support the information requirements of management systems that stress continuous process improvements through emphasis on quality

Sources: after Reed (1992) and Griffiths (1994)

Evaluation and Monitoring

Evaluation is the assessment of performance. It is crucial that heritage managers determine whether or not a plan or programme is a success in the light of its initial objectives. Indeed, it may well be the case that some goals and objectives were met while others remained unfulfilled. Moreover, some indicators may also have to be modified in order to be sure that they are the most appropriate measures of performance. The success or otherwise of heritage management is only conjecture unless a formal evaluation occurs. Furthermore, evaluation is a continuation of the control function of management and helps develop management processes and procedures for future programmes. Evaluation is therefore a valuable means to learning from the mistakes and the successes that have been realised throughout the management process, while also providing important information for improving relationships with stakeholders such as government or private industry in the future (Griffin 1994).

In its application to strategic planning, monitoring develops a body of information and knowledge that helps determine the effectiveness of a programme in meeting its objectives. The appropriateness of a plan or programme may change over time. A number of methods are available for evaluating the success of a heritage management programme, such as cost-benefit analysis, goals achievement matrix, environmental and social impact assessment, limits of acceptable change, and goal-free evaluations (see Chapter 9).

Decisions and Non-Decisions

The final component to be noted in the strategic heritage planning framework is that of decisions and non-decisions. The adoption of a strategic approach to heritage planning does not negate the need for decision making. Indeed, its adoption is itself the outcome of a decision. The planning framework is a tool rather than a substitute for the decision-making process that managers must engage in. Following the monitoring and evaluation of the decision-making process, decisions must still be made about how the various elements of the process should be revised and restated – if at all. In addition, as part of the evaluation and monitoring process, decisions may also have to be made about the need to adapt or change institutional arrangements and organisational structures and to retrain staff in order to meet strategic goals. Heritage managers must recognise that there is no such thing as a non-decision. The do-nothing option is a decision to do nothing!

Advantages of Strategic Planning for Heritage Management

While distinguishing between planning, monitoring and evaluation may be seen as worthwhile, distinguishing the different planning levels – e.g., vision, missions, goal, objectives, strategies and actions – may be seen as somewhat pedantic by some readers. However, it must be emphasised that the success of any strategic heritage management exercise is dependent upon a clear understanding of terms and issues. As Table 2.3 indicates, there are a number of advantages in adopting a strategic approach to heritage management:

- it provides a sense of purpose and the foundation of criteria for the formulation of new projects;
- it stresses the need for both short- and long-term objectives that can accommodate changing circumstances – e.g., a change in the level of government funding for heritage;

- it gives stakeholders a clear indication of the current and long-term level of support required for heritage management programmes;

- it provides potential for the integration of stakeholder objectives into an organisational or programme strategy, thereby increasing the likelihood of success;

- it encourages strategic thinking and an increased receptiveness to opportunities in the external environment;

- it can give staff a sense of ownership and involvement in an organisation's goals and objectives, with a consequent likely increase in morale and performance; and

- it can make organisations more effective and efficient in attaining programme and/or organisational goals.

Table 2.3 The advantages of a strategic approach to heritage management

Elements that strategic planning provides	Setting requires	Example
Strategic thinking at the upper management level and in specialist functions, e.g. interpretation, facility management, and archaeology	Staff at all levels to be involved in the strategic heritage planning process, plus the involvement of community groups and site visitors	Awareness of strategic information and its communication to relevant managers, e.g. an interpretation officer who receives negative feedback regarding the relevance of interpretive signs
The significance of visitor and owner objectives	Attention to the range of interests involved in heritage management	Providing experiences for a range of visitor preferences and abilities, e.g. provision of child-oriented activities and facilities for the disabled
		Incorporating the perspectives of special-interest groups in the heritage planning process, e.g. historical societies, and conservation and outdoor recreation groups
Precise objectives that offer clear direction for future actions	The delineation of long-term objectives that allow for flexibility in achievement of an agency's mission statement	The regeneration of a disturbed environment within a national park by allowing natural processes of succession to occur over a fifty-year time period
	The identification of short-term objectives that establish immediate goals for the agency to accomplish	The completion of a specific interpretation project, e.g. a self-guided walking trail, within a set time frame
New major projects	Experimentation and modification of existing plans	Use of project proposals
		Review of the effectiveness of relevant previous and currently operating projects
	Anticipation of the changing circumstances within which heritage management occurs	Identification and evaluation of the expectations, motivations and values of new and potential user groups
Mid- to long-term commitment of resources	The integration of a succession of short-term projects in a comprehensive heritage management strategy	The development of a cooperative partnership between agencies through the signing of a Memorandum of Understanding which provides for the sharing of resources

Source: after Hall and McArthur (1996c)

A Comprehensive Approach to Strategic Planning

This book advocates a broadening of heritage management concerns to integrate stakeholders (including visitors) better within the management process. The strategic planning approach advocated in this chapter provides heritage management organisations with a basis on which to accommodate changing heritage values and stakeholder needs, as well as other changes in the management environment that will impinge not only on management systems but on the heritage resource itself. Strategic heritage planning is designed to be comprehensive. Comprehensiveness in heritage management refers to an awareness that heritage is a system of interrelated social, economic and political variables focused on a heritage resource. To be comprehensive three conditions must be met:

- functional programmes and activities must be in keeping with the wider values, mission, principles, goals and objectives of the management organisation;

- any programme or activity must be monitored and evaluated in terms that are relevant to the wider values, vision, mission, goals and objectives; and

- all relevant variables must be considered in the design of individual programmes and activities.

This chapter has outlined a process of strategic planning for heritage management. It has emphasised the importance of the initiation of strategic planning, identification of purpose, mission statements, strategic analysis, goal and objective setting, and the construction of an integrated set of goals, objectives and actions that can then be implemented over time horizons ranging from the day-to-day to the long-term (Case Study 2.3). This chapter has provided a strategic planning approach that is geared towards the stakeholders rather than just the resource itself. The following series of chapters outlines some of the key approaches and techniques that assist in meeting the goals and objectives established through such a process.

Case Study 2.3
Management Plan for the Mackinac State Historic Parks, Michigan, USA

Key point:
- Mission statements, goals and objectives need to be clearly expressed in order to become a valuable management tool.

Originally the site of a strategic British, then United States, military post at the juncture of Lake Huron and Lake Michigan, Mackinac Island State Park is one of most visited heritage sites in the United States. Mackinac was declared America's second national park in 1875, two years after Yellowstone. In 1895 Mackinac National Park became Michigan's first State Park after Congress transferred the park to state control. In the same year the Mackinac Island State Park Commission was established to manage and preserve the area.

The Commission now manages three historic parks: Mackinac Island State Park, Colonial Michilimackinac (the Village of Mackinaw City of Michilimackinac State Park, which was gifted in 1904), and Historic Mill Creek (Old Mill State Park, which was transferred from the Michigan Department of Natural Resources in 1975). Mackinac Island and Colonial

Michilimackinac are federally designated National Historic Landmarks, while numerous buildings and other aspects of the cultural landscape are listed on the National Register and the
Michigan State Register. The three historic parks and the museums, facilities and sites within
the parks are collectively known as Mackinac State Historic Parks (MSHP).

The site occupies a total of 2,435 acres (approximately 986 hectares) and includes a substantial length of shoreline. In 1994 the parks received 400,000 visitors at historical facilities
for which admission is charged and 800,000 park visitors. Visitors were recorded from all fifty
US states and from sixty-two foreign countries. The parks have received numerous awards from
architectural, engineering, historical, tourist and recreational organisations, and in 1994
Mackinac Island State Park was named by the *National Geographic* as one of the top ten state
parks in the United States. The rich heritage of the MSHP and the enormous set of demands
on the parks from the visitor and tourist industry, as well as those of local residents, require a
well-developed strategic plan by which MSHP can meet stakeholder demands. The key points
of the plan will be outlined in the remainder of this case study. MSHP's mission is:

> to enable present and future generations to understand, appreciate, and support
> the historical and aesthetic significance of the Straits of Mackinac. To accomplish this
> mission of stewardship, MHSP will collect, preserve, study, and interpret the unique
> cultural and natural resources of the region. (Mackinac State Historic Parks, Mackinac
> Island State Park Commission (MSHP/MISPC) 1995)

The mission of the MHSP is undertaken through two programme units: the Mackinac Island
State Park Commission Park Operations and the Historical Facilities System. Park Operations is
responsible for all non-historical facilities and land at the MHSP. The Historical Facilities System
consists of historic buildings, collections, museums, exhibits, research, publications and interpretive programmes, which are funded by a Revenue Bond Trust Fund that was established in
1958, as well as other revenue, including visitor fees. In addition to paid employees, the
Historical Facilities System has other internal stakeholders in the form of 330 volunteers, who
assist with Commission programmes each year and who contribute more than 26,400 hours
of service.

The mission of the Historical Facilities System is to enable present and future generations to
understand, appreciate and support the historical significance of the properties under the juris-
diction of the Mackinac Island State Park Commission. The Commission will collect, preserve,
study, and interpret the unique cultural resources of the Mackinac region in accordance with
the highest professional standards for the benefit, enjoyment and education of the public
(MSHP/MISPC 1995).

The MSHP has a series of well-articulated goals that give further direction to their management tasks:

- To preserve the natural areas and 'scenic wonders' for which Mackinac was first recognized as a National and State Park, and for which Mill Creek and Colonial
  Michilimackinac are recognized. To manage the natural features located within the
  parks for the least possible change from historic appearance, while providing for
  public safety and enjoyment.

- To seek to acquire title or scenic easements of in-holdings or undeveloped land
  adjoining the parks to advance park preservation. To promote conservation of the
  natural resources through sound environmental management, including programs
  of water and energy conservation, composting, and recycling.

- To encourage and support through park rules and law enforcement activities the
  continuation of the historic ban on motor vehicles and maintenance of the 'horse
  culture' of Mackinac.

- To interpret the natural history of the parks for the public. To facilitate safe and enjoyable public use of the parks for all, with special attention to the needs of visitors with disabilities in conformance with ADA requirements.

- To preserve and protect for future generations the historical buildings and material culture resources entrusted to Commission stewardship. To develop outstanding historical, archaeological, archival, and library collections which document the history of the Straits of Mackinac region.

- To document and preserve Commission collections in accordance with the highest professional standards. To increase understanding of the resources through programs of primary research and study, and to disseminate the results of these efforts through public programs and publications.

- To contribute to public awareness and education by interpreting and teaching about the significance of the natural and cultural resources using a wide variety of interpretive methods. To regularly evaluate the effectiveness of interpretive and educational programs and visitor service activities through visitor studies.

- To maintain accreditation of Commission programs by the American Association of Museums. (MSHP/MISPC 1995)

In order to achieve its goals the MSHP also developed some thirteen objectives. A few of these are listed as follows:

- To implement access improvements in accordance with transition plan priorities. To complete the fully accessible nature trail at Historic Mill Creek.

- To utilize the results of the National Endowment for the Humanities grant-funded research program for the British period exhibit at Colonial Michilimackinac as the basis for a complete reinterpretation of the site, including development of long-term exhibition and live interpretive program plans.

- To undertake a second season of archaeological excavation and analysis at Fort Mackinac, working at the Blacksmith's Shop site. To continue the participation of the University of South Florida as a field school in this project. (MSHP/MISPC 1995)

Finally, the management plan outlines a series of issues and programme elements with respect to the activities of the Commission's Park Operations and the Historical Facilities System. Examples include (MSHP/MISPC 1995):

Issue: Rapid development of private land on Mackinac Island is increasing pressure on the park. Land and easement acquisition efforts must be given high priority. Construction proposals and utility easement applications must be carefully reviewed for long-term impact on park lands.

Program Elements: Mackinac Island State Park Commission Park Operations Activities: Promote compatible natural area recreational use through development and maintenance of roads, trails, and bicycle paths to enable visitors to enjoy parks resources. Operate and maintain the Scout Service Camp.

Program Elements: Historical Facilities System Activities: Seek grant support from diverse sources for museum and research projects, including completion of an Institute of Museum Services General Operating Support and Conservation Support grant applications.

CHAPTER 3

Integrating Stakeholders into Heritage Management

In the late 1980s the management plans for two New Zealand conservation areas – the Tararua Forest Park and Tongariro National Park – were under review. Despite the clear relationship of Maori to these areas (Tongariro was actually given to the people of New Zealand by a Maori chief), there was little Maori involvement in the review: one person made a submission to the Tongariro plan, but no one made any to the Tararua plan, although a Maori Trust Board was involved at a later stage in discussions over the Tongariro plan. It is unlikely that such a situation would occur now, when there is much more awareness in conservation organisations about the right of indigenous peoples to exert their relationship to their traditional lands. However, this example shows that we need to ensure that stakeholders are incorporated into the heritage management and planning process in a meaningful way.

> The past, contemporary society and human culture are the property of us all and make their appeals without expert intermediaries.
> (Tunbridge and Ashworth 1996)

The concept of 'stakeholders' is becoming increasingly important in heritage management and planning. Stakeholders are the individuals, groups and organisations with an interest in a common heritage management problem or issue, which are directly influenced or affected by the actions or non-actions taken by others to resolve the problem or issue (after Gray 1989). Traditionally focused on the resource and on expert opinion with respect to determining access to – and definition and presentation of – heritage, heritage management is now more outward-looking. Several reasons can be put forward for this significant shift. First, claims to singular institutional ownership of heritage, especially with respect to indigenous heritage, have come to be challenged by other groups in society. Second, government cutbacks in the funding of heritage institutions have meant that many heritage managers have had to become more commercially oriented in order to maintain conservation and exhibition programmes. Third, and related to the second point, some heritage managers now seek active support from a range of interests for heritage programmes to improve their lobbying position with government.

Unfortunately, much discussion with respect to the role of stakeholders in heritage management has focused on the commercialisation of heritage. As Hewison (1991) noted, the recent 'independent' museums are independent of:

> the traditional educational and social welfare motivations that launched the museum movement in the nineteenth century. They perceive themselves as part of the leisure and tourism business, and have no inhibitions about charging – which they must do anyway, since they have a pressing need to generate revenue. This again means that they have to be as inventive as possible in their displays, that entertainment is an overriding consideration in their presentation, and that they have to be ruthless in extracting cash from the visitor. The need to satisfy business sponsors that they can draw the crowds is a contributing factor.

With respect to the development of the relationship between enterprise and heritage in the United Kingdom, Hewison observed that, from such a commercial perspective, 'a visit to a museum [would] ... become just another commodity. Laura Ashley and the V&A, Habitat and the Design Museum, [would] simply be competitors in the same vast cultural market-place' (1991). Similarly, in Wellington, New Zealand, the development of a new Museum of New Zealand on the waterfront was described as providing a 'cultural supermarket' to the visitor (Museum of New Zealand 1997). However, such a vision of stakeholder relationship is at odds with much current strategic thinking with respect to tourism and the development of visitor attractions. For example, Haywood (1997) has suggested that there is a shift in the existing paradigm of stakeholders as shareholders to an emerging paradigm in which key stakeholders are defined as visitors, employees, tourism enterprises and the community. Haywood's observation, which matches that contained in Chapter 1 regarding the nature and direction of strategic heritage management, is extremely significant, because it suggests that by focusing on stakeholders above and beyond the corporate and visitor sector we may well be able to embrace wider ideas of community and therefore be able to respond more effectively to the multiple demands that are placed on heritage management.

The emergence of 'other voices' in heritage management is often associated with the growing strength of indigenous peoples' movements in such countries as Australia, Canada, New Zealand and the United States. In addition, the development of cultural and ethnic tourism has also led to a direct commercial interest in ensuring that cultural heritage is both authentic and controlled by those whose heritage it is. However, the emergence of new stakeholders is not isolated to indigenous heritage. Indeed, in many urban areas, particularly those which have a substantial migrant and/or labour heritage, other histories are also finding their voice and recognition through the work of heritage managers. For example, the comments of Norkunas (1993) with reference to the heritage of Monterey, California, USA, applies to many other communities:

> Ethnic and class groups have not forgotten the totality of their own pasts. They have certainly preserved a sense of themselves through orally transmitted family stories, and through celebrations and rituals performed inside the group. But their systematic exclusion from official history fragments the community so that feelings of alienation and 'loss of soul' are experienced most deeply by minorities.
>
> What is needed is an acknowledgement that power must be shared with minority populations and that the prevailing perspective on the past must be altered. Humans' relationship with nature must be re-examined, especially as that relationship is portrayed in the tourist landscape. The changing economic structure of the community must be thoughtfully analyzed, especially as it relates to a changing national economy. The community must then have the courage to enact these new insights on the public landscapes of history and tourism.

The need for recognition of other approaches, attitudes and interests in heritage is not confined just to external stakeholders. One of the most important aspects of a stakeholder approach to heritage management is that heritage managers also need to recognise explicitly their own values and their effect on the manner in which they define, interpret and manage heritage. As Glasson *et al.* (1995) have described the situation, public definitions of heritage are still largely dominated by highly educated professionals with expertise in fine art, architecture, engineering, literature, music or design whose professional future is underpinned by generating an academic, problem-based, literature on the subject. This often places the professional at considerable remove from the visitor's need for succinct and graphic information although museums have, inevitably, responded to market needs.

The dominance of a particular set of values in heritage management is not isolated to the cultural sector alone. For example, there is substantial evidence to suggest that park managers 'are only recently competent at perceiving what experiences and values are important to tourists and visitors in general, and that they believe that visitors do not know what forests and parks are about, and that they are the expert [*sic*] who know best' (Wearing and New 1996). Magill (1988, 1992) suggests that this situation occurs at least in part as a result of the type of person who works in park management and the kind of training they are likely to receive. He proposes that, at least in the past, forest/national park service jobs tended to attract loners who preferred positions that lacked much social interaction. In addition, this situation may be perpetuated by the education and training they receive, which is often largely scientific rather than social sciences-based and people-oriented. As a result, according to Wearing and New (1996), 'they tend not to be good communicators, nor to understand park visitors (and therefore build a rather negative attitude toward them), and they approach their role as one in which it is their mission to educate visitors to their point of view.'

The challenge that has been set to heritage managers at an individual level in terms of reflection on individual attitudes also has clear implications for the way in which organisational cultures can be a factor in limiting ways of thinking about heritage management, ownership and interpretation. Indeed, for institutions, one of the implications of a strategic approach is the need to readjust to stakeholder demands. However, the dynamic nature of stakeholder relationships can be very challenging. For example, the running of *The Peopling of London* programme and exhibition by the Museum of London (see Case Study 7.2), which sought to improve links with ethnic and minority groups in the city, led to the asking of substantive questions about the museum's relationship with its various stakeholders and its interpretation of their heritage (Selwood, Schwarz and Merriman 1996, paraphrased below):

- Who is the museum seeking to represent in its displays and why?

- How can it represent them? (In particular, how can it represent the various constituencies of interest that exist within particular culturally or geographically determined communities, and how can it represent different constituencies of interest that exist across various culturally or geographically determined communities?)

- What might be the long-term effects of targeting certain groups within the community rather than others?

- What resources can the museum devote to any one group within the community, and what expectations might the museum have of the relationships generated by that?

- How can the museum maintain a relationship with its traditional audiences alongside its targeting of new audiences?

While being challenging to static notions of the nature of heritage management, responsiveness to stakeholders and the desire to communicate with them can also be extremely empowering, not only for the various owners of heritage but also for organisations and individual heritage managers, as opportunities are provided for new ways of responding and doing. For example, moves towards the implementation of an ecosystem management approach among US government natural resource management agencies has opened up new ways of thinking about heritage management. According to the US National Park Service (NPS) (1994):

> Ecosystem management is an awareness that resources and processes do not exist in isolation. Rather, living things exist in complex, interconnected systems within a broad landscape. These interconnected communities of living things, including humans, together with the dynamic physical environment, are termed ecosystems. The interconnected nature of ecosystems necessitates that NPS managers shift from a primarily park- or resource-specific approach to a wider systems and process approach to management.

An ecosystem management approach is therefore essentially collaborative and requires the development of partnerships with stakeholders:

> The NPS has complementary roles as a direct resource steward and as advisor to others through education and assistance programs. Both roles require active partnerships. Partnerships encompass two elements: formal partnership assistance programs such as heritage partnership programs ... and field-level partnerships, which are not necessarily served by a formal program. Ecosystem management is best understood as shared responsibility, and the NPS should collaborate, communicate, cooperate, and coordinate with partners. Partnerships should be pursued with all major players in each specific ecosystem, including other federal agencies, state and local governments, tribal entities, private interests, advocacy and interest groups, university and research groups, and the general public. Partners include critics. The NPS should actively develop ecosystem goals and work to achieve goals through consensus-building approaches. All stakeholders in a given ecosystem should participate in goal-setting and strategic planning to achieve the goals and should share accountability and benefits. Partnership efforts should begin at the local level, with ample public meetings and participation-building efforts. Trust, openness, cooperation, and accountability take time to develop, and the NPS should attempt to establish equity among partners.
> (National Park Service 1994)

Similarly, a seminar in Tucson, Arizona, in December 1995 on developing a framework for environmental stewardship of United States federal lands concluded: 'there is a need for broad involvement of all potential stakeholders in the resource assessment, planning, and decision making processes ... They should be prepared to participate in decision-making that trades one value for another, and to reach agreements with others that may often involve compromise' (Forest Service 1996). However, while the need for stakeholder involvement is increasingly regarded as an essential element of strategic heritage management and planning, managers also need to be able to identify stakeholders and understand the nature of the relationship that exists between heritage, management and stakeholders.

Stakeholder Audits

Stakeholder audits assist managers in understanding and confronting the complex web of relationships that surround heritage planning and management. As noted above, a stakeholder is any group, organisation or individual who can affect or is affected by the achievement of a heritage organisation's mission and objectives, and/or who has an interest in or is impacted by the management of a heritage resource. Understanding the aspirations of stakeholders through an audit process is another way of understanding and manipulating our external environment (Roberts and King 1989).

The present authors have identified seven steps in the undertaking of a stakeholder audit (Table 3.1). The audit is a useful tool for managers as it provides a framework for the identification of the various interests and values that affect the successful undertaking of organisational objectives (see Chapter 2). Managers and staff of heritage organisations often have a mental map of the individuals and groups that affect their work, and they act accordingly in their relations with them. Stakeholder analysis is a more systematic way of identifying the range of interests in a particular heritage issue or resource and their ability to affect management processes and actions. For example, step one of the audit (identification of stakeholders) can utilise the construction of a stakeholder map of all individuals and groups. Figure 3.1 provides a hypothetical example of the various stakeholders that may need to be considered in the overall management and planning of a national park.

Table 3.1 Steps in the stakeholder audit

1	Identification of stakeholders.
2	Determination of stakeholder interests, priorities and values.
3	Review of past behaviour of stakeholders to assess their strategies relating to issues and the likelihood of their forming coalitions with other stakeholders.
4	Estimation of the relative power (legal authority, political authority, resources, access to media) of each stakeholder and stakeholder coalitions.
5	Assessment of how well your organisation is currently meeting the needs and interests of stakeholders.
6	Formulation of new strategies, if necessary, to manage relations with stakeholders and stakeholder coalitions.
7	Evaluation of effectiveness of stakeholder management strategies, with revisions and readjustment of priorities in order to meet stakeholder interests.

Source: Hall and McArthur (1996c), after Roberts and King (1989)

Depending on the scale of analysis and the issue being examined, the number of stakeholders with which an organisation has to contend may be extremely large. For example, in terms of agreements with stakeholders, the United States Forest Service has developed more than 12,000 agreements with other agencies at all levels of government, universities and colleges, rural communities and organisations, and other outside interests (Unger 1994). In the state of Vermont alone, the Forest Service has working agreements with the Abenaki Nation, the Catamount Trail Association, The Nature Conservancy, Lyndon State College, the University of Vermont, the Vermont Association of Snow Travelers, the Ecotourism Society, the Green Mountain Club, Tree

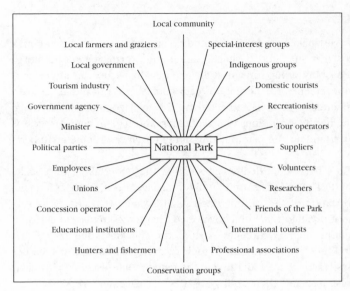

Figure 3.1
Hypothetical list
of stakeholders
in a national
park

Source: after
Hall and McArthur
(1996c)

Talk, Inc., the Vermont Department of Forests, Parks and Recreation, the Vermont Department of Fish and Wildlife, Division of Water Quality, County Sheriffs, and the Youth Conservation Corps, and numerous others stakeholders (Unger 1994).

Many stakeholders can be categorised as 'interest groups'. This term tends to be used interchangeably with the terms 'pressure group', 'lobby group', 'special interest group' or 'organised interests'. An interest group can best be defined as any association or organisation that makes a claim, either directly or indirectly, on government so as to influence policy without itself being willing to exercise the formal powers of government (Hall and Jenkins 1995). Several features of interest groups can be observed:

- Although they attempt to influence governments, interest groups do not seek government. Even if an interest group runs a single-issue candidate in an election, this is usually an attempt to gain further publicity for the group's cause.

- Not all activities of an interest group need be political.

- Interest groups will often seek to influence government policy indirectly by attempting to shape the demands that other groups and the general public make on government – e.g., through the conduct of public relations campaigns.

Interest groups operate at a number of different levels: international, national, regional and local. However, interest groups can also be classified along a continuum, according to their degree of institutionalisation, as producer groups, non-producer groups and single-interest groups (Hall and Jenkins 1995). Producer groups, such as business organisations (e.g., tourism or museum associations), labour organisations (e.g., unions and employee associations) and professional associations (e.g., professional heritage conservator organisations), tend to have a high level of organisational resources, a stable membership maintained by the ability of the group to provide benefits to members, the ability to gain access to government, and a high level of credibility in bargaining and negotiations with government, heritage organisations and other interest groups. In non-producer groups, institutionalisation has occurred on the basis of a common interest of continuing relevance to members, such as heritage and environmental conservation (e.g., the Australian Conservation Foundation, the National Trust in the United Kingdom, the Historic Places Trust in New Zealand and the Sierra Club in North America). Single-interest groups are at the other end of the continuum from producer groups and are characterised by their limited degree of organisational permanence, as they are likely to disappear once their interests have been achieved or have been rendered unattainable. This typically refers to locally based organisations that were established specifically to conserve a particular heritage resource, for example local campaigns to stop motorway development in rural areas in the United Kingdom.

The categorisation of interest groups can be extremely useful in understanding their resources, methods and effectiveness in the policy-making process. The continuing relevance of group objectives to their members and the corresponding degree of organisational permanence will clearly influence the resource base of groups and their continued visibility. For example, the Sierra Club in the United States grew from a small, local, hiking and nature appreciation society in the late nineteenth century and a regionally based nature preservation group in the early twentieth society, to what is now one of the most influential conservation organisations in the nation, whose concerns cover the full range of environmental issues. Similarly, the Wilderness Society in Australia developed from the Tasmanian Wilderness Society that was originally formed to stop the construction of the Franklin Dam in the early 1980s.

In addition to identifying stakeholders, it is also useful to note their positions on issues, their relationships with one another, and their relative strength in affecting the heritage management process. Such material can then serve as the basis for discussion amongst staff on how best to communicate with stakeholders and meet their interests. Another way of describing the relationship of various interests in heritage management is with respect to their attitudes and behaviour or involvement in heritage management. Figure 3.2 illustrates such a classification method with respect to attitudes towards visitation to a heritage site. On examination of the figure, readers

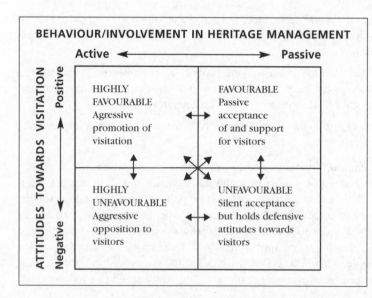

BEHAVIOUR/INVOLVEMENT IN HERITAGE MANAGEMENT

Active ◄──────────────► Passive

ATTITUDES TOWARDS VISITATION

Positive

| HIGHLY FAVOURABLE Agressive promotion of visitation | FAVOURABLE Passive acceptance of and support for visitors |
| HIGHLY UNFAVOURABLE Aggressive opposition to visitors | UNFAVOURABLE Silent acceptance but holds defensive attitudes towards visitors |

Negative

Figure 3.2 Classification of attitudes towards heritage issues

Source: after Bjorklund and Philbrick (1972)

may well be able to slot organisations and individuals into each category. However, it should be realised that much of the time of heritage managers is spent in dealing with those who are most strongly in favour of, or against, a particular policy or action. Yet, in the majority of cases, these stakeholders will only represent a relatively small proportion of the pool of stakeholders. The challenge for the heritage manager is therefore to try and accommodate not only the more extreme perspectives but also much of the middle range of interests and values into the heritage management process. Therefore, stakeholder input into the planning process is an important aspect of connecting aspirations analysis with the development of management strategies over the short and long terms.

Stakeholder Input into the Planning Process

As noted in Chapters 1 and 2, strategic heritage planning and management implies the development of an organisational and personal management philosophy that is responsive to stakeholder needs, values and interests. Sound objectives and on-going participation and involvement in terms relevant to the various stakeholders are the essence of an appropriate heritage management framework. Some of the key elements in such a process include (Hall and McArthur 1996c):

- acknowledging the 'ownership' of heritage by various stakeholder groups within the community;

- recognising that different stakeholder groups may have very different perceptions of the value of heritage and means of communicating those values;

- identifying key stakeholders and acknowledging that there is a range of reasons for stakeholder involvement, including a desire to assist constructively in heritage conservation, to express a value position or self-interest, or be kept informed;

- specifically identifying what is required from stakeholders, and what managers can be provided in return;

- ensuring that information provided to stakeholders is timely, comprehensive and comprehensible;

- developing individual strategies for each stakeholder that includes several opportunities for participation and the opportunity for 'feedback on the feedback process';

- ensuring that heritage organisations provide a commitment to act on the stakeholder's suggestions and views, if possible, given the context and constraints within which the organisation operates; and

- recognising continuous stakeholder involvement throughout the implementation of strategies.

Some of the techniques that are used to gain public input include: media advertisements, hotlines, trained personnel to deal with enquiries, public meetings (general and specific), focus group discussions, surveys, polling, and information sheets. Within each of these techniques there should be specific messages targeted to specific audiences in order to achieve clear goals and objectives. This may involve using different communication approaches and techniques for different stakeholders. For example, when indigenous peoples are to be involved in heritage planning and management it is essential to use meeting and planning procedures that are set in their terms, otherwise it is highly likely that the level of involvement in traditional Western participation exercises will be minimal and virtually meaningless (James 1991). Many of these techniques are discussed in greater detail in relation to community and visitor relationships in the following chapters. However, such techniques also apply in dealing with interest groups.

From Dissonance to Partnership: Identifying Stakeholder Relationships

For many managers, one of the greatest difficulties in dealing with stakeholders is coping with the range of values and interests that occur in relation to heritage. The interpretation and writing of history has always been replete with tension. However, as noted earlier in this chapter, the treatment of historical resources so as to create heritage products that convey specific notions of identity and their consequent commodification, in many cases for a commercial market, has heightened and extended these tensions. Tunbridge and Ashworth have described the tensions inherent in heritage as 'dissonance'. 'Much dissonance is trivial, ignorable or bearable; much is avoidable, often quite simply, and much that is not avoidable is certainly mitigable in various ways' (1996). Dealing with dissonance is a key feature of strategic heritage management. Similarly, Tunbridge and Ashworth (1996) argue for the adoption and development of active dissonance management techniques,

> involving the development of a coherent blueprint which anticipates the problem ... where possible, defuses it before confrontations develop; and simultaneously draws attention to the diversity of the potential heritage resource, as a basis for determining the particular broader or narrower strategy for its exploitation which might be deemed appropriate to particular circumstances.

As noted in Chapters 1 and 2, understanding stakeholders is integral to identifying problems of dissonance and therefore charting appropriate management strategies. However, it is important not only to identify and understand stakeholders but also to chart the relationships between them. The levels and degrees of interaction between stakeholders in heritage range from *ad hoc*, short-term, informal arrangements to highly structured formal and long-term relationships. Long (1997) recognises four distinct forms of positive relationships between stakeholders: cooperation, coordination, collaboration and partnership. The four categories can be conceived as moving along a continuum between 'loose' and 'tight' relationships. These forms therefore provide useful categories with which to analyse the nature of stakeholder linkage and also assist in the determination of the preferred nature of linkages in the light of organisational goals and objectives.

Cooperation refers to stakeholders working together towards a common end or resolving a shared problem (Case Study 3.1). Coordination is a more formal description of a stakeholder relationship in which two or more stakeholders create and/or use rules that have been established to deal collectively with their shared management problem or environment. Collaboration refers to the interaction of stakeholders with one another in the context of a common management problem or environment, in which they use a shared set of rules and/or structures in order to act or decide on issues which relate to that problem or environment. Partnership refers to a more formal relationship than either coordination or collaboration, in which there are typically 'added dimensions of cross-sectoral representation and the definition of geographical boundaries' (Long 1997).

Case Study 3.1

The Relationship between the Maori and Recreational Use of the
Whanganui River, New Zealand

Key Points:

- Taking the initiative to consult may be all that is required to reach consensus.
- Consultation is vital to the development of a cooperative relationship between stakeholders.
- Failure to consult may lead to conflict between interest groups.

The Whanganui River on the North Island of New Zealand has been a source of conflict between the traditional Maori inhabitants and Europeans since the first moves for the colonisation of the area by European settlers from the middle of the nineteenth century. To the Maori the river is a *taonga* (treasured possession) that provides for both physical and spiritual sustenance. For many Europeans the river has also served as a water supply and a recreation area, but it has also been used to dump effluent, assist with irrigation and has become a major source of tourism revenue for some operators because of the river's overall attractiveness.

In 1987 the upper reaches of the river and some of the surrounding lands were declared a national park. In ecological terms the park is highly significant because it contains some of the largest remaining tracts of lowland forest in New Zealand.

The renaissance of Maori culture since the early 1970s and the consequent assertion of rights under the Treaty of Waitangi have led to many Maori seeking to redress the misdeeds of the past, with particular emphasis on the return of lands that were wrongfully taken from them. In the case of the Whanganui they have taken both legal and direct action to ensure that their claims receive attention. For example, they have claimed a number of areas in both the national park – where they have occupied land in order to rebuild *marae* (meeting houses) on old *marae* sites – and the surrounding region. The re-assertion of Maori sovereignty over their land and water has also meant that Maori seek appropriate respect for their *taonga*. Where this has been lacking, aggrieved Maori have taken direct action. For example, in 1995 the Whanganui elder Niko Tangaroa and a group of Maori in nine canoes disrupted jetboat racing on the river, giving as reason that the organisers had not consulted them first.

In 1997 jetboat racers competing in the world championships on the Whanganui River agreed to follow protocols set down by the local *iwi* and *hapu* (tribe and subtribes). In October of that year sixty boats raced up the river as part of a six-day marathon on six North and South Island rivers.

Niko Tangaroa said the marathon's organisers had agreed to respect the cultural, spiritual and physical aspects of the river: they would keep noise levels down and take care not to cause erosion of the banks and not to spill oil. 'This time they approached us, so we set out these protocols. They've had a good attitude, the talks have been very positive' (Morgan 1997).

The Jet Boat River Racing Association's president, Robert Thompson, said the consultation had been 'pretty straightforward. We are very happy to respect the things that are important to them. A lot of what they asked we already had in place.' According to Thompson, there was 'not even a suggestion' that the cooperation of the Maori should be paid for; 'In fact I am sure they would be insulted if money was offered.' He went on to say:

> I am sure the Niko Tangaroa portrayed on TV is a result of media manipulation. We have had several meetings. You lay your cards on the table, say this is your problem, and he lays his cards down and says this is what we've got to deal with, and you just work through it.
>
> What could be better? This way we all win. (Morgan 1997)

Waddock (1991) identified three different forms of partnership: programmatic, federational and systemic.

A *programmatic partnership* is a technical or an operational partnership that tends to be short-term and focused on products or outputs – e.g., the joint provision of staff by stakeholders.

A *federational partnership* is a partnership of organisations according to sectoral and/or regional interests and problems. According to Long (1997), such a partnership 'tends to adopt a proactive stance towards coalition building, issue identification and purpose formulation and in consequence is a more complex arrangement than in programmatic partnerships'. Examples include museum federations and associations which act to lobby government, and conservation groups which join forces over a regional environmental issue.

A *systemic partnership* is concerned with issues of process and outcomes in the overall heritage management system rather than just products or outputs. The emphasis is also geared more towards benefits to the system overall rather than to individual stakeholders. The ecosystem management approach that is being adopted by federal resource management agencies in the United States, discussed above, is an example of such a partnership.

One area of heritage management where the importance of partnership development has been given greater recognition concerns the relationship between heritage managers and indigenous peoples, especially in national parks. Often under colonial forms of national park conservation, indigenous peoples were typically regarded as unnatural and were excluded from the parks. Apart from the enormous environmental impact such policies had, because of the removal of traditional hunting and harvesting activities that had become an integral part of ecosystem dynamics such measures also had major economic, cultural and dietary effects on the traditional landowners.

Many protected areas around the world are increasingly pressured by growing populations of local people who are forced to increase their use of their immediate environment, through such measures as poaching, in order to improve their condition or even just survive. Not surprisingly, national parks were typically seen by indigenous people as an unnatural, imposed structure, which divided them from what was rightly their land. An example of a positive response to this type of situation, which is common in many African, Asian and South American countries, comes from South Africa.

For several years, the Natal Parks Board has actively sought to develop a dynamic neighbour relations policy with the objective of transforming previously neutral or even negative attitudes into healthy, mutually beneficial relationships. This policy has progressed far beyond the Board's former, more traditional, approach of providing neighbours with access to natural resources, such as wood and thatch harvested in protected areas, on an *ad hoc* basis. Today the Natal Parks Board's Neighbour Relations Policy aims to develop joint participation in conservation programmes and appropriate shared responsibilities between the Board itself and the communities whose homes are adjacent to protected areas. The key elements of the Board's policies are illustrated in Table 3.2.

In addition to the four forms of relationship identified by Long (1997), a fifth form may be offered, that of non-cooperation. Although such a relationship is negative, it is still a relationship that implies interaction between stakeholders. Indeed, in some cases non-cooperation may be a deliberate strategy by a stakeholder to encourage other stakeholders to reinterpret or change their definitions of structures, rules and problems before a more positive relationship can be developed between parties. What is clearly important in the development of positive relationships between stakeholders is the determination of common ground between the parties. From such a basis further negotiation, compromise and agreement, even if only to disagree, can be reached.

Table 3.2 Key elements of the Natal Parks Board's neighbour relations policy

Neighbour Liaison Forums

To encourage participation in protected area management and planning, a network of Neighbour Liaison Forums has been set up to:

- resolve issues relating to problem animals;
- provide controlled free access to protected areas; and to
- formalise and honour mutual commitments.

These forums comprise leaders and members of local communities, as well as Natal Parks Board field staff at various Board stations. The Board's participation is generally to facilitate the achievement of objectives through discussion, the accent being on empowerment of community members themselves.

Economic and social development

To help improve the standards of living among deprived rural communities on the borders of protected areas, the Board strives to promote their economic and social development by:

- helping to identify and address basic social needs;
- encouraging preferential employment;
- involving local entrepreneurs;
- developing surrounding wildlife resource areas; and
- undertaking internal staff training in skills required for neighbour relations projects.

Enhancing environmental awareness

In order to create a greater understanding of the need for sound environmental use and the role of natural ecosystems, the Board is committed to assisting in the development of environmental awareness, education and interpretation programmes.

Source: Natal Parks Board (nd)

The set of relationships between stakeholders, as throughout the heritage management system itself, is highly dynamic. Relationships change over time and problems. Case Study 3.2 on the Malpai Borderlands Group provides a good example of how the collaboration between stakeholders over the problem of fire management in a range ecology grew into a partnership with individual and systemic benefits. It is also useful to note that relationships change according to different levels of organisations and different divisions or jurisdictions. For example, within federal systems it is not unusual for different levels of government to be in conflict over heritage policy while at the operational level staff continue to maintain close contact and exchange information. Organisational stakeholders should therefore be seen not just as unitary wholes but also, where applicable to certain issues and problems, as a series of individual stakeholders. Indeed, as Tunbridge and Ashworth (1996) observed with respect to interest groups in heritage management, 'The implication that such interest groups may consist only of unrepresentative activists is not only wildly "incorrect" to the supposed orthodoxy of the 1990s but raises a serious issue for us: the greatest heritage dissonance applicable to these groups may be internal to their supposed memberships.'

Case Study 3.2
The Malpai Borderlands Group, New Mexico and Arizona, USA

Key points:

- Stakeholder partnerships are best initiated through establishing some sort of common ground.

- Stakeholder relationships can change over time, requiring flexible management systems.

- Systemic partnerships operate as effective tools to deal with problems of ecosystem management.

> From the beginning, we have been committed to bridge-building and to creating a different approach to working with public land agencies and private property owners, giving them an equal role in protecting the landscapes we all have a stake in. (Malpai Borderlands Group Status Report, December, 1994 in Malpai Borderlands Group 1995)

In southern New Mexico and Arizona, private landowners and public land management agencies are working together in the development and implementation of a natural resource management plan on approximately one million acres (approximately 400,000 hectares) of land on the border between the United States and Mexico. The land is owned by a number of bodies, including thirty-six private landowners, the Animas Foundation, the Forest Service, the Bureau of Land Management, and the states of New Mexico and Arizona. Leadership for the project comes from the Malpai Borderlands Group, which includes the private landowners, The Nature Conservancy, the Animas Foundation, the Hidalgo Soil and Water Conservation District in New Mexico, and the Whitewater Draw Natural Resources Conservation District in Arizona. The Natural Resources Conservation Service (NRCS) and the Forest Service have each assigned full-time staff to provide technical assistance for the project.

The private landowners and other participants in the Malpai Borderlands Group were originally drawn together through a common recognition of the ecological importance of fire in the borderland ecosystems in environmental conservation, economic and cultural terms. Using this commonality as a starting-point, the Group has evolved to develop a more comprehensive agenda. The Group's goal is:

> To preserve and maintain the natural processes that create and protect a healthy, unfragmented landscape to support a diverse, flourishing community of human, plant, and animal life in the borderlands region. Together we will accomplish our goal by working to encourage profitable ranching and other traditional livelihoods which will sustain the open space nature of our land for generations to come.
> (Malpai Borderlands Group 1995)

One example of actions undertaken by the Malpai Borderlands Group is a 'Grass Bank Program', which allows ranchers in the Group to make grass on one ranch available for grazing by another rancher's livestock, thereby increasing ranchers' management options, particularly in terms of resting pastures when needed. In return, the rancher who utilises grass on the other ranch agrees through a conservation easement to not subdivide or develop his land for housing.

The work of the Malpai Borderlands Group is an example of how private landowners can work with public agencies to achieve various economic, social and environmental goals, at both local community and national levels. One of the interest aspects of the Group is that there is a realisation by its members that a static environmental management plan is not the answer to the problems that the region faces. Instead, all are involved in the development of long-term participatory partnerships that provide for the exchange of knowledge and that provide a capacity to adjust to changing socio-economic, political, and environmental conditions by the various parties involved.

Understanding and Integrating Stakeholders: Conclusions

One of the essential ingredients of a strategic approach to heritage management is the recognition of the role that stakeholders have in the management task. Stakeholders set definitions of quality that managers work towards (Chapter 1), directly influence all aspects of the management and planning process (Chapter 2), and increasingly make demands with respect not only to policy settings but also access and ownership of their heritage (see above). However, more traditional resource-focused approaches to heritage management have only given passing reference to the role that stakeholders have in the day-to-day reality of managing heritage.

This chapter has provided an introduction to the role that stakeholders play in heritage management and the need for greater reflection on their roles, interests and values with respect to heritage. It has also suggested that managers need to reflect on their own values and interests, as they too are stakeholders who also have the great responsibility of mediating and reconciling the range of stakeholder interests. The chapter has also identified a process by which stakeholders can be audited so that managerial relationships can be clearly laid out and addressed. The particular role and characteristics of interest groups were also discussed. Finally, the chapter has addressed the nature of relationships between various stakeholders. The identification of the different types of relationship between stakeholders is important, as it provides a basis that can help managers to determine the likelihood of obtaining certain desired results from relationships with stakeholders and the strategies and techniques that may improve relationships.

It is to the realm of strategies and techniques that this book will now turn, with reference to two major categories of stakeholder in heritage management – the community and the visitor. Chapter 4 looks at understanding and working with the community, an area that until recently has not received the attention it deserves in heritage management. Yet such a focus is crucial in terms of ideas of ownership of heritage. As Glasson *et al.* (1995) observed, 'in identifying and designing revised or new heritage "experiences" the local population upon whom such proposals will impact must be considered, not only because of the physical inconveniences which may result in the short or long term, but because it is their local identity which is being manipulated.'

CHAPTER 4

Involving the Community

I still remember standing at the base of a waterfall in Tasmania with two national parks staff. We had been discussing various options for upgrading a walking trail, and my suggestions had been based on extensive visitor research and discussions with various special interest groups. Their body language suggested they were unhappy with the feedback and ideas I was sharing with them. In the end they turned to me and said 'Of course, it's our land, and we're responsible for it. So at the end of the day, it will be us that make the decisions.' Thankfully, this attitude seems to have retreated to the poorly funded, remote sites and will continue to dissipate with the pressures for internal and external reform.

Introduction

There are still heritage managers in the field who consider that their supporting legislation, their scientific training and their years of fighting fires, building tracks and restoring buildings gives them the responsibility, and perhaps the right, to make all the critical decisions. Heritage managers need to understand the community because it is the community that owns the heritage. The community may not always be aware that its members are stakeholders, but they nonetheless provide the support required to look after heritage. Every day the communities supply political support through its general endorsement of heritage management and heritage managers. The most obvious endorsement of this support comes via direct and indirect taxation contributions, which fund the substantial expenses associated with heritage management. Other major endorsements come indirectly through the acceptance of the opportunity costs associated with alternative uses of a heritage resource.

The level of community support for heritage management is to a certain extent dependent upon the community's confidence in current systems and outcomes. In the past there has been greater compatibility between the roles of technical experts and the public in decisions about heritage management. However, the assumed compatibility between the traditions of democratic participation and technical expertise has now been called into question. As citizens have frequently become more polarised and adversarial in their politics, and experts have often been bought by the highest bidder, the objectivity of both has been put in doubt. The result has been a growing distrust by many citizens of scientific experts and vice versa (De Sario 1987). The confidence of a community is generated through some degree of involvement in heritage management and through the degree of responsiveness by heritage managers to this involvement, which may range from being generally informed to assisting in decision-making. Consequently, those sectors of the community which provide the greatest support for heritage management and heritage managers are those which:

- have gained positive and enriching experiences from heritage;
- share similar values to those involved in the heritage management process;

- have witnessed constructive outcomes from their input into the heritage management process; and

- derive the greatest personal benefits from the current form of heritage management.

Therefore, support can be maximised by providing high-quality visitor experiences, rich insights into heritage, and genuine involvement in heritage management.

For anyone who is still not swayed by the argument above, there is of course one other very practical reason for understanding the community. It is the community that represents both actual and potential visitors. Visitors form the basis of the heritage management paradox (see Case Study 4.1). We need to understand visitors to understand how we can manage the paradox. Understanding these people before they become visitors will enable a better understanding of them as visitors. The earlier we can understand the values and expectations of people, the earlier we can respond to them. The earlier we respond to them, the more effective we can be in managing heritage. This argument is dealt with more fully in Chapter 5.

Case Study 4.1
The Tarahumara Indians in Mexico's Copper Canyon

Key points:

- A lack of community involvement disempowers people.

- A lack of community involvement creates conflict between different sectors of the community.

- A lack of community involvement can reduce the integrity of a culture.

The Copper Canyon in central Mexico is a natural feature three times the size of the Grand Canyon. It is home to 40,000 Tarahumara Indians (Plate 4.1). These people have a rich and long history that represents one of the few remaining traditional cultures still being practised in Mexico. The Copper Canyon has a high biodiversity of native plants, many of which are used by the Indians for medicinal purposes.

The Mexican government has invested significant funds into developing the Copper Canyon. The train trip from the coastal farmlands into the canyon is a spectacular experience. The air-conditioned tourist train stops only briefly at stations and does not allow locals to sell produce to passengers. The economy-class train is not marketed to tourists, though those who discover it spend the ticket savings on local food and crafts.

The Tarahumara Indians rarely have much input into the development of tourism or other industries in their region. A poor level of education prevents them from expressing their views effectively where major industrial development is concerned. The Mexican government and World Bank have been undertaking a US$91 million development project that will, in the words of the World Bank Fact Sheet, 'affect a small but significant part of the temperate forests'. Those lobbying against the project claimed that the logging plan failed to consider the region's rich biodiversity, thin soil, steep terrain and heavy seasonal rains. As an afterthought, the lobbyists mentioned that there had been little or no input from the Tarahumara Indians.

Despite their culture being used as part of the marketed product of the Copper Canyon, the Tarahumara Indians fail to receive a fair economic distribution from tourism. Most of the tours in the Copper Canyon, particularly the ecotours, are dominated financially and physically by Americans. Therefore, when considering the impact of a development, government planners come to Americans for comment. The lack of cooperation between operators and the

Plate 4.1 Tarahumara Indians in Mexico's Copper Canyon

Tarahumara Indians again restricts the Indians from becoming involved. For example, when they enter the Canyon, visitors are approached to pay an entrance fee that the Tarahumara Indians claim is reinvested in the upgrading of walking trails. However, Mexican tour guides claim that the fee is a scam and tell tourists not to pay the Tarahumara Indians.

Chapters 3, 5 and 7 cover the process and methods by which the community and markets such as visitors may be identified. This chapter will focus on how to involve the community in heritage management. For this purpose, the term community has been defined as 'a social group of any size whose members reside in a specific locality, share government, and have a cultural and historical heritage' (Macquarie University 1991). It can be noted that this definition implies a more defined market than 'the general public', which may now be seen as derogatory in its generalisation. This change reflects a cultural shift to deal with people as individuals with distinctive, yet related, values and needs that must be acknowledged, understood and worked with cooperatively. This cultural shift from general public to individuals forms the basis for the rest of this chapter.

Community Involvement

The involvement of the community has, in principle, become an integral component of planning and decision-making. In developed countries consulting the community is now central to most public sector management practices (Kennedy 1993a; Environment Protection Agency 1996; Thomas 1996). Some of the reasons for involving the community are to:

- increase the quality of planning;
- reduce the likelihood of conflict;
- conserve time and costs;

- ensure that sound plans remain intact over time;
- enhance a general sense of community;
- increase the community's ownership of its heritage; and
- enhance the community's trust in heritage management.

These reasons are expanded on in Table 4.1.

Kennedy (1993a) took a more methodological approach to determining reasons for involving the community. She suggested that these reasons could be broken into: the giving of information; the receiving of information; the sharing of information; and participating in decision-making. The progression from the first to the last of these methodological reasons indicates that participatory decision-making is the purest form of community involvement because it generates the greatest understanding, support and input into the decision-making process (as outlined in Table 4.2). Community consultation generally fits into the sharing rather than participatory form of involvement. Consultation will allow people some influence on the assumptions and decisions to be made but is not as comprehensive as true participation, where people are involved from so early on that they fully understand how assumptions were identified and decisions reached.

Moves to establish the involvement of the community in heritage management began in the 1960s, developed in the 1970s and became common in the early 1980s. In the 1960s there was tacit recognition that heritage decisions involved public value judgements. Later in the decade this recognition developed into specific requirements. For example, the US's National Environmental Policy Act of 1969 required analysis and disclosure to the public of the environmental effects of every major decision made by the United States federal government that affected the environment (Daniels *et al.* 1996). In the 1970s guidelines and then regulations were produced that resulted by the late 1970s in public involvement becoming a central part of the analysis of all significant federal natural resource decisions.

However, community involvement in heritage management generally remains immature in its development and accountability. After an extensive review of the literature Daniels *et al.* (1996) found a 'generally unimpressive application of public participation principles and low levels of public satisfaction ... there has been surprisingly little progress over the last 20 years'. The lack of progress has not been so much in the techniques for involvement as in the culture in which they are applied. Community-driven reforms can only really begin to occur when heritage managers shift the involvement focus from the sharing of information to the sharing of decision-making. The narrow scope of community involvement currently restricts the community's input to tactical rather than strategic input. The determination of heritage values is largely based on scientific constructs that keep other values held by the community out of the process (see Chapter 3). There is still some way to go before genuine participatory decision-making is achieved. Until this occurs, fundamental reforms to heritage management will be limited in scope.

Principles for Community Involvement

It is vital to decide why the community should be involved before deciding how to involve it. In deciding why, it is useful to consider some principles that embody true community involvement. The degree to which these principles are recognised, understood and adopted tends to suggest the underlying agenda for involvement in the

Table 4.1 Underlying reasons for involving the community

Reason for involvement	Explanation
Increase quality of planning	There is a wealth of skill and experience within any community waiting to be tapped. Heritage managers need fresh input to be as creative and innovative as possible. The combination of perspectives and ideas can be extremely productive, improving management efficiency and effectiveness
Reduce likelihood of conflict	Conflict is most likely to occur when individuals are denied freedom of expression and lack accurate information needed to be rational. Involving people from the outset and sharing information diffuse the likelihood of conflict or focus the conflict on more specific issues that can be resolved
Conserve time and costs	Inadequate consultation can lead to conflict, which can in turn slow down the decision-making process. This can impose major human and financial costs on programmes and developments ready to be implemented. Sound involvement will thus improve efficiency and effectiveness of heritage management
Ensure that sound plans remain intact over time to the medium- to long term	Heritage managers come and go, leaving their policies, plans and programmes open to renegotiation, alteration or cessation. Effective consultation can shore up sufficient support to continue an initiative into the medium- to long term
Enhance general sense of community	Involvement can act as a catalyst to bring together and bond a community. This in turn helps it to define common interests that can lead to the development and refinement of a community culture
Increase community's ownership of its heritage	Involvement exposes communities to the notion that heritage is being looked after for their benefit and that heritage needs to be owned, otherwise it will not be looked after and benefits will not be forthcoming
Enhance community's trust in heritage management	The enormous trust the community places with heritage management is always subject to performance, particularly in relation to issues. This trust can be topped up with genuine consultation

Table 4.2 Tactical reasons to consult the community

Technique	Tactical reason
Give information	• To stimulate the consultative process • To check and refine throughout the consultative process • To inform that a decision has been made at the conclusion of the planning, i.e. once the policy, plan or programme has reached an operational stage
Receive information	• To stimulate the planning process • To develop the consultative parameters and techniques • To obtain feedback on existing and preferred situations
Share information	• To generate greater insights from the giving and sharing of information • To develop a degree of trust and support among participants • To develop some involvement in the planning or operating environment
Participate in decision-making	• To further enhance the results of sharing information • To develop long-term fundamental support and involvement in the planning, operating and reviewing environment

first place. Some principles for involving the community are outlined in Table 4.3.
A set of practically oriented principles suggested by Kennedy (1993a) include:

- respect the views of all parties;
- be willing to listen;
- seek points of agreement;
- work creatively through points of disagreement;
- work towards the best option for all parties, rather than just a compromise; and
- ensure each party gains something meaningful from each transaction.

Perhaps the most important principle in effective consultation is sound planning
that is designed to achieve all of the principles listed above.

Table 4.3 Principles of community involvement

Principle	Explanation
Involve the public early and throughout the process	People should be involved as soon as possible, rather than reviewing decisions already made. Involvement should also include the monitoring and evaluation aspects of heritage management
Involve people in policies as well as projects	Policies drive the more tactical planning and therefore are the most essential element for community input
Public involvement should not be limited to legislative obligations	Voluntarily taking steps to involve the community in decision-making is likely to generate more positive and constructive responses than involvement through obligation
Enshrine community involvement into organisational culture	Continuing commitment to community involvement needs to come from all levels of heritage management. This helps to demonstrate that the initiative and the implementation of the input is genuine. The organisation also needs to be able to demonstrate past benefits of involvement to all those concerned
Present the principles for involvement to the community at the first stage of involvement	When people understand the principles and rationale for community involvement they can shape realistic expectations and are more likely to be satisfied with the final result
Ensure adequate human resources are available before commencing	Involving the community requires people with sound interpersonal and communication skills, and people with personalities that are friendly, non-confrontational, good listeners
Present the involvement process in context with the wider planning and management process	People like to know the context and stage in which their involvement fits into the broader scheme of things
Select an involvement technique that reflects the objectives of community involvement and the type of people required to be involved	No one technique suits all situations. Different techniques should be selected to meet different needs. In addition, any involvement programme should have additional techniques on stand-by, should the situation change
Determine a target audience, but be prepared to involve any interested party	Targeting particular groups will help in selecting the most appropriate technique and will maximise the positive outcomes from the initiative. Nonetheless, some flexibility should be maintained to accommodate others who have a desire to be involved

Planning Steps to Generating an Initiative for Community Involvement

There are a number of crucial steps in planning an initiative towards community involvement. These include:

- identifying the issue or problem;
- defining the objectives for involving the community;
- identifying key stakeholders for targeting;
- selecting techniques according to objectives and stakeholders;
- maximising the ability of stakeholders to participate;
- determining the timetable and resources available;
- checking the decisions made against original objectives;
- determining participant feedback mechanism(s);
- implementing the techniques; and
- evaluating the process.

These steps are further explained in Table 4.4.

Identifying the issue or problem and defining the objectives for involving the community are the most crucial steps. Several models have been created to avoid subjective assessment (Daniels *et al.* 1996; also note the ecosystem management approach discussed in Chapter 3). For example, the Vroom–Yetton Model offers some general guidance regarding the appropriateness and type of broad approach to involvement that should be used (Thomas 1996). The Vroom-Yetton Model requires a yes or no response to seven sequential questions about the problem that has arisen. Answering the questions results in one of five scenarios. The model has been presented as a dichotomous key in Figure 4.1. The first scenario implies that management makes the decision alone without community involvement (an autonomous managerial decision). The second scenario implies that management seeks input from the public but makes the decision alone (modified autonomous managerial decision). The third scenario has management sharing the problems separately with segments of the community, getting ideas and suggestions and then making a decision that reflects the influence of the groups (segmented community consultation). The fourth scenario has management sharing the problem with the public as a single assembled group, getting ideas and suggestions and then making a decision that reflects the influence of the groups (unitary community consultation). The fifth and final scenario involves management and the community sharing the problem and the solution (community decision).

The objectives for community involvement set the context for what can be termed 'the rules of the game'. These 'rules' guide the way the input is taken on board and processed. They can state explicitly the 'givens' or bottom line in the planning framework. For example, community input into the Plan of Management for Australia's Wet Tropics World Heritage Area commenced with a set of six guiding principles covering land management and seven guiding principles covering community relations (Wet Tropics Management Authority 1995). The principles served as 'training wheels' while more elaborate management objectives were crafted.

Another variation on providing 'rules of the game' is to provide criteria against which input will be assessed. The assessment criteria for submissions can cover what is required for comment to be considered, adopted or rejected. For example,

Table 4.4 Planning a community involvement process

Steps	Questions to consider
Develop a 'first cut' of the issue or problem	• What is the nature and origin of the issue? • What are the potential contentious issues? • What are the potential options? • Are there any genuinely non-negotiable issues?
Define the objectives for involving the community	• What can be achieved by involving the community? • Why is the initiative occurring at this point in time? • What sort of criteria could be monitored to evaluate the initiative?
Identify key stakeholders for targeting	• Who should be involved and who must be involved? • Do different sectors have different involvement expectations or capabilities? • Do different sectors reflect different experiences with involvement? • Are any previous involvement experiences likely to help or hinder this initiative? • What sort of agendas might each sector have and how is this likely to be manifested?
Select techniques according to objectives and stakeholders	• What involvement techniques are available? • Which techniques best reflect the objectives of the initiative? • Which techniques are likely to work with the various stakeholders? • Which techniques can be evaluated against the objectives?
Maximise the ability of stakeholders to participate	• What are the constraints upon stakeholders to effective participation, e.g. timing, cultural, comprehension and language impediments, venue access? • What can be done to reduce the constraints? • What are the most appropriate methods to advise participants of the initiative? • What are the most appropriate methods to prepare participants for the technique?
Determine the timetable and resources available	• Is the initiative a one-off or on-going? • Is the timetable realistic? • What resources and personnel are required? • Is there a need for staff training or consultants? • Have funds been allocated to meet anticipated costs? • Have staff and funds been allocated to evaluate the initiative?
Check the decisions made against original objectives	• Are the desired outcomes clear and defensible? • Do the target sectors, techniques and resource outlays reflect the objectives? • Are participants likely to want to redefine the issue or problem? • What sort of results are likely to be achieved?
Determine participant feedback mechanism(s)	• How will the outcomes of the initiative be conveyed to participants and other stakeholders?
Implement the techniques	• How can the techniques be improved as they are implemented? • How can the satisfaction of participants be improved further? • Can participants rework the problem or issue (if they feel it is warranted)?
Evaluate the process	• How do the outcomes compare with the objectives? • How do the outcomes compare with previous involvement initiatives? • Did the initiative attract a representative sample of those targeted? • What feedback on the initiative was gained from participants? • What improvements could have been made to the initiative, e.g., selection of stakeholders, choice of technique, timing and staffing? • How will the results of the evaluation be recorded and utilised in subsequent initiatives?

Source: adapted from Kennedy (1993b)

Figure 4.1 Dichotomous key for determining nature of community involvement

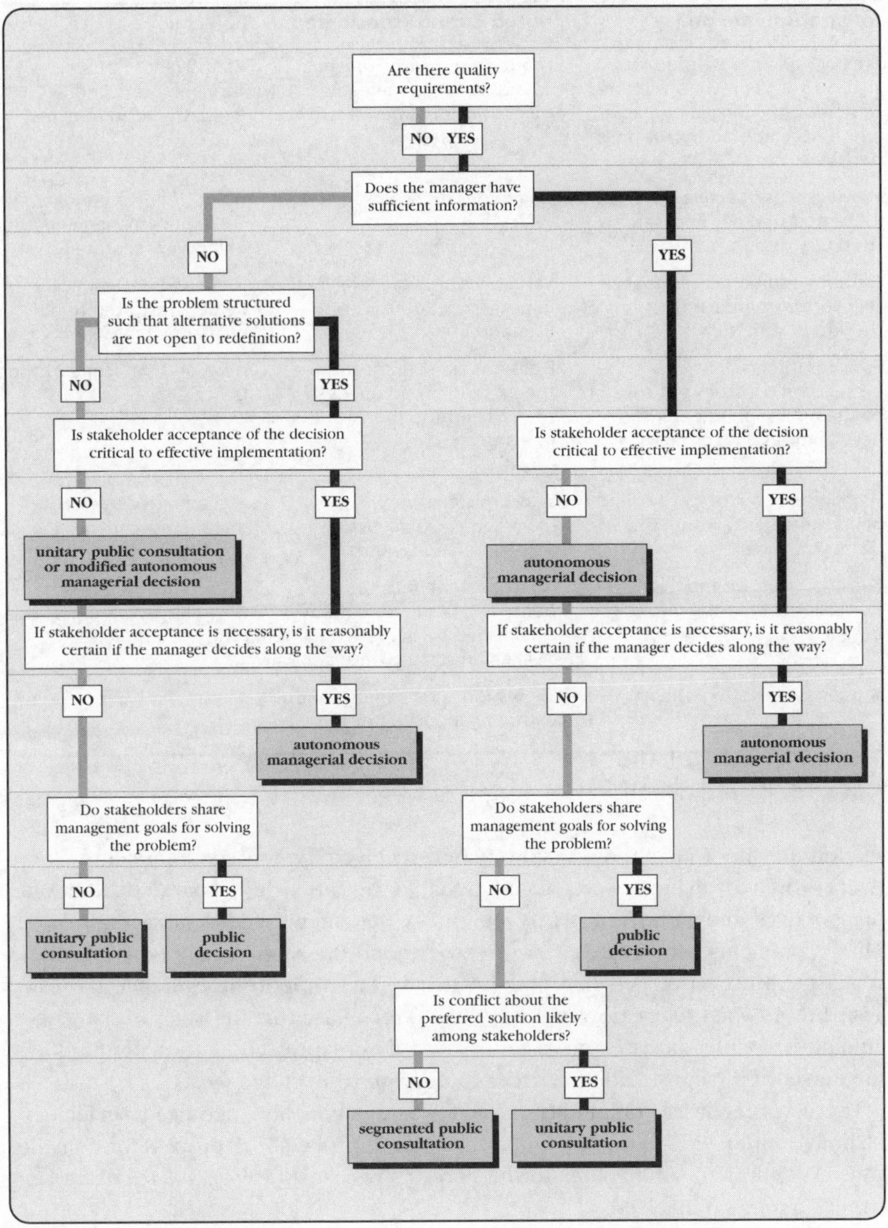

Are there quality requirements?

NO   YES

Does the manager have sufficient information?

NO   YES

Is the problem structured such that alternative solutions are not open to redefinition?

NO   YES

Is stakeholder acceptance of the decision critical to effective implementation?

NO   YES

unitary public consultation or modified autonomous managerial decision

If stakeholder acceptance is necessary, is it reasonably certain if the manager decides along the way?

NO   YES

autonomous managerial decision

Do stakeholders share management goals for solving the problem?

NO   YES

unitary public consultation

public decision

Is stakeholder acceptance of the decision critical to effective implementation?

NO   YES

autonomous managerial decision

If stakeholder acceptance is necessary, is it reasonably certain if the manager decides along the way?

NO   YES

autonomous managerial decision

Do stakeholders share management goals for solving the problem?

NO   YES

public decision

Is conflict about the preferred solution likely among stakeholders?

NO   YES

segmented public consultation

unitary public consultation

Source: adapted from Thomas 1996

submissions for a discussion paper on policy for tourism in Tasmania's State Forests were assessed using the criteria outlined in Table 4.5. Submissions that were given the highest consideration incorporated the input of a representative proportion of any interest group demonstrating a stake in tourism within state forest, while submissions that did not provide any comment on options for dealing with policy issues were considered as a neutral response. An example of the subsequent reporting generated from this process illustrates its superior accountability. The background

Table 4.5 Criteria for assessing submissions for tourism policy

Integration into policy	Noted but not considered	Rejected
Provides additional information that was not known at the time of writing the discussion paper, which has implications for policy decisions	Is out of line with Forestry Tasmania's management objectives for state forest	Contravenes Forestry Tasmania's existing legislative requirements
Provides a perspective on issues presented that has implications for policy decisions	Is not considered cost-effective	Is out of line with Forestry Tasmania's management objectives for state forest
Provides additional information that further clarifies the status of tourism in state forest	Stimulates unavoidable impacts upon other forest uses and users	Is queried and cannot be demonstrated to be factual by the writer
Provides information or a perspective on issues not covered by the discussion paper, which have implications for policy decisions	Does not assist in meeting the existing broad needs of tourists and the tourist industry	Is beyond the scope of the policy
Highlights a lack of clarity in policy statements within the discussion paper	Is inconsistent with management objectives for adjoining land tenures	Is adequately dealt with in the discussion paper
Corrects errors or improves expression within the discussion paper	Is inconsistent with tourism policy and planning initiatives established by the federal and Tasmanian state government	Represents the minority view and lacks supporting evidence
Supports an existing option	Expression is personal opinion without supporting evidence	

Source: after Forestry Tasmania (1994a)

section of the tourism discussion paper received twenty-six comments, some twenty-three of which were accommodated because they provided additional perspectives and improved clarity on policy statements and general expression. Three comments were rejected: two were beyond the scope of the policy and one was an expression of personal opinion that lacked supporting evidence (Forestry Tasmania 1994a, 1994c). However, it is vital to recognise that the 'rules of the game', guiding principles or assessment criteria must be expressed to the community at the outset of the consultation in order to develop respect and trust.

The assessment of community input for integration into heritage management planning requires extreme care and a transparent process. The process for collating and responding to submissions to the Forestry Tasmania (1994a, 1994c) discussion paper on tourism involved:

- undertaking a general review of all submissions;
- establishing criteria for assessment and codes for designating the rationale for each response;
- preparing a matrix to accommodate submissions (submission writer on vertical axis, structure of document – i.e. policy issues – on horizontal axis);
- testing a representative sample of submissions against criteria;
- modifying criteria and codes if unrepresentative of submissions;
- entering summarised submissions into the matrix;

- reviewing submissions to gain an overall perspective on each policy issue, as well as any similarities or differences in the perspectives of each stakeholder;

- developing the first draft of a policy using the review;

- re-assessing submissions to determine the extent to which each one was accommodated within the draft (allocating response code to each accordingly);

- seeking comment on draft from key stakeholders and refining policy to final draft; and

- preparing a summary of the overall treatment of submissions for each component of the discussion paper.

This planning example greatly enhanced the accountability of the initiative and organisation and led to a far more productive on-going relationship with stakeholders (Forestry Tasmania 1995).

Community Involvement Techniques

There are a number of techniques for consulting with the community. This chapter will address briefly some of those which are used most regularly but will focus on those of a more participatory nature.

Draft Documents (Plans and Policies)

One of the most conventional forms of community consultation is to take the planning internally to a state of near completion, then present it for comment as a draft document. The community is then invited to read the document and prepare some form of submission in response. This approach has been the mainstay of the resource-based approach to heritage management and is frequently used for plans of management and development. This level of advancement provides plenty of 'meat' on which to chew, but limits significantly the degree to which it can be 'chewed'. The laws of planning authority are maintained within the heritage management organisation by virtue of limiting the range and nature of input that can be made. Conceptually, this is done by ensuring that input is focused on the details of implementation rather than on the policy. For example, the heritage manager focuses on limiting access to a particular activity at a given site, rather than determining which activities may be appropriate in the first instance. Specific techniques for maintaining control have been achieved by making sure the document:

- is only available from limited sources, in limited numbers, or at a cost (ensuring only very interested persons access copies);

- overwhelms the reader using extensive amounts of background information, underpinning concepts and technical terms (subliminally suggesting the author knows what they are talking about and can thus be trusted);

- is fairly dry and dull (ensuring the reader never gets through the document to make overall comments);

- does not outline the context in which input will be judged (allowing personal values of the planner to generate the final judgements); and

- does not publish how input was acted upon (preventing the opportunity for external review of the consultative process).

Input to this form of consultation thus comes in limited supply and rarely makes an impact into real shifts in policy and decision-making.

Discussion Papers

Discussion papers tend to take one step back from draft plans, policies or proposals in that they do not presume to know the most appropriate direction to take. Instead, they set up context, an issue for consideration and, sometimes, a range of solutions to consider. This approach provides the community with some power through choice between options. Of course, the choice may be as narrow and preconceived as is imaginable, but it is nonetheless choice. Choosing and framing the questions are the most critical parts of preparing a discussion paper. Input is usually expected in the same form as a draft plan, but is slightly easier to assess because the framework for assessment becomes the degree to which the respondent has addressed the questions and selected an option. After the feedback is received and analysed a draft document is usually prepared. A discussion paper is therefore marginally more participatory than a draft plan but shares most of the same consultative issues and is thus equally open to abuse by the planner.

Information Sheets and Brochures

In response to the lack of representative input to draft plans, most heritage management organisations generate more user-friendly 'summary publications'. Information sheets, brochures and posters are generated voluntarily by heritage managers to provide potted versions of the main document. They usually provide the reader with:

- a discussion of the need for a study;
- a discussion of likely issues to be addressed;
- a discussion of possible solutions;
- a discussion of how individuals can participate;
- a contact name and number; and, sometimes,
- a formal submission form.

If the involvement is scheduled to run for some time, a newsletter may be established. Information sheets and brochures are sometimes generated as a series, covering a range of themes as per chapters in the original document. Of course, the summarising of any document is a value-laden exercise, since it requires the author to judge which information stays, which information goes, and which information should be altered to make it more user-friendly. The re-created documents often get relegated to a publications officer or interpreter, as these individuals are considered to have the more 'user-friendly' skills. They are, however, are generally unfamiliar with the context and issues of the subject and therefore struggle to maintain the original focus and emphasis of the document. These generalised publications reach a wider audience but do not necessarily increase the level, nature or source of feedback.

Assessment of the Political Climate

An assessment of the political environment can provide a range of indicators on the community's current level of interest, emotion and activity on the heritage and its management. For example, a review can be conducted of recent public requests for information, correspondence, questions in parliament and even demonstrations. An assessment of the number of letters or telephone calls received is a practice commonly used by politicians to measure public interest in or attitudes about a particular issue. In addition, a study can be made of political issues of a similar nature to determine the likelihood of a similar situation occurring for other heritage management scenarios. For example, an assessment could be made of community interest in a similar subject or planning process or other activity in a similar region. Unfortunately, assessments that reveal the level of conflict or apathy have sometimes been used to justify the level of community involvement. (See Case Study 4.2.)

Case Study 4.2
Workshopping to Co-manage the Rooftop of the World, Central Karakoram, Pakistan

Key points:

- The presence of high-quality visitor experiences reduces the likelihood of other human-induced impacts upon heritage.

- Community involvement helps heritage managers to understand management issues.

- Community involvement helps to preserve natural heritage and cultural practices.

The Central Karakoram includes several of the largest glaciers outside the polar regions and four of the world's fourteen 8,000-metre mountains – including the world's second-highest mountain, K2. Each year approximately 3,000 people climb K2, including the Pakistan military, who perceive the area as having high strategic importance. The mass movement of supplies and people has resulted in unsustainable firewood cutting, abandoned garbage and a collection of socio-cultural impacts on the remote communities. Using local legislation, the International Union for the Conservation of Nature and Natural Resources (IUCN) and Pakistani government declared a section of the region a protected area, put forward a nomination for World Heritage significance, then began a consultation process to explore the needs and interests of the local Balti villages (Fuller and Hussain 1996). Relationships between these groups and the national parks had been so poor that substantial perceptual barriers stood in front of the proposed consultation. A national park had been imposed and a proposal to eliminate grazing put forward, with little to no consultation. The results had been passive resistance to park management. To stimulate a formal planning exercise, the local Rural Support Program was seconded to assist park management in organising a new consultation initiative centred around a two-day intensive workshop. The first critical milestone was in accessing the right participants, which included representatives from the Khunjerab community, tour operators, the Pakistani Ministry of Food, agricultural cooperatives, the Environment and Urban Affairs Division, the Ministry of Tourism, Northern Areas Administration, the World Wildlife Fund Pakistan and the Belour Advisory and Social Development Organisation.

Early in the process community representatives were given the opportunity to state their concerns. It was quickly revealed that local land tenure rights and traditions would be threatened under the current proposal and that the definition of a national park under national legislation was a major impediment to a cooperative approach. Several major decisions were then made which set up a degree of certainty and thus trust that both parties could rely upon for on-going planning and management. First, it was agreed that the local community should be the main recipients of the benefits of the proposed World Heritage Site, and that they should be involved in critical planning and management. From these principles the workshop was able to define the boundaries for the proposed World Heritage Area, a tentative outline of the planning process and an advisory board to direct the process. Although the redrawn boundaries for the park reduced its size, it was ensured that local traditional practices could be maintained outside the park boundaries, thus eliminating the main stumbling block to a cooperative partnership. Trust was built when the IUCN Pakistani staff demonstrated an understanding of the issues and frustrations and openly discussed them (IUCN 1995). Decisions were able to be made because the people responsible for making and implementing them were present throughout. The timing of the workshop to coincide with local government elections helped to strengthen community identity and add credibility to the process.

Displays and Computer Simulations

Displays are often used as another means of presenting the original planning document in a more user-friendly form. They typically provide the same information as that printed on information sheets or in brochures but differ in being more visual (predominantly maps and photos) and in being located in a public place. Models or computer simulations are sometimes used to make the information more attractive and comprehensive or to provide the individual with the opportunity to vote or comment on an issue or option. The effectiveness of displays and computer simulations is greatly enhanced when they are staffed. This provides an opportunity for further elaboration, adjustment to individual interests and capabilities and, of course, feedback. Unfortunately, such positions are often given to people who have good public contact skills but limited experience in preparing or implementing the plan. The responsible planners and decision-makers are often perceived as being too precious too spare, or are too busy preparing the next planning initiative.

Information Hotlines

Telephone hotlines are typically used as information receivers. A dedicated telephone, facsimile or email number is set up to record enquiries or requests for information. This may be nothing more than a simple facility whereby a person may leave an address for material to be posted to them, or it may provide an electronic or personalised service for accessing information about a given subject of interest. Many hotlines are pre-recorded systems with an additional service for special enquiries. Their level and nature of use can be monitored and assessed, making them a useful barometer for other consultative mechanisms. It takes some time to raise community awareness and use of information hotlines; they should therefore be run for several months, which is often much longer than the planned involvement period. Consequently, hotlines work best as a long-term venture offering a range of services that can be modified or exchanged over time.

Media Campaigns

The media can be an effective means of communicating relatively simple messages to a large proportion of the community. The most popular print media are newspapers and magazines, while the most popular electronic media are radio, television and the World Wide Web. The message may simply be a promotional one leading people to an alternative consultation technique. For example, the media are frequently used to advertise a forthcoming meeting or workshop, the availability of a plan, or the location of an exhibition. The media may also be used by heritage managers to reach specific segments of the market. For example, the context and contents of a section of a plan of management on caving might be rewritten and placed in various caving magazines. Alternatively, the media can be used by the community as a means of voicing opinions and thoughts on an initiative. This may be in the form of a letter to the editor, or as an advertisement, or as part of a specially prepared article by a journalist. Individuals will be more likely to utilise print, whereas organisations and some experienced individuals will seek out the electronic media. The media are a reflection of the community's short attention spans and hunger for controversy and conflict. Therefore, heritage managers must have sound media skills and experience. Planning out a staged campaign helps to increase the likelihood of constructive outcomes.

Guided Tours

Guided tours are occasionally undertaken to gain input from the community at the heritage site in question. Misconceptions about the current state of a heritage resource can be reduced. Tours often begin by drawing on one or more specialists to outline the nature of the situation, during which time participants may walk, or be driven in a bus, around the site. The group then stops at a reference site for feedback and general discussion. Sometimes the tour is adapted from an existing interpretive tour and sometimes it is generated from scratch. If this version is successful, additional tours may be run or, alternatively, the tour may be turned into a guidebook (perhaps containing a map, written interpretation, photographs and a series of questions to stimulate participants' expression of their feelings and thoughts). Prizes are sometimes offered as a means of guaranteeing that the forms in the guidebooks are completed and returned within a designated time frame. (See Chapter 8 for more detail on interpretation; see also Case Study 4.3.).

Case Study 4.3
Integrating the Community into the Management of Tortuguero National Park, Costa Rica

---

Key points:

- The presence of high-quality visitor experiences reduces the likelihood of other human-induced impacts upon heritage.

- Community involvement helps heritage managers to understand management issues.

- Community involvement helps to preserve natural heritage and cultural practices.

Tortuguero National Park in north-western Costa Rica offers visitors a large and diverse range of habitats, including lowland tropical rainforest, swamp forest, wetlands and beaches. The network of waterways provides excellent opportunities for viewing wildlife such as sloths, anteaters, manatees, peccaries, tapirs and the white-faced monkey. It is the wildlife, particularly the turtles, that provide the main attraction and daily challenge for visitor management. Several species of turtle choose Tortuguero to come ashore and lay their eggs. Tortuguero is the most important breeding ground in the Caribbean for the green sea turtle. The regularity of the event and the close proximity and slow speed at which it occurs provides an ideal ecotourism opportunity while concurrently providing the ingredients for a lose/lose situation through poor visitor and heritage management. The turtles themselves are extremely sensitive to human presence, let alone interference.

Visitor-induced impacts include large and noisy crowds, the use of torches to spot the turtles (and even the tears in the creatures' eyes), camera flashes and interference with the turtle's movements. To mitigate these problems, rangers offer guided tours during the peak season. The presence of properly trained tour guides seems essential in managing visitor behaviour outside the peak periods, and could be marketed as the only sure way to find and understand the experience.

Another major form of impact upon the turtle population is the sometimes indiscriminate removal of turtle eggs from the easily visible nests. The local community considers egg eating as a part of its culture, but the removal of eggs is not as connected to cultural events and practices as it once was. Today the removal reflects partly tradition and partly a growing desire to eat a delicacy, free of charge, whenever the urge is felt. During peak tourist seasons the number of eggs removed is limited. Locals recognise the obvious economic benefit that tourists coming to view the turtles bring, and rangers enjoy a high profile from the interpretive activities. However, during the off-peak period turtle eggs are plundered. The lower number of visitors reduces the importance locals place on the turtles, the tours become unfeasible and the profile of rangers decreases accordingly.

In response to the locally-induced impact, heritage managers have spent considerable time integrating the community into the management system. Regular meetings on weekends between park management staff and locals were conducted to explore the relationship between the random removal of eggs across the year and the number of turtles and subsequent visitors. The rangers were able to demonstrate a relationship that then gave the meetings the impetus to explore the critical versus desirable demand for eggs. Agreement was reached on the removal of a set small number of eggs per person as a means of maintaining cultural traditions. A voluntary code of practice was established and is coordinated and monitored by the community. Regular meetings have been maintained and are always well attended. The critical turning point appears to have been the preparedness of both parties to trust each other. The local community trust the suggested relationship between turtle and visitor numbers. The rangers trust the code of practice and the way that it is monitored and policed. The trust and apparent success in this venture has increased local interest for involvement in other park management decisions.

Telephone Polling and Surveys

Market research techniques such as telephone polling and surveying are very useful for gaining moderate to large samples of structured input from the community. The rigour used to collect the results often allows them to be a strong marketing tool for an organisation needing to gain the political high ground. Telephone polls and surveys can be used to undertake targeted sampling to ensure adequate representation and are therefore more effective for broader contextual information, such as attitudes towards the environment, awareness of the heritage management organisation and awareness of general issues (see Chapter 5 for more detail on these techniques). One of the weaknesses of such techniques is that on their own they do not provide sufficient background information specific to heritage for respondents to provide perceptive comment. This can be partially overcome when participants are provided with the information prior to the survey, although this opens up issues relating to bias if there is no guarantee that the respondent has read the entire document.

Review of Related Plans and Publication

In many instances, considerable planning on a related topic may already have taken place and may have involved some consultation with the community. It is therefore wise always to consider reviewing these plans as a legitimate form of preliminary consultation. The plans may have already identified values, objectives, issues and solutions that can be considered further. In addition, the reports may contain lists of stakeholders already involved, which may permit some direct consultative techniques or at least conserve human resources. Finally, the assessment may also suggest what types of consultation have been used in the community and what sort of insights they generated. This type of investigation contributes to what is known as a stakeholder analysis, which was covered in Chapter 3.

Public Meetings

Public meetings are one of the most common, well-established and conventional consultation techniques. In general, they are advertised by open invitations in the media, on leaflets dropped through the letterbox or on public notice-boards. A public meeting usually involves two or three individuals providing a brief outline of the heritage in question, the issues and some of the proposed solutions. The meeting is then open for any of the audience to comment on what they have heard or on a related matter. Ideally, a facilitator coordinates the questions and comments and ensures that the meeting runs smoothly. However, it can be extremely difficult to facilitate public meetings because they can attract too many people to ensure a fair distribution of speakers and a fair code of practice for addressing speakers. As a consequence, certain individuals and their personal agendas dominate and create conflict that cannot be resolved adequately within the time available. Heritage managers are often the first to avoid public meetings.

One means of reducing problems commonly associated with public meetings is to run a scoping meeting earlier in the planning process. A scoping meeting is conducted at the outset of a study or planning exercise and typically seeks to identify critical issues and stakeholders in an attempt to limit later criticism. The meeting may result in the call for written submissions to gain further comment before commencing. Scoping should be a natural part of the planning for community involvement, which was covered earlier in this chapter.

Small Stakeholder Meetings

The principal difference between public and small stakeholder meetings is that the group of participants in the latter is smaller and they have a stake in the management of the heritage. They are thus more likely to be aware and involved in the issues being addressed. The structure of the meeting can therefore avoid some of the background context and be more focused on issues and solutions. Nonetheless, individual agendas can still dominate proceedings and make it difficult for the less forthright participants to generate meaningful input. One response is to generate a series of meetings for stakeholders with similar interests. For example, a plan of management may have one meeting for walkers, one for tour operators and one for apiarists. This can provide further focus for the meeting and reduce competing interests. The small size of the group allows for open dialogue, which helps to generate productive and perhaps even trusting relationships. The trade-off is that these meetings are not a forum for the resolution of conflict between different groups of stakeholders.

Individual Interviews with Stakeholders

Individual interviews with stakeholders provide a greater depth of insight because the session is totally focused on one individual. The structure may still be similar to a that of stakeholder meeting – e.g., general introduction to the purpose of the interview, introduction to the topic, issues to cover and solutions proposed. Alternatively, the interview may be more investigative, using a series of targeted questions to focus on retrieving feelings, perceptions and ideas. Some interviews are based around SWOT analyses of a heritage site or its management system (Strengths, Weaknesses, Opportunities and Threats). The technique is particularly useful for politically sensitive subjects that require a degree of discretion. The trade-offs to obtaining such rich information are the human resources required to collect it and the smaller sample size that can be achieved with these resources. Nonetheless, interviews can be one of the most effective techniques for the early consultative stages.

Focus Groups

Focus groups are a market research technique designed to explore a subject with a designated small market sample. They are often used to explore fundamental feelings and ideas about a subject in the early stages of planning. Consequently, they tend to be a little looser in their structure than a meeting or an interview. Focus groups may also be used to generate market segmentation systems for recognising and working with particular sectors of the community. The sessions yield large amounts of qualitative data and require highly skilled market researchers to analyse and interpret the data effectively. Consequently, focus groups are relatively expensive to operate and should therefore be used sparingly once considerable preparation has been undertaken (see Chapter 5 for more detail on focus groups).

Workshops

Workshops have become one of the most popular mechanisms for community consultation. They typically involve one or two facilitators and an invited group of twelve to twenty-five individuals. The group spends between three hours and one day in intense discussions of particular aspects of heritage management. Most planning exercises run two or three workshops during the planning process. In the case of a plan of management, the first workshop typically outlines the planning process then quickly moves on to the identification of values, a vision and objectives (or desired outcomes). Issues may need to be brainstormed in this first workshop, as many participants come with nothing else in mind but to voice a concern. In the second workshop there tends to be more sharing of information, with the facilitators reporting back on how they have assimilated the input from the previous workshop, followed by the participants providing input on what should be done to achieve the objectives and address the issues. The third workshop is almost entirely centred on obtaining feedback on the draft document. There are many secrets to a successful workshop, including:

- ensuring a representative sample of participants;
- using a comfortable and stimulating environment;
- generating a range of interactive communication techniques;
- sharing information throughout each session; and
- ensuring energy levels are high and a positive mood is maintained.

Some workshops are run over one or several days, which can create a strong sense of community ownership of the planning process. The positive atmosphere generated by such a successful workshop needs to be checked against the expectations of the participants. These expectations are sometimes dashed when the group is brought together again and discovers that in the interim much of their work has been rejected or significantly modified. (See Case Study 4.4.)

Case Study 4.4
Defining the Character of Sumner, Washington, USA

Key points:

- The most effective community involvement uses a combination of techniques at the very beginning of the planning process.

- Techniques that empower the community to become more aware of the issues increases their ability to generate innovative solutions.

The city of Sumner is located 35 miles south-east of Seattle in Washington, USA. Sumner faces a dramatic increase in population, urban sprawl and congestion. In recognition of the complexity of what may be causing these problems, the City adopted an integrated approach to involving its community. An extensive part of the community was integrated into the planning process in the very early stages of a planning. These initial stages featured a variety of planning and participation techniques that included visioning, town meetings, walking tours, workshops and surveys. The city also undertook a Visual Preference Survey™ (VPS). The VPS helped the community to evaluate a variety of design features for future development. The VPS involved asking participants to view and evaluate between 40 and 240 slides. In this instance the slides were of a wide variety of streetscapes, land uses and densities, site designs, roadways, building types, civic and public spaces, parking lots, parking and recreation areas, pavements, landscapes and open spaces. Each participant viewed each slide and assigned it a score according to whether they liked it and thought it appropriate to the community. Scoring was on a scale of −10 to +10, zero being rated neutral. The results presented the collective opinion of participants and could be determined on a computer during a tea break for reporting back and further discussion.

As an educational tool, the technique provided valuable community input into the planning process by helping people define what they liked and disliked about what they saw around them. The process heightened awareness about the trade-offs inherent in heritage management. As a participatory device it empowered people to develop a common vision that could be fully understood. The initial results included a set of the most and least favoured attributes. However, the real results were the increased awareness that led to further constructive discussion and visioning. The input was used to develop a visual plan that summarised what the community believed to be the most important issues relating to planning and design in their community. The innovative update to the City Plan was achieved with relative ease and general consensus.

Advisory Committees

Advisory groups or committees are often established to provide independent involvement in the decision-making process and an on-going consultative mechanism to monitor performance and provide general feedback as required. They usually function as groups of independent experts responsible for reviewing technical information or recommendations made by heritage managers. They may function in an advisory capacity or be given direct decision-making powers. The most crucial aspect of an advisory group is the selection of individuals and their terms of reference. Small groups of four to five individuals usually provide a sufficient balance of diversity and productivity. The terms of reference need to be endorsed by all participants before commencement of planning and then reviewed regularly. The use of an advisory group need not be based around meetings. An efficient chair will maintain regular contact with individuals and circulate material for comment as required. It is vital to ensure that the individuals have a moderate to long-term commitment to avoid turnover and associated losses in productivity. The chair of the group must ensure that the agenda remains relevant to members and that any tangible benefits of their efforts are regularly marketed internally and externally. Some form of reimbursement for the members may be required, because most people find their time limited and valuable.

Assessing the Effectiveness of Community Involvement Techniques

The success of involvement techniques is largely dependent upon the application of involvement principles, the level of supportive planning, the resources available and the time and context in which the technique is practised. Nonetheless, it is possible to compare the strengths using qualitative assessment. Table 4.6 examines the degree to which the various techniques give, receive and share information, and how well they generate participatory decision-making. It also assesses the degree to which each technique makes contact with the community, handles specific community interests and generates two-way communication. Interpretation of the table suggests that all of the techniques have the capacity to give information, most have the capacity to receive information, but less that half can truly share information, and even fewer generate participatory decision-making. The techniques that provide the best overall performance are: stakeholder interviews and meetings; focus groups; workshops; and advisory committees. The results suggest that it may be possible to position the main techniques on a form of matrix according to the degree to which they reflect legitimate trust on behalf of the heritage manager and stakeholders, and the degree to which they provide legitimate community involvement in heritage management decision-making. The positioning of these techniques is shown in Figure 4.2, which again suggests that advisory/consultative committees and small

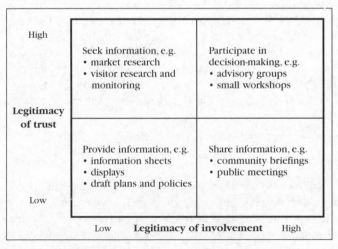

Figure 4.2 Relative degrees of trust and involvement in various forms of consultative objectives and techniques

Table 4.6 Assessment of community involvement techniques

Techniques	Objectives				Assessment			
	Information giving	Information receiving	Information sharing	Participatory decision-making	Level of contact with community	Ability to handle specific interests	Level of two-way communication	Ability to resolve conflict
Information sheets and brochures	•				√√	√	√	√
Displays and computer simulations	•				√	√	√	√
Media campaigns	•				√√√	√	√	√
Draft documents (plans and policies)	•				√	√	√	√
Review of plans and publications		•			√	√	√	√
Political environment assessment		•			√	√√	√	√√
Information hotlines		•			√√	√√	√√	√
Discussion papers		•			√	√	√	√√
Individual stakeholder interviews		•			√	√√√	√√√	√√
Telephone polling and surveys		•			√		√	√
Guided tours		•	•		√√	√√	√	√√
Public meetings		•	•		√√	√	√√	√
Stakeholder meetings		•	•	•	√	√√	√√√	√√√
Advisory committees		•	•	•	√	√√√	√√√	√√√
Focus groups		•	•	•	√√	√√√	√√√	√
Workshops		•	•	•	√√√	√√√	√√√	√√√

• Most appropriate for achievement of objectives; √ Limited performance; √√ Reasonable performance; √√√ Good performance

Source: adapted from Kennedy (1993b), Environment Protection Agency (1996) and Munn in Thomas (1996)

interactive workshops are most capable of generating legitimate involvement. It must be stressed that no single technique will be particularly successful and that the best approach is to integrate several techniques.

Constraints Against Community Involvement

There are enormous constraints against the transition from sharing information to genuine community participation in heritage management. Kennedy (1993b) identified the constraints facing heritage managers on the one hand and those facing the community on the other, as shown in Table 4.7. The objectives of heritage managers in being involved in consultation are usually different from those of the community. Sewell and Phillips (1979), for example, found that the managing agency provided pragmatic, agency-oriented objectives, whereas the community had a broader set of objectives. Specifically, they found that the management agency aimed to develop programmes with broad public acceptance, enhance performance and improve the image of the agency; in contrast, the community was concerned to influence the design and implementation of policy and reduce the power of bureaucracy and its planners.

Furthermore, the culture of most heritage management organisations remains resistant to a total embracing of community consultation. Popular perceptions contributing to this culture are that:

- the time is not right (premature to begin);
- in terms of commitment to human resources it takes too long or costs too much;
- it stirs up opposition;
- it raises expectations beyond what management can deliver;
- only the extremists or the articulate contribute; and
- the community would not understand the real depth and complexity of the issues.

Molesworth (in Thomas 1996) suggests the following underlying reasons for resistance among heritage managers as being notions that:

- only those with scientific or technical training are able to contribute to positive and constructive decision-making;
- it is more efficient to have a small number of people involved in making decision (efficiency of time and decisiveness);
- members of the public tend to be subjective, whereas professionals (technical or bureaucratic) are thought to be objective;
- the existing political process works to take into account public opinion – public participation is almost interference;
- third parties should not be allowed to interfere with another person's democratic right to do something;
- public participation is not truly representative of public opinion;
- public participation encourages litigants to disrupt the proper processes of government/administration; and
- the public cannot appreciate the importance of many affairs of state (which only government or its agencies can fully understand).

Table 4.7 Constraints against greater community involvement in heritage management

Heritage management	Community
Lack of an established working relationship with consumers and representative groups due to previous limited consultation	Inexperience in consultation practices
Personnel are inadequately briefed and/or have insufficient delegated authority to respond effectively to customers' questions and requests	Lack of understanding of political processes, technical skills and knowledge
Rigid, bureaucratic approach	Lack of ability to influence policy or agenda
Unclear or conflicting consultation objectives within or between organisations or sections of an organisation	Lack of an appropriate customer representative structure
Lack of human or financial resources	Diverse and conflicting community opinion
Difficulties in obtaining a representative sample of views	Cost to participants in being involved
Cultural constraints, such as believing the community is not interested in or capable of providing useful input	Cultural constraints, such as the preference not to expose special values, traditions and beliefs, or limitations on the way communication can be undertaken

Source: adapted from Kennedy (1993b)

These points support the perception that the public cannot contribute anything useful to decision-making processes and that the best decisions are those made by experts. However, it is important to note that while most of these points have an element of truth, even collectively they present no case for downplaying the role of community consultation. Instead, they indicate the need to develop consultation further to be more effective and accountable. This can only be achieved with a positive shift in culture.

Gaining Adequate Representation

A major issue constantly dogging initiatives in community involvement is the need to be representative. What constitutes representativeness has been based around a diversity of roles rather than a diversity of interests or perspectives. This has typically been reflected by a focus on stakeholder or special-interest groups rather than individuals (see Chapter 3). Inherent in this focus is that each group will be able adequately to reflect a wide range of interests because of its role – e.g., a conservation group will encompass a broad range of interests and perspectives on conserving the environment, and a walking group will encompass a broad range of interests and perspectives on walking. This is rarely the case, since special-interest groups usually narrow their focus to achieve greater success in satisfying their main aims (and members). In the examples provided, a conservation group may focus on preserving more of a site rather than how it is managed, while a walking group may focus on preventing the closure of any tracks rather than improving a short interpretive walk. A question that is rarely considered is whether representativeness should also consider the diversity of positions on – or even the diversity of solutions to – an issue. Such an approach could greatly enhance the potential for fresh perspectives. There has been a lack of debate about whether representation should come from key stakeholders, all stakeholders, or all of the community.

Some of the consequences of not achieving an adequately representative group may include:

- a narrowing of the scope of the initiative;
- simplification of the issues and solutions; and
- domination of certain stakeholders' political agendas over sound planning principles.

Many involvement initiatives have tried to gain representative input from the broader community, but have not met with success, one of the reasons being that many community members were unavailable, not interested or not able to be involved at the time their involvement was sought. There will always be a proportion of people with other commitments that genuinely preclude their involvement, but involvement initiatives can be adjusted to make it easier for people to become interested and involved. The involvement technique itself will play a critical role in influencing the type of people who participate. For example, staffed displays and guided tours are more likely to attract general community members than a meeting of stakeholders or a public meeting. A range of techniques will increase the likelihood of achieving a wider range of community members. Often the timing of a programme is arranged to suit the convenience of the management rather than what might be convenient for the community. The timing of the initiative may need to be adjusted to accommodate the community's work and leisure patterns, since the location of the initiative needs to reflect where the community feels most comfortable. Sometimes the initiative is located close to the heritage site or in the wrong suburb or township, or its promotion may have been limited in time or scope. Promotion needs to get into the nooks and crannies of a community and needs to give people sufficient warning to respond. This time frame is dependent partly on the issue and partly on the scale of the community and its own decision-making system.

Perhaps the fundamental restriction on greater representativeness is the scope of the involvement that is offered to the community and the question of whether the involvement that is being offered is relevant to the community's decision-making process. There are two dimensions to scope: the nature of the task, and the level of development to which it has been or will be taken prior to or after involvement. In the first instance, involvement may be offered in regard to shaping:

- an on-going community involvement programme;
- heritage values;
- management policy;
- strategic plans that reflect policy; and
- a development initiative.

Each of these reflects different levels of 'givens', beginning with the least number of givens at the top of the list and ending with the most at the bottom. In addition, any of these components may be offered to the community at stages that range from no previous planning being undertaken to a completed draft for comment. The bottom line is of course a trade-off. On the one hand, the community may rightly request participation with the least number of givens and the greatest opportunity to shape the involvement programme to suit its needs. On the other hand, it may need a position that is tangible enough for it to comment on. In addition, cultural differences between heritage managers and the community must be understood before community involvement can be considered genuine and effective (James 1991). Determining the position in this trade-off is best undertaken in a stakeholder analysis prior to developing the involvement programme (see Chapter 3).

The other dimension influencing the perception of scope offered is the way in which the input is processed, integrated and then reported back to the community. This has to some extent been covered earlier in the chapter, but it does raise the question of who should have the final right of veto in the decision-making process. Should final decisions be made by the heritage managing authority, those participating in the involvement programme, the elected government or another body? This issue is critical because it raises a more fundamental question of who has the right to balance different interests and, in particular, those of a local versus global scale (see Case Study 4.5).

Case Study 4.5
Bringing Opposing Parties to Consensus at Willandra Lakes World Heritage Area, New South Wales, Australia

Key points:

- The most successful planning occurs when planners focus on being facilitators and all parties are prepared to compromise.

- Plans need to be broken down according to their function, audience and lifespan.

- The real test of a plan is the degree to which stakeholders continue to work together after it has been completed.

The Willandra Lakes region World Heritage Property (the Willandra) is located in the Australian state of New South Wales. It was given World Heritage status, both for its natural values (of being an outstanding example of major stages of the earth's evolutionary history, on-going geological processes, biological evolution and human interactions with the natural environment) and for its cultural values (because its landforms held unique evidence of continuous habitation by Aboriginal people for at least 40,000 years). Most of the area comprises pastoral stations and a large part of the Mungo National Park. The Willandra was placed on the World Heritage List in 1981, but its boundary did not reflect the landscape elements for which it was inscribed. The other major land management issue was the fourteen-year delay in preparing a plan of management. The inappropriate boundaries and long planning delays frustrated many stakeholders, particularly the pastoralists who were unable to make critical farming decisions until a plan was prepared. In 1995 Manidis Roberts Consultants were contracted to prepare a plan of management for the region that would: provide a framework for consistent decision-making; develop a government–community partnership for on-going management; satisfy Australia's obligations under the World Heritage Convention; and develop a process that would serve as a model for preparing plans of management for other World Heritage Properties (Manidis Roberts 1996).

The greatest strength of the planning process was the stakeholder involvement process. The planners took the view that preparing the plan required a combination of involvement techniques underpinned by facilitation rather than direction. The first step was to prepare and call for public submissions on a strategic directions document. Small interactive workshops were then held with local landholder and Aboriginal groups to develop a consensus within each group on the issues of greatest concern. The small workshops also provided an opportunity for the groups to familiarise themselves with the interactive workshop process. The workshops were backed up by extensive discussions with individuals to determine potential conflicts and common ground. The principal involvement technique was a five-day on-site workshop involving forty major stakeholders. The aim of the workshop was to produce the first draft of the plan of management through the active participation of all major stakeholders, using a combination of whole-group and small-group sessions. Whole-group sessions were facilitated to understand and resolve the conflict between major stakeholders. Small-group sessions were used throughout the workshop to develop the various components of the plan. The workshop required the planners to give up most of their control and trust the directions established by participants. The high level of interaction and trust freed participants to express deeply held views, many of which were incorporated into a set of guiding principles. These principles functioned in a similar way to a bike's training wheels by giving participants the security that their core needs were recognised and would be fundamental to the plan's development. All the participants also agreed that any changes in content to the draft plan after the workshop would involve input from all those who had attended the workshop.

A values-based planning approach was developed to ensure that the things which made the Willandra special were not diminished. The values were supported by a vision and a set of desired futures that, when combined, formed the first part of the plan known as the Basis for Management. This part was developed for decision-makers and designed to have a lifespan of twenty to thirty years. The second part of the plan consisted of management issues and strategies. The issues were identified according to whether they were likely to diminish the values, while the strategies were developed to realise the desired futures and address the issues. The strategies were developed for federal and state governments and had a five- to ten-year lifespan. The last part of the plan was an operational plan that prescribed detailed measures for on-ground management of the national park and each pastoral property. This was developed for site-based national parks staff and pastoralists and is reviewed annually.

A final plan was agreed upon in early 1996. Significant agreements were achieved between conflicting stakeholders that have made this plan a milestone in Australia. One major agreement reached was the decision to reduce the World Heritage Property to 240,000 hectares, as well as to reduce the number of pastoral properties and include a number of small previously excluded areas that contained World Heritage values. However, the greatest achievement is that more than two years later stakeholders continue to constructively work together to form new cooperative agreements.

Conflict Resolution

Conflict can be positive or negative, constructive or destructive. It is a regular occurrence in public involvement and commonly shows itself among participants as discomfort, misunderstanding or tension. The first step in resolving conflict is to regard it as an opportunity. There are a number of key ways of approaching conflict: withdrawal, suppression, win/lose, compromise and win/win. These approaches are shown in Table 4.8. Although a combination of approaches is often required, the single most effective is the win/win approach. The steps required to establish a win/win situation are to:

- define everyone's needs;
- determine why each party needs what they say they do;
- identify similarities and differences;

- design creative options to consolidate the similarities and link the differences; and

- agree to cooperate to agree on the best option.

Successful outcomes are often limited when a problem is not clearly defined or mutually agreed upon.

Table 4.8 Various approaches to resolving conflict

Type of visitor information

Approach	Examples	Advantages	Limitations
Withdrawal	• Stop talking • Leave the room or entire process • Shift the focus of attention	• Keeps one to one's own business • Helps draw attention to an area of neglect. • Forces people to change their mind	• Leaves problem to grow out of proportion • Leaves remaining parties feeling abandoned
Suppression	• Act as if nothing is wrong • Plough on regardless • Say nothing at the time but scheme later on	• Avoids people hearing what they are not ready to hear • Reduces likelihood of unnecessary minor distractions • Allows points to be represented at a more convenient time	• Others are not aware of situation • Others cannot help • Others can interpret silence as endorsement
Win/lose	• Demand that a course of action be followed for a greater good • Manipulation • Overpower through verbal or physical force	• Provides a sense of order • Protects a person from the pain of being wrong • Opportunity for one person or party to come out 'on top'	• Losers may not support a decision they were not involved in making • Later on the loser may refuse to cooperate or may sabotage the process
Compromise	• Divide opportunities and constraints as equally as possible • Spread power as evenly as possible	• Everyone gains something • Simple principle for all to recognise and thus endorse	• The notion of equality is difficult to ascertain • All parties may feel like losers
Win/win	• Mutual ties to a solution	• As per compromise, only more productive outcomes that are more widely endorsed • Stronger relationships	• Requires considerable negotiation skills • Requires considerable time to develop and implement

Source: adapted from Cornelius and Faire (1994)

The development of an orderly, systematic approach is essential to achieve a win/win situation. One of the ways in which this can be done is the use of a map. Maps have a number of advantages to conflict resolution. They can:

- provide a neutral point for conflicting stakeholders to focus on;

- reduce sidetracking and emotional responses by structuring the conversation;

- generate group work that creates a more cooperative atmosphere;

- give participants confidence in the participatory process by acknowledging and presenting all points of view;
- organise points of view on an issue; and
- help detect similarities that lead to solutions.

It must be stressed that the map concept has been largely derived for use in Western countries. Other cultures have radically different decision-making conventions that must be recognised and respected. For example, in some cultures contact must be made with the community's men, after which they have to be given time to return and consult with their women or other elders.

The first step in generating a map for a Western country is to define the issue in a general, open-ended statement. The second step is to determine who the major stakeholders are (see Chapter 3). The third step is to determine each stakeholder's needs and fears relevant to the issue. Needs could also mean wants, values, interests or things people care about. Sometimes people will prefer to address solutions immediately. This is counter-productive as it puts pressure on other stakeholders, which in turn limits the alternatives that can be generated later. This problem can be avoided by restating their comment as: 'Your answer to the issue is to do this, but what sort of need might this answer help you achieve'. Fears can reflect concerns, anxieties or worries. It is important to have all fears listed. If the stakeholders get sidetracked, take their points down on a separate sheet of paper and return to the map.

To analyse the map while the stakeholders are present requires great skill. The first step is to look for common ground, such as similar needs or interests. These can be simply marked or connected with lines. The connections can then be combined to form a common vision or set of desired outcomes, which can be written to the side of the map. It is then useful to look for different values and perspectives that can be accommodated into the vision if they do not impair it. From this point in the analysis it is often possible to look for insights that were not previously obvious. These insights may serve to expand or further colour the vision, or they may be used to develop response strategies to the vision. At this point the facilitator needs to adjust their behaviour to make the participants feel that the insights are raising the group's energy and cooperative spirit. One method of achieving this is to emphasise the wins that come from these insights and their potential benefits. The facilitator can then harness this change in atmosphere to integrate the unconnected elements into the vision. Elements that cannot be addressed by the main strategies can then be linked into separate groups for specific strategies to be developed. The underlying objective with the mapping is to ensure that everyone has contributed and everyone has achieved some form of win. An example of a map is shown in Table 4.9.

The next step to turning conflict into a win/win situation is to develop options. There are three distinct stages to options development: creating options, choosing the preferred option, and taking action on the chosen option. The options need to be created using the needs already identified. One of the favoured methods for options generation is brainstorming. Brainstorming typically involves a facilitator, a scribe and a group of two to fifteen participants generating as many ideas as possible within a designated time. A free-falling atmosphere is created with all ideas welcomed, regardless of how immediately relevant they may appear. If the problem appears very large and complex, the facilitator may break the brainstorm into a series of smaller parts.

The second stage in options development is to choose the preferred option. There are many selection methods, and selection criteria must also be available. These

Table 4.9 Example of a conflict resolution map

Background: redevelopment of historic hotel into fast-food restaurant (fictitious)

- Arnott Street residents were unhappy because the owner of the Arnotts Hotel wants to build a fast-food restaurant franchise in its place
- Two spokespersons for the residents and two staff from the restaurant chain went to a conflict resolution course; the residents felt very angry and helpless and the employees felt the owner was in for a session of verbal abuse
- Participants saw the value of mapping the needs before seeking a solution
- Participants mapped the situation and left the workshop deciding they could work together to arrive at a mutually beneficial solution
- Other residents joined with several staff from the restaurant chain and an architect, landscape planner and heritage planner to use the conflict resolution map as the basis for a Memorandum of Understanding (MOU) between the restaurant chain and the residents
- MOU was established. The restaurant chain agreed to keep and restore the hotel façade and major internal features, limit promotional signs to small ones at an agreed location, and fund 50% of the development of a youth recreation activities centre upstairs, the local council providing 30% and the residents 20%. The residents agreed not to hold an anti-development campaign and supported a restaurant chain-driven publicity video outlining the successful MOU

Stakeholder	Needs	Fears
Residents	• Maintain heritage streetscape • Enhance deteriorating fabric of Arnotts Hotel • Improve vibrancy of lagging commercial district • Avoid children loitering; give them something to do	• Arnotts Hotel would be demolished • Streetscape would look too commercialised • Sense of community would deteriorate
Restaurant chain	• Large property on main street • Community support for public profile • Local government support for development application	• Would not get another property large enough within street to develop • Would not be able to operate in the locality • Public campaign would damage profile • There would be boycott of restaurant once open • Mishandling of social contact

criteria could include: stakeholders impacted, cost effectiveness, feasibility, degree of impact, versatility, operating life and maintenance requirements. The most relevant criteria are those based around the needs already generated. Some brainstorm facilitators set up a matrix that has a small set of one stakeholder's needs listed down one side with another stakeholder's set listed across the top of the matrix. Options are then inserted into the cell that best meets the individual needs. Another method is to get participants to rank the options using categories, such as 'very useful', 'lacking some elements' or 'not practical'. Another method is to allocate each participant three ticks, allowing them total freedom in their allocation (i.e., all three votes to one option, two votes to one option and one to another, or one vote to each of three options).

The final stage in options development is to implement the chosen option. If the option has been generated and refined via community involvement, there will be a number of people (participants) expecting quick and accountable implementation. This can be enhanced by getting participants to assist in developing the implementation plan – for instance, identifying what tasks are required, who will undertake the tasks and when each task will commence and be completed. The participants' involvement has the added benefit of ensuring that they leave the initiative with realistic expectations of the implementation process. There will always be a greater chance of effective implementation if stakeholders own not only the option but also the process used to derive it.

While processes form the bricks of conflict resolution, a wide range of negotiation skills form the mortar. These skills are too numerous to cover in detail, but some deserve mention and illustration. Table 4.10 lists some of the key skills and corresponding examples to assist readers in recognising and implementing them.

Conclusion

Conflict over what is heritage and how it should be managed often occurs because of a lack of community involvement in the planning process. This chapter has explored some of the principles and practices associated with community involvement in heritage management. It has also briefly examined some of the processes and skills associated with conflict resolution. Community involvement is fundamental to ensuring heritage management is fair and accountable. True involvement goes beyond making people aware of an initiative, seeking comment on an initiative and seeking endorsement of an initiative. True involvement means allowing people to share in fundamental policies that shape initiatives and allowing people to contribute in a manner that reflects their interests and capabilities. It means being prepared to share responsibility. Other chapters will continue to explore the use of responsibility as a fundamental dimension of the heritage management culture.

Table 4.10 Key negotiating hints for conflict resolution

Hints	Example
Ask questions to steer the negotiation	• Is this plan going to get us where we want to go? • Has the issue or problem been properly defined? • Is there another aspect to the issue or problem? • Is the identified issue or problem relevant to you?
Ensure participants qualify generalities	• I know you said you wanted the best outcome, but what would be the best outcome for you? • You said it was too expensive. How much is too expensive?
Avoid participants using rigid statements	• You said it was impossible. What would it take to make it possible?
When feeling defensive, become an active listener, then ask a win/win question	• What could we do to fix up the situation, then?
Separate the person from the problem	• Use a board to write people's ideas down and focus attention on the board rather than individuals.
Acknowledge all points of view	• Thanks for that comment, I can see your point of view.
Continually restate common ground	• You may remember that everyone agreed the building needs repair.
Shift unrealistic expectations	• Wasn't weed control last April very time-consuming because of the weather?
Be flexible	• Predetermine a range for a solution could be considered appropriate.
Identify cultural dimensions beforehand	• Identify whether there are any dimensions to the issue that participants may not be able to discuss. • Identify any cultural limitations that the location, venue and timing may have on participants.
Know when to stop	• Call a break if emotions run too high, an impasse is reached, an unfair tactic throws the facilitator off balance or information appears to be being withheld.
Let some hostile remarks pass	• Ask the participant to rephrase the statement to make it clearer. • Re-frame the hostile remark into something more constructive. • Facilitators do not have to deal with everything that is thrown at them.
Disempower troublemakers	• Make the troublemaker aware that you are aware of their efforts. • Identify another participant who is popular with the group and can be depended on to tone the offender down in a humorous manner.
Do not address side issues until appropriate	• Place side issues on a separate sheet of paper and mention when it may be more appropriate to address it. • Transcribe comments directly on to paper.
Write exactly what participants say	• If a comment is unclear, ask for clarification. • Ensure facilitator can practise humility against some of their more basic skills (e.g. clear writing or spelling).
Use humour	• When people are tiring, ask a participant to tell a joke. • If there is more than one facilitator, develop an informal relationship which may involve retelling an amusing story about them.

Source: adapted from Cornelius and Faire (1994)

CHAPTER 5

Understanding the Heritage–Visitor Relationship

'This place is boring, Mum - there's nothing to do. I'm going to go and play with my football.' Peter trudged off from the museum displays that his parents were studying. A short walk later he found an old stone wall with enough courtyard space to let him kick his ball against it. The courtyard had no roof and made a fantastic echo when the ball struck the wall. Peter noticed that the top bricks of the wall were loose. After a few kicks he had managed to hit one of the weaker bricks. It broke away and fell backwards on the other side of the building. Twenty minutes later Peter had managed to dislodge two other bricks before his parents called him to return to the car and head home. On the other side of the wall lay the remains of a broken drinking fountain. The fountain had withstood a civil war, fire and 400 years of natural decay, but not the impact of a bored boy kicking a ball.

Introduction

In some respects, visitors derive the greatest benefit from heritage conservation through the direct experiencing of it. When people visit heritage sites they receive obvious recreational outputs, such as relaxation and stimulation. Perhaps more profoundly, people who visit heritage sites have a greater opportunity to use heritage as a means of contemplating, reflecting and discovering what is important to them than people who never visit. The interactions of visitors and heritage increase the role that people play within the heritage management system because they introduce a fundamental challenge: how to help visitors experience heritage in a manner that helps them to enjoy and celebrate heritage without loving it to death.

The visitor–heritage relationship is intrinsically symbiotic. As identified in Chapter 1, an item, place or practice becomes heritage because people ascribe value to it. This value is clarified and enhanced by direct experience - an experience that is undertaken as a means of gaining enjoyment and adding meaning to life. Therefore, the closer the contact visitors have with heritage, the more meaningful and enjoyable the heritage becomes, and the more value is ascribed. Paradoxically, the closer or greater the contact with heritage, the greater is the potential for impact upon that heritage. If the impact changes the distribution, function or aesthetics of the heritage, it may well also cause it to lose its integrity and value. Once this has occurred, satisfaction from experiencing the heritage site may deteriorate and interest in experiencing it may wane. This in turn can lead to reduced support for heritage and heritage management in general.

Visitors also present one of the closest relationships that a heritage manager can forge with the community and stakeholders. The standard of management, as formal custodian of heritage, is judged by the standard of the heritage and the heritage experience. When the heritage is in excellent condition and the visitors' experience richly rewarding, the visitors praise management and are happy to support it through contributions to resourcing and compliance with responsible behaviour. A deteriorating quality of heritage and visitor experience will generate a deteriorating respect and support for heritage managers. This will generate lower profiles and lower resourcing, which in turn will further reduce the capacity of management to improve the situation.

Therefore, the visitor-heritage relationship presents great opportunities and challenges to the heritage manager. Management must be able to work with the heritage-visitor relationship by having a sound understanding of the characteristics and status of heritage and visitors. Clearly, information about that relationship needs to be collected, assessed and integrated into the strategic planning process. This chapter will examine the principles and practice of collecting, sorting and presenting such information. It will contrast visitor monitoring and research, then present a range of techniques to collect and analyse information.

Principles for Collecting Information About the Heritage–Visitor Relationship

Although there are texts on designing general social research studies, there are few publications covering principles, standards or approaches specific to heritage or visitor management (Harrison 1994; Glasson *et al.* 1995). Nonetheless, some of the principles that appear to be regularly practised in the field of heritage-visitor studies advocate that:

- information should be collected from a range of reputable sources, using a range of techniques, as a means of minimising bias and maximising the reliability of data;

- information should be collected from sample sizes that reflect the scale of the actual population or setting;

- information should be collected in a way that minimises disruption to the heritage and visitor experience;

- participants should always be advised who is collecting the information, what the purpose of the collection is and whether individual responses are to be publicly displayed; and

- participants and other stakeholders should be offered the opportunity to access key results relevant to them, as a means of sharing benefits and establishing trust.

However, it is also possible to collect so much detail that priority information, trends and relationships become hidden. In addition, some decisions will have to be made on the basis of intuition, guesstimating or loose forecasting.

Information Needed to Understand the Heritage–Visitor Relationship

The most critical type of information that can be generated for managing the heritage-visitor relationship concerns trends and relationships between causes and effects. Some of the key information includes: basic contextual characteristics, values, condition, visitation, visitor profile, visitor behaviour, impact, and management activity. Table 5.1 provides examples for each of these groups.

Monitoring and research are the two main approaches to collecting information on the heritage-visitor relationship. They can be distinguished by the nature of their objectives and the time frames within which their programmes operate. Research generally seeks to assist with policy development and planning, and its objectives

Table 5.1 Key information needed to understand the heritage–visitor relationship

Type of information	Examples
Basic contextual characteristics	• Location • Scale • Components • Age • Ownership • Management responsibility
Values	• Intrinsic, environmental, cultural, economic and use values • Formally recognised values across international, national and State legislation and policy • Values informally recognised at the regional and local levels • Values informally held by stakeholder groups and individuals
Condition	• Pre-visitation status • Past deterioration trends • Current state of deterioration • Forecast state of deterioration • Resistance and resilience to deterioration
Visitation	• Number of visitors (annual, monthly, weekly, daily, hourly) • Visitation patterns (peaks, troughs and predictable versus unpredictable periods)
Visitor profile	• Demographics (e.g. gender, age, place of residence, income and education) • Psychographics (e.g. motivations, expectations and satisfaction)
Visitor behaviour	• How heritage is directly experienced (activities undertaken, transportation used)
Impact	• Visitor-induced • Development-induced • Global-induced • Potential threats
Management activity	• Revenue • Expenditure • Staffing levels • Nature and degree of activities undertaken • Organisational profile • Level of support from critical stakeholders

may well include a desire to explore a subject in order to develop notions and principles that can become fundamental building blocks of heritage management. Monitoring is typically used to detect and observe long-term trends in the state of the resource and visitor experience or the profile of the visitor, or as a method of assessing particular issues of management concern, such as visitor impact.

Research

Research has been defined as 'the diligent and systematic inquiry or investigation into a subject in order to discover facts or principles' (Macquarie University 1991). There are three main approaches to research: pure, applied and tactical. The more academic pure research explores basic concepts that contribute to fundamental understandings. Applied research balances a tangible outcome against some basic conceptual understandings. Tactical research is typically issue-driven and therefore provides basic information of a practical and short-term nature. These classifications serve to remind heritage managers of the distinction between 'once-off' research and on-going research. The prevalence of 'once-off' research has caused many heritage managers to 'reinvent the wheel' and miss major opportunities for innovation. Some of the objectives of research are to:

- further explore existing information to derive more meaning or make pre-dictions;
- test the validity and strengthen underlying assumptions of information already being monitored;
- explore completely new areas to establish a basic level of understanding (benchmark studies);
- explore completely new areas to determine the nature and extent of mon-itoring; and
- provide focused information that will assist with evaluation programmes. (McArthur and Hall 1996a)

There are three more subject-based forms of research commonly used to help understand the heritage–visitor relationship: market research, visitor research and impact research. The first can be defined as the gathering, analysing and interpreta-tion of information to identify marketing opportunities and link an organisation with its marketing environment (Aaker and Day 1990; see Chapter 7). The second can be defined as the identification and investigation of demographic, psychographic and behavioural characteristics of visitors and the nature of their experience. The third explores the nature and extent of impact upon the physical, social and cultural value of heritage and, to some extent, upon the visitor experience. Impact research is some-times used as a precursor to the development of impact monitoring, which often needs exploratory work done to determine what should be measured over the medium- to long term. A common example of this is baseline studies, which are undertaken to establish benchmarks (see below).

Monitoring

Monitoring is 'a process of repetitive observation of one or more elements or indicators of the environment according to pre-arranged schedules in time or space' (Selman 1992). The World Heritage Committee noted that monitoring should be undertaken in collaboration with stakeholders, and has defined monitoring as:

> a process of repeated comparison of the current status of a site against the original baseline information about its physical, social and administrative con-dition, undertaken with the collaboration of local authorities and institutions ... a process of continuous cooperation between site managers, States Parties and the World Heritage Convention and its partners involving the continuous/repeated observation of the condition(s) of the site, identi-fication of issues that threaten the conservation and World Heritage characteristics of the site and the identification of decisions to be under-taken; and reporting the results of monitoring and recommendations to the appropriate authorities, the World Heritage Bureau and Committee and the cultural and scientific communities. (UNESCO 1993)

Within a strategic approach to heritage management, monitoring goes beyond the selection of indicators and the process of observation to assist in determining the relevance of management decisions and actions. Some of the objectives for under-taking monitoring are to:

- determine the level and nature of use that a heritage site or facility is receiving;

- determine demographic characteristics of visitors and their satisfaction with the experience;

- ensure that activities are carried out in accordance with regulations or permit requirements;

- identify and quantify environmental changes linked to visitor activity;

- identify and quantify changes to the quality of the visitor experience that are linked to other activities within the region;

- check the validity of management assumptions; and

- predict potential impacts and management actions.
  (McArthur and Hall 1996a)

There are perhaps two main areas of monitoring, which are continuously used to understand the heritage–visitor relationship: the monitoring of visitor numbers and characteristics; and the monitoring of visitor impacts. Visitor numbers are the most frequently collected pieces of information and often serve as a critical political tool in arguing for resources. Impact monitoring measures the nature and extent of impact upon the physical, social and cultural value of heritage and, to some extent, upon the visitor experience.

The World Heritage Committee recognises three types of monitoring as being systematic, administrative and *ad hoc* (World Heritage Centre, UNESCO, 1994). The Committee defined systematic monitoring as the continuous or regular process of observing world heritage sites, the identification of threats to conservation and World Heritage values, and the identification and reporting of decisions and actions that subsequently need to be made. The Committee recommends that systematic monitoring and reporting will have to apply to all sites on the World Heritage List and should also include an appreciation of the overall implementation of the World Heritage Convention at the national level (UNESCO 1993). Administrative monitoring was defined as follow-up actions to ensure implementation of recommendations and decisions of the World Heritage Committee and Bureau, either at the time of inscription or at a later date. *Ad hoc* monitoring was defined as reporting on the state of conservation of certain World Heritage sites that are under threat, in exceptional circumstances or where work is being undertaken that may affect the state of conservation of the sites. (See Case Study 5.1.)

Case Study 5.1
Integrating Monitoring into the World Heritage Convention

Key points:
- The level of monitoring undertaken for World Heritage sites has been insufficient.

- Internationally driven efforts are now under way to raise the level and standard of monitoring for World Heritage sites.

- Monitoring is being integrated into the nomination and renomination of World Heritage sites.

The World Heritage Committee is placing increasing importance on monitoring as a critical component of the management of World Heritage sites. In late 1993, at a conference concerning the protection of the world's cultural and natural heritage, the committee recommended that all heritage management organisations:

- put systematic monitoring programmes and supporting organisational structures into place;

- establish guidelines for baseline information and its collection and management;

- revise the nomination and evaluation procedures and process to secure baseline information at the time of the inscription of the site on the World Heritage List;

- establish a format for reporting;

- commission the World Heritage Centre jointly with the International Centre for the Study of the Preservation and Restoration of Cultural Property, the International Council for Monuments and Sites (ICOMOS) and the International Union for the Conservation of Nature and Natural Resources (IUCN) to determine the needs and format for training in methods required; and

- report to the United Nations Educational Scientific and Cultural Organisation (UNESCO) World Heritage Centre on progress in achieving the above steps. (UNESCO 1993)

The monitoring initiative commenced through the collection of baseline data that defines the site's character, universal significance and condition. The importance of undertaking monitoring at the earliest moment possible is being strengthened through the requirement for rigorous monitoring programmes within the nomination process and revised nomination and evaluation procedure. In other words, monitoring must be integrated into the management procedure for new and existing sites. The data must be reviewed and updated every five years and must result in a state of conservation report. Sites under specific threat or on the 'World Heritage List in Danger' will require annual reporting. Regional monitoring, resulting in a regional state of conservation report, is being encouraged to optimise impact and efficiency. Every twenty years a more comprehensive re-evaluation will be undertaken to determine the degree to which sites still meet inscription criteria.

The baseline data must now be collected using international standards. The regulatory initiative will be backed up with training in monitoring for operational heritage managers. Though no evaluations had been published on the implementation at the time of writing, reflections by some individuals suggest only limited success.

Monitoring models

Before deciding which type of monitoring or research technique(s) to use, one should first select the type of monitoring programme that is most appropriate. The mere selection of data collection techniques does not constitute a monitoring programme. A monitoring system or programme is the means by which information is collected, stored and analysed. Monitoring systems may be a part of a broader heritage or visitor management model or may act as a separate unit. It may therefore be helpful first to decide how the information will be used and whether the integration of a monitoring programme into a broader model will be useful – a growing number of heritage managers are adopting this approach (McArthur and Hall 1996a). (Chapter 6 describes several visitor management models – e.g., the Visitor Impact Management Model, the Visitor Activity Management Program and the Tourism

Optimisation Management Model.) The analysis of the data should be integrated into the initial design of the monitoring programme. Some of the monitoring models that have been designed to process and analyse information in areas relating to heritage management are outlined below.

The Decision Feedback Model

The Decision Feedback Model is an extremely simple monitoring analytical model. It generates a simple feedback loop between all decisions and monitoring. The scheme recognises that the environment is affected by heritage management decisions and that the environment itself changes over time (Goldsmith 1991). The simplicity is both a strength and a weakness – highlighting the need for some form of monitoring for all decision-making, yet failing to account for other environmental or organisational influences that must be integrated into a model.

The Ecological Effects Detection Monitoring Model

The Ecological Effects Detection Monitoring Model focuses on obtaining quantifiable levels of precision data using statistical methods to increase reliability and reduce the level of monitoring required and thus reduce monitoring costs (Table 5.2).

Table 5.2 Criteria for selection of environmental indicators

Critical criteria for performance assessment	Desirable criteria for performance assessment
• Measure correlates strongly with changes in ecological processes or other unmeasured components	• Indication of a response to resource use in a measurable way
• Application is possible over a broad range of regional ecosystems	• Indication of widespread change
• Unambiguous and monotoxic relationship to an identified issue	• Presence of a standard measurement technique
• Qualification can be achieved at a low cost	• Low measurement error
• Functionality	• Historical database is available
	• Cost-effectiveness (relative to value of information)
	• Can be used in existing application in policy models

Source: adapted from Hunsaker and Carpenter (1990)

The model (adapted from Hinds 1984) has several stages:

1 define objectives;

2 determine whether specific taxa are to be used:
   • if they are, the taxa are selected and multiple-plot field work is undertaken for variance estimation;
   • if they are not, particular ecological processes are selected;

3 variance is then measured between different plots being measured;

4a if variance is not detected, multiple-plot field work is undertaken for variance estimation;

4b if variance is detectable, a decision is made whether precision and power are adequate for the objectives;

5a if they are not adequate, the findings are documented and the programme design reworked; and

5b if they are adequate, the cost per unit precision and power of the data is determined to be successful or unsuccessful and the monitoring is deemed acceptable (again, if it is not, the results are documented and the design reconsidered).

The Heuristic Kinetic Modeling Model

The Heuristic Kinetic Modeling Model attempts to generate a cost-effective model for determining environmental effects. It is based on first-order kinetics to represent relevant features of baseline monitoring sites and involves:

1 defining the system and monitoring objectives;

2 developing a conceptual model;

3 designing a sampling design;

4 designing a mathematical model;

5 collecting field data;

6 running the model;

7 comparing results; and

8 modifying the monitoring system design. (Wiersma *et al*. 1991)

The model is heuristic in the sense that it enables researchers to describe the relevant features of a system and the interactions between them as a basis for system comprehension, and because information collected in one stage is directly used in the next stage. The model can, however, be limiting in its ability to identify process relationships and accurate descriptions of ecosystem dynamics.

The Integrated Land Management Monitoring Model

The Integrated Land Management Monitoring Model reflects the interrelated nature of scientific and management monitoring components by integrating them together in the one model. It involves:

1 defining users and types of information required;

2 defining the region to be covered;

3 specifying land management objectives;

4 establishing an inventory of basic resources;

5 identifying dynamics of changes relevant to objectives;

6 determining how changes may be measured;

7 designing and implementing a monitoring system;

8 interpreting and evaluating data; and

9 implementing revised management practices.

While the monitoring system is being developed, a decision-making framework for using the information is also determined (Friend 1987). Unfortunately, the emphasis is more on the scientific than the managerial elements. The structure operates at a range of scales but provides limited delineation between indicators and management actions.

The Monitoring and Evaluation Model

The Monitoring and Evaluation Model was developed in a response to a need to evaluate the efficacy of numerous tourism initiatives in the United Kingdom to address business management concerns (Saleem 1992). The model involves:

1 preparing a programme description statement (mission, goals, objectives and strategies of heritage management);

2 carrying out a programme evaluability assessment of the micro- and macro-environment;

3 setting monitoring goals and objectives;

4 establishing performance criteria for the objectives;

5 determining units of measurement for the criteria; and

6 conducting the monitoring, analysing data and drawing conclusions.

The approach relies on identifying clear and measurable objectives and selecting the most appropriate performance criteria available.

The Filter–Signal Monitoring Model

The Filter–Signal Monitoring Model proposes the use of an 'up-front' filtering system to clarify the focus of monitoring in relation to management objectives. It involves:

1 analysing site characteristics;

2 identifying key indicators;

3 designing monitoring methods;

4 undertaking monitoring;

5 analysing the data in relation to the indicators; and

6 management action. (Goldsmith 1991)

The strengths of the model are that it identifies the key features that led to heritage values, then identifies indicators that reflect the state of the values, then monitors status in relation to management actions and natural changes to the heritage. One limitation is the difficulty in distinguishing between incipient and extrinsic change.

Indicators

It can be very difficult to establish a monitoring programme that captures reliably the most appropriate information needed for an understanding of the heritage–visitor relationship. There is an enormous range of information available for collection, so making the right choice of information is critical. The use of indicators helps in part to address this problem. Indicators reflect some form of parameter that is representative or indicative of the state of the heritage being monitored. Indicators will not necessarily describe a situation fully, but they can suggest critical aspects and changes in it. It is vital not to import indicators used in other studies without thoroughly examining their applicability to the heritage site, organisation and stake-holders. P. Middleton (1994) suggests that financial indicators should focus on:

> how well they can be related back to the organisation's stated strategic object-ives (objectives which may often be only partially quantifiable); and the degree of ownership amongst staff and directors trustees of those objectives and hence of beliefs in reference to the measures as an aid to management decision making.

Table 5.3 identifies indicators to detect operational performance of a heritage management organisation while Table 5.4 identifies potential financial performance indicators.

Table 5.3 Potential indicators of operational performance (excluding finances)

Visitor-based indicators	Staff indicators	Overall operational performance
• Visitor numbers by type (e.g. full-price adults, child admissions, school groups) as a proportion of total annual admissions • Proportion of days open per annum with attendance of less than (say) 25% of peak daily attendance • Repeat visits as a proportion of total visits • Visitors with journey times of up to 30, 60 and 90 minutes and of more than 90 minutes to site from home, holiday base, etc.	• Numbers of staff (expressed as FTEs) by functional category (e.g. sales, curatorial, finance) • Proportion of staff with less than one year's service and with more than five, ten and fifteen years' service • Voluntary FTE staff as a percentage of total FTE staff	• Customer complaints as a percentage of letters of compliment • Average number of days taken to reply to customers' letters

Source: adapted from P. Middleton (1994)

Table 5.4 Potential indicators of financial performance

Revenue indicators	Expenditure indicators	Overall financial performance
• Gross admissions revenue per annum • Net contribution from retail, catering etc. per annum • Gross income from other trading sources (e.g. conferences, services etc.) per annum • Average admission receipt per person per annum	• Gross secondary spend (retail, catering) per annum • Cost of retail, catering and other sales per annum • Cost of collections management per annum • Cost of visitor services per annum • Cost of marketing per head of admission per annum	• Annual profit (or deficit) • Gross annual income as a proportion of gross annual costs (or vice versa) • Cost of fund-raising as a proportion of funds raised per annum • Cost of loans servicing as a proportion of total costs per annum • Net monthly cash flow and cumulative monthly cash flow

Source: adapted from P. Middleton (1994)

One means of helping to choose the right indicators is to develop criteria from which to assess the merit of each one. For example, a monitoring report for Australia's Wet Tropics Management Plan listed selection criteria for indicators as being:

- ease of comprehension by all parties;
- requirements for flexibility;
- need to avoid political bias;
- need to meet international comparative standards; and
- need to be capable of integration into 'index' (aggregate) measures of environmental condition. (University of New England 1993)

While indicators suggest what is to be measured, the resulting data will ultimately need to be compared against some sort of reference point for analysis. A benchmark is an indicator's point of reference against which to compare new monitoring data. A benchmark can be identified for each indicator before the monitoring or research techniques are developed and the information collected. In this instance, benchmarks can be established with reference to past studies. If no information is available, benchmarks need to be established, either by estimating what the situation might be or by assuming that the first data set collected represents the benchmark.

It is unrealistic to expect information being collected to remain static; the data will change over time at varying degrees around the benchmark. Therefore, it is also useful to add to the monitoring programme an acceptable range within which the data can be expected to shift. An acceptable range is an ideal yet realistic range in which an indicator should be performing to reach management objectives. Like the benchmarks, the development of acceptable ranges for each indicator may draw on previous studies or estimations from those with experience and expertise in the given field. After their applicability and value have been tested, acceptable ranges and indicators may therefore have to be modified during the start-up phase.

Monitoring and Research Techniques

Once a research or monitoring programme has been developed from objectives, been integrated with a relevant monitoring framework and considered indicators, it is then time to select research or monitoring techniques. Many different techniques can be used to collect information about the heritage–visitor relationship. Common research techniques include questionnaires, interviews, focus groups, needs assessments, environmental impact assessments, environmental audits, and economic assessments. Common monitoring techniques include counting, observation, measurement and community polling. However, many of these techniques float across the dividing line between monitoring and research.

Questionnaires

Questionnaires are a set of printed questions for people to read and respond to. They are either mailed or handed out, or they can be offered in some sort of distribution box. They typically feature multiple-choice and scaling questions and a few closed questions, and some include one or two open-ended questions or places to add comments towards the end. Scaling tests greatly assist visitors to provide information. These can employ a wide range of psychological parameters, such as levels of agreement, interest or satisfaction. An even simpler technique is to represent emotion by means of visual expression, such as asking visitors to represent their feelings via a series of faces showing different expressions or bodies with different postures.

Questionnaires are one of the most frequently used methods of accessing information from visitors (McArthur and Hall 1996a). This is largely because they are believed to produce the greatest volume of information for the least investment in staff resources. Questionnaires can cope with vast ranges in sample size and can be completed at any time, often without any assistance from staff. The saving in staff resources has, to some extent, been transferred to the visitor, who must read and understand the question, then formulate an answer according to a pre-determined style and structure. All of this has to be done at a time when, theoretically, the visitor is on holiday, relaxing or engaged in a leisure activity. However, many visitors have great difficulty in verbalising feelings, issues and ideas about their experience, let alone the management of heritage. Unfortunately, questionnaires are often not designed by people with expertise in social research, and the resulting style and format of questions can often confuse, or ask too much of visitors, or provide little usable information for managers.

Interviews

Highly structured interviews are in some respects like a face-to-face verbalised questionnaire. However, the personal contact of the respondent and interviewer typically generates a more relaxed atmosphere that frees up questioning and the nature of responses. Interviews usually involve a set of topics or questions. The interview begins by introducing the interviewer, the study and the intended use of the information collected. Unlike the questionnaire, this introduction tends to be refined for each interviewee to ensure they are comfortable and prepared to answer questions. Most of the questions tend to be open-ended, but begin with relatively straightforward queries, develop into deeper and more insightful probing, and then end with one or two more forthright queries. This mirrors the comfort and attention span of the interviewee. The interviewer usually has a template to refer to and write notes into. The interviewer may ask follow-on, probing questions if an answer is vague or suggests more insight could be forthcoming. The notes are usually expanded after the interview to include additional comments or even the perceptions of the interviewer. Interviews are very dependent on human resources and therefore tend to have smaller sample sizes than questionnaires. However, the respondent feels more comfortable with them and therefore yields more information and more insight (Forestry Tasmania 1994a).

Focus groups

A focus group has been defined as 'a small, temporary community formed for the purpose of the collaborative enterprise of discovery' (Templeton 1987). Such groups are ideal at exploring complex ideas that cannot be anticipated and structured into an interview or questionnaire. Focus groups are extensively used in product- and service-based market research and increasingly in heritage management (Rubenstein 1991).

The conduct of focus groups is best undertaken by experienced professionals, but the process can be simply outlined in six stages. The first stage involves selecting appropriate participants by screening them via a series of discrete questions pitched over the telephone. The researcher then produces a 'discussion guide' to provide a preview of the way the discussion is likely to proceed. A typical session usually involves:

- a short warm-up period, where individuals introduce themselves and the moderator introduces the ground rules;

- a predisposition discussion, where the moderator provides context to the topic;

- the body of the session, where a series of questions is used to stimulate discussion about a topic;

- a collective and comparative discussion, where the answers are assimilated to form links and broader discussion; and

- a wrap up, where participants are given the opportunity to make any additional comments or ask relevant questions of their own to the moderator. (McArthur and Hall 1996a)

During the body of the session, the moderator will often use objects and audio-visual presentations to assist with context and stimulate thoughts. Relatively unstructured sessions usually rely upon some form of recording to be made for later qualitative analysis. Semi-structured sessions may utilise workbooks for participants to write their thoughts down prior to discussing them with the group. This can enhance the quality of comment but rarely negates the need for a back-up audio recording to be made. The final stage is a brief post-mortem and the preparation of a report.

Needs Assessments

Needs assessments have become an integral part of many recreation planning processes. They identify the needs of a defined group of people before, during or after a plan, facility or service is implemented. Ideally, needs assessments are undertaken periodically and cover what currently exists, what the market-place needs and, thus, the areas of under- and over-supply. Tools employed include inventories of facilities and services, telephone polls for general information and workshops or focus group sessions for more detailed insights. Many needs assessments are limited to collecting demographic rather than psychographic information about constituents. Unfortunately, many heritage managers in local government have become overly focused on demographic information collected by telephone polling. Alternative systems, such as market segmentation, are often shunned as being too risky, one reason being that their typically smaller sample size and qualitative data generate perceptions that they are less credible. The other reason is an underlying fear of focusing on particular markets as opposed to being all things to all people, which is actually preferred by politically sensitive managers.

Environmental Impact Assessments

Environmental Impact Assessments (EIAs) are an analytical procedure for predicting and evaluating the environmental impact of proposed development programmes and projects, terminating with a written report to prescribe environmental safeguards; and a legally defined administrative procedure for involving major interest groups in the decision-making process and for informing the public and resolving potential conflicts caused by multiple uses of the community's resources (James and Boer 1988). In this way the EIA is a reactive form of research that is not initiated until something is proposed. It usually involves some five stages across the construction and operational periods of the proposal (Selman 1992). The first stage of an EIA is to describe the proposal itself, the expected quantity of resources used and wastes generated, the existing environmental conditions and any information gaps in knowledge of the conditions. The second (main) stage of the EIA involves forecasting the probable impact of development and the relative importance of each impact to scientific benchmarks and the needs of stakeholders. The third stage involves checking for compliance with environmental policies, plans and regulations. The fourth stage is to examine then compare the relative impacts of alternative proposals to the main one. The last stage is to convert the main findings of the EIA into a report called an Environmental Impact Statement (EIS).

The research typically consists of environmental investigation of particular habitats to determine biodiversity, dependent relationships, sensitivity and resilience to impact. It may also involve social research through consultation with proponents, specialists and stakeholders. This research is more effective when the stakeholders are kept well informed of the proposal and major findings, since the greater awareness typically leads to greater insight and thus more descriptive accounts of perceived impacts. EISs can be limited in their ability to prevent or modify undesirable initiatives. One reason for this inability is that the timing of an EIA creates uncertainties in its forecasting and prevents it from assessing cumulative impacts (Buckley 1991). Another, more fundamental, reason is that EISs are considered too complex and too bureaucratic to respond to the more dynamic economic and political momentum established by proponents of ventures being assessed.

The same sort of approach is also applied to Social Impact Assessments (SIAs), which focus on forecasting impacts upon stakeholders from a proposal. SIAs are more likely to generate more qualitative data than EISs and are therefore more difficult to use to make comparisons between alternative proposals. The fact that SIAs are not taken on as regularly or extensively as EISs has raised questions about how heritage is valued and whether physical environmental dimensions sometimes dominate over socio-cultural attachment to heritage. (See Case Study 5.2.)

Case Study 5.2
Visitor Impact Management Model for Youghiogheny River, Maryland, USA

Key points:

- Research that addresses simultaneously the quality of the heritage and the visitor experience can generate fundamental understandings about the heritage–visitor relationship.

- Research can reveal methods of making visitor management more flexible to minimise impact and maximise visitor satisfaction and the viability of tourism operator.

The Youghiogheny River in western Maryland is one of the premier whitewater boating rivers in the north-eastern United States. Since the commencement of commercial river running in 1980, the number of operators and visitors has grown substantially. In response, in 1989 the managers of the river, the Maryland Department of Natural Resources, imposed a limit of seventy-two visitors per day and various boating regulations. Two years later the Department decided to determine the degree of environmental and social impacts that were occurring as a result of the increasing visitation (Graefe 1991). The study identified: hydrological character-istics of the river; existing recreational use; environmental impacts; and the capacity of the river for whitewater boating. The hydrological assessment measured the travel time characteristics of hydro-power releases to identify navigability limitations for various types of vessel. The envir-onmental impacts were determined using a combination of past studies, field observations and interviews with visitors and landowners. Existing use and capacity were determined through a series of on-site interviews before and after the river experience. Questionnaires were mailed out to adjacent landowners and visitors after their experience to access more detailed information and reflection.

Results of the research suggested that slight impacts existed but were confined to a few access points along the river. Visitor satisfaction was continually high but decreased with the combination of increasing numbers of boats and lower water levels. The study suggested that the minimum water release period of two hours created lengthy periods for boats to pass through low-water areas, which in turn increased perceptions of crowding and decreased satisfaction. It concluded that higher user limits could be accommodated during periods of higher flow and that it was unrealistic to set a carrying capacity because of the varying water levels. The principal implication was that more flexible limits on boat numbers and visitor behaviour needed to be adopted.

Environmental Audits

Auditing involves testing the accuracy of predictions made in past plans or assess-ments against those actually occurring (Selman 1992). Environmental audits are often made to assess the changing state of an environment or, occasionally, the effective-ness of a policy or programme: 'an audit should cast light on the accuracy of forecasts [and] the performance of measures to mitigate impacts, and should indicate the effectiveness of monitoring, surveillance and environmental practices' (Selman 1992). Audits differ from EIAs in four respects: auditing is usually not mandatory, whereas the EIA is usually mandatory; auditing requires documented evidence, whereas the EIA uses opinion based on professional judgement; audits focus on envir-onmental performance, whereas the EIA focuses on preconditions of development; and audits that involve a comparison are more concerned with whether the process of impact prediction is performing satisfactorily (Ding and Pigram 1995). The audit typically begins by establishing a set of benchmarks from which to make compar-isons with the actual state of affairs. Research is then employed to detect how close the current state of play of each indicator is to its benchmark. The current status is also compared with compliance levels or forecasts. The reporting then simply involves identifying and reporting on gaps and inconsistencies.

The basic act of comparison between predicted and actual affairs has manifested itself in a wide number of audits. Compliance audits ensure that regulations are not being breached. Site audits use spot checks upon known problem areas. Corporate audits examine the performance of an entire organisation. Issues audits respond to specific environmental issues. Associate audits involve the extension of vetting an environmental action to an organisation's contractors, agents and suppliers. Activity audits evaluate policy in activities that cross business boundaries, particularly distribution and transport networks (Selman 1992).

Although audits can help an organisation to identify weaknesses and establish a green image, they have been widely criticised for lacking rigour and comprehensiveness (Selman 1992). One of the main contributors here is the lack of reliable benchmarks from which to make comparisons and forecasts. Often heritage managers have never established benchmarks nor collected sufficient data to allow statistically valid interpretations of cause–effect relationships. This is obviously a problem for most monitoring and research techniques.

Economic Assessments

With growing competition for limited public funding, heritage managers are increasingly turning to economic assessments to justify resourcing. Perhaps their most profound use is in determining the economic value of a heritage site (Mathieson and Wall 1982). This form of research is considered highly specialised, and because of the scale of economic and subsequent political issues consultants are usually employed. There are a number of methods of undertaking an economic assessment of the value of a heritage site. One of the most frequently used is calculating the income generated from tourist activity. Typical indicators used in assessment models include: visitation; number of beds or nights spent by visitors in a locality; expenditure by visitors; and income earnt from tourist operations. A critical factor in making an assessment is the use of a multiplier effect (the amount of follow-on activity indirectly resulting from visitors). Many assessments have not included the economic value that non-visitors place on heritage and the multiplier effects generated by the mere presence of heritage. To assess these opens up enormous debates that typically fall back into competing values and the inability to cost opportunity or intrinsic value (Aukerman and Thomson 1991).

Counting

Counting is the simple process of determining how many objects or people exist or how many times something occurs over a period of time (McArthur and Hall 1996a). One of the most frequently used forms of counting in the heritage–visitor relationship is the counting of visitors to establish visitation patterns. The simplest system asks visitors to register themselves in a visitors' book. Managers of natural heritage have expanded the books for visitors to enter their route or intentions. In heavily visited places devices are used that count the number of vehicles, pedestrians or sales. Vehicle counters are typically activated by pressure hoses located on or under the road surface. Standard counters log the time and date of each entry, and more elaborate models can determine the direction and speed of the vehicle, as well as differentiate between standard cars, cars with trailers, mini-buses, coaches and trucks. Managers responsible for facilities such as visitor centres, museums and art galleries use counting devices more focused on the individual visitor. Electronic beams common in shops are popular, though other systems such as turnstiles and pressure pads are also used. Facilities and experiences that charge an entrance or use fee now build monitoring into the computer within their cash registers. Like the vehicle counters, these also monitor time and date, but can be further programmed to record the type of visitor – i.e., adult, child, student or pensioner. A facility can have a monitoring device fitted to it, which may include anything from switches attached to the lids or seats of toilets, to programs that monitor decisions and correct responses made within interactive computers. The challenge in monitoring the use of facilities or experiences is to ensure that the visitor either is unaware of the device or does not abuse it. However, despite all of the technological advances, the reliability of monitoring visitation is still heavily dependent on restricting visitor access to a minimum number of points.

Observations

Observations can be a simple and cost-effective means of collecting information. They can also help validate other data sources, such as visitor intentions. They can even be used as alternatives to over-burdened techniques, such as questionnaires, which have been known to ask visitors for information that is easily observable. Observations can be structured according to the level of variation expected. A narrow level of variation may permit categorising into types (e.g., gender, age group and activities) or levels (e.g., noise, use of facilities and attentiveness). A wide or unknown level of variation may require observations to be purely descriptive (e.g., type of equipment used, clothing worn and expressions displayed). The more observations that can be categorised, the more cost-effective they become to make and analyse. Visitor behaviour can also be observed using maps for movement and stops to be chartered on (often referred to as flow diagrams). Aerial photography can also be used to observe the distribution of vegetation and location of wildlife.

Environmental Measurements

Environmental measurements are typically used to measure the physical, biological or chemical condition of heritage. They share some overlap with counting and observations. Environmental measurements typically involve the use of electronic equipment or chemicals to measure specific aspects of the environment. They include:

- gauges to measure rain, wind, pressure, tides and currents;
- thermometers to measure temperature;
- probes to measure conductivity, dissolved oxygen and pH;
- theodolites to measure heights;
- geometers to measure distances;
- radio tracking devices to follow animals; and
- carbon dating equipment to measure age.

Measuring impact on heritage is difficult because of the complexity of the natural and cultural environment. Many heritage managers lack a solid benchmark from which to measure from – e.g., knowing what the condition of the resource was before visitation occurred, making it difficult to identify natural oscillations and reflect legitimate change. While initial direct impacts can be measured, it is the indirect, secondary and follow-on effects that may pose the greatest challenge and tend to make the results of most research programmes indicative at best. As a consequence, most measurements of impact are tied to major tourist infrastructure, such as accommodation or transport systems, rather than the impact caused by the visitors themselves, though this general rule is broken in instances where an individual's behaviour can cause a readily identifiable impact, such as walking on a coral reef (McArthur and Hall 1996a). (See Case Study 5.3.)

Case Study 5.3
The Wildlife and Visitor Relationship at Kakadu National Park, Australia

Key points:

- Research that addresses simultaneously the quality of the heritage and the visitor experience can generate fundamental understandings about the heritage–visitor relationship.

- It is difficult to prove direct disturbance of wildlife from visitor activity, but research can identify indicator species for monitoring programmes to detect warning signs.

- Well-managed ecotourism experiences can provide high-quality, sustainable visitor experiences.

Kakadu National Park in far northern Australia has cultural and natural features of World Heritage significance. Nature-based tourism operators provide a vast array of visitor experiences, but perhaps most famous are cruises along the Yellow Waters. Significant efforts are being made to make these tours ecotourism based; the tours operate in a natural area, have interpretation as a core part of the experience, contribute to the management of the local area and its indigenous population, and are attempting to be ecologically sustainable. To help achieve these objectives a research study was undertaken to explore the relationship between the quality of the environment and the visitor experience (Braithwaite *et al.* 1996). The study simultaneously measured visitor responses to a variety of experiences and environmental impacts accrued to the experiences. Some 195 cruises were monitored over twelve months and across six different times of the day. Surveys examined the nature of visitor expectations and the degree to which they were fulfilled. Environmental impact was determined by measuring the observed number of animals and their behavioural responses to tourist activity. The strongest causes of disturbance were identified and assessed against each disturbance actually observed. Data were recorded on each cruise whenever the guide pointed out a species of plant, bird or animal (these segments of the interpretation were called focus events). Data included: the duration of the focus event; the species; the number of individuals; whether the approach by the boat was powered or unpowered; the speed and angle of the approach; and the behavioural disturbance observed. The analysis of the impact data per species began by narrowing the range of causes of disturbance using a sub-set regression analysis, then by identifying the principal cause for each species using $r2$ and Mallo's Cp statistics (Seber 1977).

Visitor satisfaction did not appear to be derived from one major event but from the cumulative effect of different biological, climatic and social characteristics. The greatest lowering influences on satisfaction were the absence of animals and high levels in temperature, humidity and water. No strong evidence of environmental impact was found, though disturbance of fauna by tour boats was weakly related to such variables as monthly rainfall and water levels. The tolerance of each animal was indicated by the closeness of the approach, the time-length of the presence and the intensity of the response that it allowed. Tolerance to the approach of boats gradually increased with successive experiences. However, the study identified a point at which disturbance may become so frequent or intense that the animal's response causes it to lose energy and weight, followed by reduction of, and potential cessation in, breeding. A number of species were identified as being vulnerable to human disturbance and were therefore identified as indicators for on-going monitoring to focus on.

Community Polling

Community polling is a cost-effective technique for gaining broad-scale information about attitudes and values towards heritage and heritage management. The technique typically involves a market research company being contracted to carry out a telephone survey of between 500 and 1,000 respondents. The procedure basically involves the development of a short and simple questionnaire featuring closed questions of a yes/no, true/false or multiple-choice variety. Respondents are rung up, introduced to the purpose of the study and then asked four or five basic questions. The results can be quickly tabulated and dispersed among stakeholders. Polling tends to give scale to results gained from more intensive research efforts. When this is not the case, such as when it is used to determine voting intentions, it is taken with no more than a grain of salt. However, like questionnaires and interviews, the design of questions for use in polling will have a fundamental influence on the response. It is possible to achieve radically different responses just by seemingly minor alterations in the question.

Conclusion

This chapter has introduced the need to understand more about the intimate relationship between heritage and visitors. By understanding more about visitors it is possible to develop more proactive initiatives that assist heritage management planning and programmes to work with, rather than against, the visitor. This chapter has stressed the need to determine what the critical information needs are and how they relate to broader visitor and heritage management before selecting monitoring or research techniques. The chapter has outlined a number of models that help address information needs and how data can be integrated into the decision-making process.

A number of constraints currently work against the more widespread adoption of monitoring into heritage management. Ding and Pigram (1995) suggest that these include:

- lack of relevant legal requirements, policies and standards in tourism;
- lack of mechanisms for the implementation of an environmental auditing process in tourism development;
- difficulties in defining the explicit boundaries of an environmental auditing process for the tourist industry;
- lack of necessary authority and ability to undertake environmental auditing for the development of tourism;
- the absence of up-to-date environmental monitoring data; and
- the absence of examples and comparative studies.

One of the key challenges in understanding more about the heritage–visitor relationship is to collect information that is needed for critical decision-making but that also contributes to fundamental concepts about visitor behaviour. At present there remains a gulf between the short-term, issues-based tactical research undertaken by heritage managers and the occasional applied research undertaken by academics and postgraduate students. Another challenge is to begin developing visitor profiles that can be applied across disciplines and stakeholder groups. In this way, heritage managers will be able to track the needs and behaviour of visitors across such practices as marketing, interpretation, recreation and tourism planning. The challenge in impact monitoring is to develop and get endorsement of an effective monitoring system that satisfies a range of stakeholders, before more rigorous and mandatory compliance measures are imposed. Imposed compliance may seem attractive to some heritage managers, but it will reduce the opportunity for cooperative partnerships between heritage managers and stakeholder groups.

Once we understand all key stakeholders, particularly visitors, we are in a position to undertake visitor management. This is the subject of Chapter 6.

CHAPTER 6

Visitor Management

Our good friends had arrived the previous day and talked incessantly about wanting to visit the locality and find out more about its history. We'd had a tough time finding a place to go to. The tourist information centre was full of brochures on hotels, motels, flats, restaurants and golf courses. The staff recommended a place but didn't sound as though they'd been there. As we arrived, we realised the estimate of one hour's drive was about an hour short; now the tank was low, and we'd have to watch where we drove. The three signs we saw read: 'No littering. Penalty $500'; 'No hunting or shooting. Penalty $300'; and 'Visitors leaving their valuables unattended do so at their own risk'. We no longer felt as keen to get out. But we did, and the staff were right: there was a lookout point and a monument. However, there were no signs about the view, no information about what to do, and we weren't even sure we were in the right place. We couldn't get close to the monument because two bored boys were throwing stones at it. We left and contemplated a game of golf for the rest of the afternoon.

Introduction

Chapter 3 outlined the range of stakeholders in heritage and the reasons why they need to be involved in as many aspects of management as possible. Chapter 5 suggested that it is visitors who derive the greatest benefit from heritage conservation through their direct experiencing of it. Close visitor contact with heritage makes it meaningful and enjoyable, which increases appreciation. Yet close contact also increases the potential for impact upon the heritage and the visitor experience. Visitor impact can reduce the integrity and value of heritage, which in turn may reduce visitor satisfaction and interest in experiencing heritage and, ultimately, support for heritage and heritage management. This situation is known as the heritage management paradox (Hall and McArthur 1996b).

Heritage managers find in visitors a ready market for communicating to them what they value about heritage and how they would like it managed. They can also share with the visitors the values and issues associated with heritage, and even the opportunities and limitations of having them experience that heritage. Visitors have been known to translate impressions of their experience into general impressions of heritage management and the heritage manager. This is not surprising if the visit is their only direct experience of heritage management. Therefore, the visitor–heritage relationship is a symbiotic one; the heritage manager needs the visitor to help justify the way heritage is being managed, and the visitor needs the heritage manager to look after the heritage and provide a high-quality experience. Visitor management is about managing this relationship; it has been defined as 'the management of visitors in a manner which maximises the quality of the visitor experience while assisting the achievement of an area's overall management objectives' (Hall and McArthur 1996c). In the case of heritage management the number-one overall management objective is the conservation of the heritage resource.

This chapter will outline and contrast some of the ways in which visitor management is undertaken, concentrating on how well the various techniques conserve heritage and improve the quality of the visitor experience, as well as the extent to which they are used by heritage managers. The reader should note that some of the more fundamental visitor management approaches have been covered in separate chapters. These include strategic planning, research and monitoring, marketing, interpretation and education and evaluation. The chapter will then present a number of models for integrating and driving some of the techniques. The authors propose that all visitor management techniques and models can be valid, but stress that an integrated approach will always be more capable of reflecting the complexities that typically exist in the visitor–heritage relationship.

Visitor Management Approaches and Techniques

There are a host of approaches or techniques available to undertake visitor management. Table 6.1 lists some of these and provides examples where they have recently been or are still being utilised. The approaches listed in the table are briefly outlined further below.

Table 6.1 Applications of visitor management techniques

Visitor management technique	Application
Regulating access by area	• All visitors are prohibited from visiting some highly significant Aboriginal sacred sites in Australia. • Different types and levels of use are regulated through zoning at the Saba Marine Park in the Netherlands Antilles.
Regulating access by transport	• The only way to explore the Royal Chitwan National Park in Nepal is by foot or by elephant. • The only way to explore the Keoladeo National park in Nepal is as a pedestrian or by bicycle. • The only way to explore Plitvice Lakes in the former Yugoslavia is by buses provided by the Parks Service. • Centennial Park, Sydney, Australia has several 'car free days' each year in which alternative ways to enter and move about the park must be found.
Regulating visitation by numbers and group size	• Regulations on total visitation per year, day or at any moment have been generated for sites in the United States such as Yosemite Valley and Boundary Waters Canoe Area, Angkor World Heritage Site in Cambodia, Green Island and Wilson's Promontory in Australia, Waitomo Caves in New Zealand and in Bermuda. • Group size restrictions have been implemented in Antarctica, various mountain trails in Nepal (particularly on Mount Everest) and in the United States in areas such as the Sylvania Recreation Area (Ottawa National Forest, Michigan, and the Boundary Waters Canoe Area. • Only one group of visitors per day can visit a family of gorillas at Kahuzi-Biega Park, Zaire, and the maximum group size is eight visitors.
Regulating visitation by type of visitor	• The Banc d'Arguin National Park in Mauritania has a limit on visitation and the type of visitor, who is required to be 'well informed' about the traditional fishing culture, before being permitted to enter. • Cyprus targets older high- and middle-income groups and actively discourage other segments by using strict controls on all accommodation and services, keeping prices high and scrutinising all marketing to maintain consistency.
Regulating behaviour	• Zoning on Great Barrier Reef Marine Park, Australia, allocates different types of use to specified areas.

continues

Table 6.1 continued

<table>
<tr><td></td><td>
<ul>
<li>Zoning at the Tatry National Park, Poland, allocates different types of use to specified areas with a strong emphasis on buffer zones.</li>
<li>A carry-in, carry-out policy for rubbish has been generated by rafters within the Grand Canyon National Park, United States.</li>
<li>Walkers along the Milford Sound in New Zealand can only stay one night in the designated huts provided along the route.</li>
<li>The International Association of Antarctica Tour Operators has a detailed set of guidelines of conduct for visitors to Antarctica.</li>
<li>Visitors viewing sealing seals at Seal Bay, Kangaroo Island, South Australia, must visit with a guide and the group must not get closer than five metres from any seal.</li>
</ul>
</td></tr>
<tr><td>Regulating equipment</td><td>
<ul>
<li>Off-road/highway vehicles are generally not permitted to leave formed roads within most of the world's national parks.</li>
<li>In Tasmania's World Heritage Area, Australia, open fires are not permitted; fuel stoves are the only legal alternative form of cooking.</li>
<li>Motorised river vessels are prohibited in wild sections of the Chatooga River, United States.</li>
<li>Zoning at Angkor World Heritage Site, Siem Reap Province, Cambodia, limits levels of tourism development.</li>
</ul>
</td></tr>
<tr><td>Implementing entry or user fees</td><td>
<ul>
<li>Most heritage managers responsible for highly visited heritage now charge fees to access the site or use facilities at the site, influencing some visitors to choose whether to visit or find an alternative destination.</li>
<li>Some heritage sites offer days during low season when residents are offered free entry, e.g. Port Arthur, Tasmania, Australia.</li>
<li>Machu Picchu, Peru, requires tourism operators to pay for a permit or licence to access the heritage site, and operators must also collect entrance fees from each of their clients.</li>
<li>A portion of user fees collected in Kenya's parks is returned to local stakeholders as a means of demonstrating the value of conserving wildlife.</li>
</ul>
</td></tr>
<tr><td>Modifying the site</td><td>
<ul>
<li>The Valley of the Giants in the Walpole–Nornalup National Park in Western Australia has a 60-m-long, 40-m-high steel boardwalk built through the tree tops to reduce compaction from trampling and to provide a unique visitor experience.</li>
<li>The Castlemaine Jail, Victoria, Australia, is privately run as a heritage tourism venture, with the prison workshops providing a conference venue, the dungeon kitchen providing a wine bar, the mess hall providing an à la carte restaurant, refurbished cells providing accommodation, and remaining cells being presented as they were originally used for guided tours to access.</li>
</ul>
</td></tr>
<tr><td>Undertaking market research</td><td>
<ul>
<li>A study of eleven representative summer holiday brochures of overseas destinations targeted at a cross-section of the British public explored the proportion of images depicting tourists mixing with local communities, and the way in which indigenous tourism workers were depicted to suggest a level of responsible marketing.</li>
<li>A study of postcards of indigenous people from many different places across the world was used to reflect on how the marketing of indigenous heritage has changed, yet continually focused on the exotic, and to suggest the need for more accurate and accountable marketing.</li>
<li>A study of the New Zealand international visitor survey was conducted in order to identify the market segments most likely to visit wildlife tourism attractions.</li>
</ul>
</td></tr>
<tr><td>Undertaking visitor monitoring and research</td><td>
<ul>
<li>The Norfolk Coast Project in the United Kingdom asked visitors to complete special 'day diary' forms to identify their motivations for visiting and the activities they undertook.</li>
<li>River boaters on the Salmon River Wilderness Area, United States, were asked for their attitudes towards their experience and the performance of the respective heritage manager as a means of improving visitor management strategies.</li>
<li>Visitor impact monitoring and research has been widely undertaken across the United States, such as in Sequoia and Kings Canyon National Parks, the Sierra Nevada in California, the Great Smoky Mountains National Park in North Carolina/Tennessee, and Boundary Waters Canoe Area, Minnesota.</li>
</ul>
</td></tr>
</table>

continues

Table 6.1 continued

	• A study of recreation users in the Rattlesnake National Recreation Area and Wilderness, United States, explored whether the designation of an area as a reserve inevitably led to an increase in visitation, by comparing visitation before and after the designation.
Undertaking promotional marketing	• Visitation pressure in the Lake District National Park, United Kingdom, is being relieved through the development and marketing of value-added alternative destinations and incentive schemes by Furness and Cartmel Tourism. • Forestry Tasmania joined with Tourism Tasmania to generate a set of photographs of visitors to Tasmania's State Forest, Australia; both organisations endorse the market profile, activity and destination.
Undertaking strategic information marketing	• Coach drivers can avoid sensitive areas within the Dartmoor region of the United Kingdom by using a specially designed map and pictorial guide that also identifies the best vantage points for attractions. • A 'trail selector' (brochure and map) was developed to provide information on lightly used trails in Yellowstone National Park, United States, to redistribute use away from heavily used trails.
Providing interpretation programmes and facilities	• Corfu in the Ionian Islands is generating greater levels of visitor respect for living culture through the provision of opportunities such as learning to cook with a Greek family and spending a night with a local shepherd. • Visitors to the Canyon de Chelly National Monument in New Mexico are taken on guided tours by the local Indian tribe which also spends the summer and grazes animals in the reserve. This level of authenticity greatly enhances the quality of the visitor experience.
Providing education programmes and facilities	• Grand Cayman's Ramada Treasure Island Resort created an underwater snorkel trail in an artificial pool to educate visitors about correct diving and snorkelling procedures. • The educational campaign 'Tread lightly on public and private land' has been so successful at promoting minimal impact behaviour across various recreational activity that it now operates across the United States, Canada, Australia and New Zealand.
Modifying the profile of heritage management	• Most museums position security staff strategically in corners and corridors to to create a high profile when visitors are moving between exhibits and low profile when they are studying an individual exhibit. • The United States Parks Service employs track rangers each summer to roam busy tracks in sensitive areas and generate positive profile for the organisation and sustainable behaviour by visitors (such as Yellowstone, Grand and Bryce Canyon National Parks, and the Colorado and Chattooga Rivers).
Encouraging and assisting alternative providers – the tourist industry	• Rara Avis, Costa Rica, provides ecotourism accommodation and tours by guides who are highly trained in heritage and interpretation, with profits being reinvested into the development of sustainable industries for the local population. • The Sunungukai Tourism Camp in Nyagande Village in Zimbabwe uses local villages to provide ecotourism accommodation and indigenous activities that maximise returns from marginal land.
Encouraging and assisting alternative providers – volunteers	• The management plan for selected Gwaii Haanas sites in Haida Gwaii requires traditional resident guardianship and interpretation for visitors during summer months. • The Kaori Wildlife Sanctuary in New Zealand is a private trust with a membership of several thousand people. A sizeable proportion of members volunteer to help build trails and act as guides, allowing the Trust to reinvest funds into activities such as pest control and building a strong community base.
Concentrating on accredited organisations bringing visitors to a site	• Australia's National Ecotourism Accreditation Program is being used by several heritage management organisations to check on the appropriateness of tourism operator practices. • The Austrian Association of Green Villages requires accommodation providers to meet criteria and market cooperatively with others.

Regulating Access by Area

Regulating access is often, at first sight, the simplest method of minimising visitor impact. (Without the presence of visitors it is hard to have visitor impact!) Regulating access can be done by passing legislation directly (through an Act) and/or indirectly (through a plan endorsed by government) prohibiting people from visiting a site. Access restriction is usually confined to small and well-specified heritage sites that are generally accepted as having national or international significance and have little to no resilience to visitor impact. The total exclusion of all visitors specifically to protect heritage is rare to non-existent in most countries. Instead, managers regulate access on given terms, such as certain days or times of the day, or for certain activities. For example, seasonal or annual closure of camping grounds is common practice to reduce impact.

Two major drawbacks of regulating access are that it often creates visitor discontent and sometimes fails to manage demand. In consequence, alternative sites receive additional visitation, and as soon as the problem site is reopened it may receive an increase in average visitation.

Regulating Access by Transport

Controlling visitor access within a heritage site can also be done less directly by regulating the type of transport permitted. The most common approach is a negative one: regulating against certain types of transport, such as off-road vehicles, power-boats, horses, mountain bikes, helicopters, planes and, of course, motor cars. Alternatively, heritage managers can use a positive approach: requiring visitors to arrive on foot or to use certain types of transport, such as a public shuttle bus, or a boat. Either approaches can be directly or indirectly enshrined in law and can form part of a zoning system.

Regulating Visitation by Numbers and Group Size

Ceilings or caps on the total number of visitors (at any one time, per day or per year) are becoming an increasingly common way of regulating visitation. The strength – and weakness – of the technique is its simplicity. It can be easily understood by managers and stakeholders, but it assumes each visitor will have the same demands and create the same impacts. Another problem with setting limits is that it encourages dishonesty among visitors. For example, people required to book for use of a camping ground in summer may book for the following year in advance or book under another name, thus monopolising the experience. An alternative to limits on numbers is to restrict the maximum size of the group. This technique is often applied for constricted spaces, such as caves, river corridors, buildings and specialised facilities. It is frequently used on guided tours because the guide monitors the number and prevents more people from joining. Just as in setting caps on overall visitation, the many variables influencing an ideal group size make generating a single number extremely difficult. Regulating overall visitation or group size can generate significant conflicts between heritage managers and stakeholders, particularly if the means by which the optimum figure was generated is unclear.

Regulating Visitation by Type of Visitor

It is possible to regulate to ensure a certain type of visitor utilises a heritage site (positive approach) or, conversely, to prevent certain types of visitors from accessing a heritage site (negative approach). Examples of the positive regulatory approach include requiring a visitor to be of a specified gender, be of in certain age category, have undergone certain education or training, or hold a certain status within the community. Examples of a negative regulatory approach include preventing loud, obnoxious or intoxicated people from visiting and preventing women who are currently menstruating from entering sacred sites. However well-intentioned the rationale, the approach is a volatile one that raises equity issues relating to the rights of an individual versus the rights of the greater community.

Regulating Behaviour

Regulating behaviour is becoming a common method of managing visitors. The most common form is to favour certain activities over others at sensitive sites. This is typically undertaken using a negative approach whereby certain activities are prohibited (e.g., mineral prospecting, hunting and shooting, off-road driving, mountain-bike riding and horse riding, fishing, campfires and the removal of any living or non-living material). The approach can be phased according to the level of sensitivity. Some of these activities may be permitted in designated areas of semi-sensitivity under certain conditions, while at more resilient sites the activities may be permitted but not encouraged.

The classic way in which this form of regulation is implemented is through zoning, which is a geographically based approach to evaluating, classifying and controlling activities across different sites. Ideally, zoning is a graded system representing the nature of an area and the extent to which it can be utilised (Scherl 1994). It identifies: a core area, which reflects the highest conservation value; a buffer zone around the core; and development or utilisation zones surrounding the buffers. In this way zoning establishes conservation areas and separates incompatible recreational activities by allocating the most appropriate use to the most appropriate area, typically based on conservation values (Ceballos-Lacuarain 1996). To achieve this, zoning requires that the use of adjacent land or water be complementary rather than conflicting. Zoning is not an end in itself; it needs to be flexible and backed up by management plans. Some of the problems experienced with zoning include:

- a need for extremely high-quality information about the heritage resource and associated uses;
- considerable spatial and temporal variance;
- a generalist, compromising nature, which reduces accuracy in achieving management objectives and creates conflict; and
- limited capability to justify on-going management decisions.

Nonetheless, zoning is increasingly being used as a planning control to regulate access because it provides a simplistic and relatively clear-cut system for managers to implement and visitors to follow. Prohibiting certain activities can be an equally blunt approach to managing visitors and their impacts. Each activity undergoes varying levels of use over varying time periods. Variation can even occur in the way the activity is undertaken among visitors with different interests, abilities and equipment.

The second, less common, form of behavioural regulation concerns the way in which an activity is undertaken. For example, heritage managers may regulate against damaging exhibits in a museum or gallery, how to walk in trackless areas, times of the day in which it is permitted to swim, how a visitor may address an indigenous person, sources of wood for campfires, how to extinguish a campfire, and how to dispose of human waste and personal refuse. These behavioural regulations are less likely to be enforced because they are difficult to apply to individual circumstances and because they may seriously diminish the image of the heritage manager. Imposing any sort of limitation often runs against visitors' need for freedom, self-expression and escape. Experiences that include a high degree of regulatory behaviour tend to be time-consuming and generate various inconveniences.

Regulating Equipment

Some heritage managers have regulated the type of equipment that is permitted (positive approach) or not permitted (negative approach) to experience heritage. The negative approach is more common. Two examples are:

- the banning of equipment required to undertake a banned activity (e.g., off-road vehicles, horses, firearms, axes and chainsaws, explosives and cameras with flashes); and
- prohibiting equipment that is part of a permissible activity but is not deemed appropriate at a heritage site (e.g., generators, tape recorders and players, bags (which could aid purloining or souveniring) and clothing deemed offensive.

Positive approaches occasionally employed include requiring the use of:

- fuel stoves instead of campfires;
- soft shoes at heritage sites;
- a sash or scarf at religious sites; and
- helmets when riding a horse, motorbike or trail bike.

Even positive approaches to regulating equipment are not common because they can impose considerable inconveniences on visitors. For example, visitors may have to purchase equipment that they may never use again, or they may have to learn how to use the equipment before visiting the heritage site.

Implementing Entry or User Fees

The initial concept of 'user pays', as represented by entry and use fees, is based on the notion that those who benefit the most should pay the most. Most visitors deriving benefit from heritage are not opposed to paying for the experience, provided that the money can be directly reinvested into managing the heritage and the heritage experience. In addition to raising revenue, entry and user fees can also be used to deliberately change the number and type of visitors. The fee tends to stimulate visitors to think more about why they are coming and what they expect from the experience. People who do not value the heritage experience enough to pay for it may elect not to visit. This implies that fees increase the proportion of visitors who are supportive of heritage management and are prepared to adjust their behaviour accordingly. Entry fees are typically collected at heritage sites where access can be controlled, such as museums, historic sites, art galleries and natural areas with only one or two road access points. Heritage managers may require tour operators to collect the fee from their clients, and this is usually done by incorporating the fee within the overall package price. Use fees are charged for the use of specialised infrastructure, such as recreational facilities, or services, such as guiding and interpretive activities.

Use fees are also levied on tourist businesses operating on the heritage site, such as providers of accommodation, shops, restaurants and tours. These use fees are typically veiled within a licence or permit. Fees can give rise to a number of visitor management problems: they can only be collected from sites where it is economical to do so; they can displace visitation and associated visitor management issues to other sites where fees are not collected; and sites that cannot collect fees may not have the resources to address visitor management issues. Perhaps the most pressing concern resulting from the imposition of fees is the way they can raise visitor expectations of products and services. If improvements are not clearly obvious and on-going, then visitors may quickly become dissatisfied with heritage managers and interpret the fee as yet another unsubstantiated charge or tax. (See Case Study 6.1.)

Case Study 6.1
Resourcing and Value for Money at the Tikal World Heritage Site, Guatemala

---

Key points:

- Some of the world's most significant heritage is being managed on a shoestring budget.

- The application of 'user pays' comes into question when visitors perceive they are not getting value for money.

The ancient city of Tikal is one of the most mystical and attractive Mayan ruins in Central America. Tikal is located in a relatively remote part of Guatemala, close to the border of Belize. The Tikal national park contains 575 square kilometres of tropical rainforest and thousands of separate Mayan ruins. The central city of Tikal occupied about sixteen square kilometres and contains some 3,000 separate buildings. The Mayan civilisation at Tikal dissipated in 900 as part of a mysterious general collapse of lowland Mayan civilisation. Today towering pyramids still rise up to forty-four metres above the forest, which rings to the sound of howler monkeys and is full of the colours of macaws and toucans.

Tikal was inscribed on to the World Heritage List in 1979 and is part of a biosphere reserve created in 1990. The road from Flores crosses the national park boundary about fifteen kilometres south of the ruins. At this point visitors pay US$6 per day to enter the park, then US$2 to enter the ruins, and an additional US$2 to visit the museum. Food and accommodation prices are between two and three times those of prices paid in nearby Flores. There are no information brochures, no interpretation and no English-speaking guides. The Guatemalan National Parks Department spends ninety-seven per cent of its annual budget of US$11,111 on salaries. Works programmes are generated for archaeological sites with high profiles like Tikal from additional funds allocated by conservation groups. For example, the Centro de Estudios Conservacionistas donates US$50,000 and the Instituto de Archaeologia Historia US$1,500,000 to the protection of Guatemala's archaeological sites (McNeely *et al.* 1994).

Modifying the Site

The heritage site can be modified as a form of coercive control in order to change the way the site is used by visitors (see Plates 6.1 and 6.2). This can be undertaken

Plate 6.1 Visitor impact caused by rafters accessing a river, Tasmania, Australia

Plate 6.2 Modifying the site to minimise further impact from rafters, Tasmania, Australia

at a site-specific level or as part of a regional approach. The most common form of change is to make a site more resilient to visitor impact and more comfortable for visitors to experience. This is known as 'hardening'. After regulation, hardening is the most popular approach to visitor management. The site is hardened by surfacing access routes and associated facilities with materials that are highly resilient to impact yet relatively sympathetic to the heritage. The hardening usually makes the surface more comfortable by avoiding topographic variation, obstacles, water and elements perceived as making the going more difficult.

At a regional level, modifications may create a 'sacrificial site'; one that takes the brunt so that others within the region may continue to be relatively unvisited and undisturbed. The sacrificial site will have the number and range of facilities increased and hardened. Use is then concentrated within the sacrificial site because most visitors willingly choose the more comfortable option that appears to be established for them. The choice is further ensured through subtle promotional and strategic marketing.

There are several issues in using hardening at the site-specific level. First, hardening is very expensive. Major site modifications represent a significant drain on human and financial resources and are often only made possible through one-off grants. The inevitable upgrading and replacement represent a significant expense and potential impact upon the heritage resource, yet replacement is rarely considered during the planning stages. Second, despite the best design and use of 'environmentally sound' materials and construction techniques, heritage values may be compromised when the hardening fails to blend with the surrounding environment. The more sympathetic materials and design can be expensive to purchase, transport and build with, sometimes forcing heritage managers or tourism operators subsequently to focus on the more affluent visitors and clients. Third, hardening changes the nature of the experience by confining the flow of visitors to the point where the experience becomes generic to most visitors and crowding is therefore increased.

The main limitation of hardening at a regional level is that it attracts promotion by the tourist sectors over which heritage managers have very little influence. An increased level of promotion can be evidenced by increased use of photographs of, and text about, hardened sites in standard regional brochures and advertisements. The change in the nature of promotion is evident when tourism operators start to associate heritage with their own attraction or service. These two changes can increase visitation, intensify peak periods and change the type of visitor. When original visitors are exposed to the changed visitation, they move elsewhere to find an alternative site not that has not yet been subjected to the promotion. This move helps create 'recreational succession' or 'displacement' – a process by which tourists or recreators 'accommodate an unsatisfactory experience, by changing venues and times, or not undertaking the experience at all, or by re-imagining the unsatisfactory experience in new ways' (Kearsley 1995). When the original visitors move elsewhere, they may well introduce new impacts and stimulate succession at another site.

Undertaking Market Research

Market research involves the gathering, analysing and interpretation of information to identify marketing opportunities and link an organisation with its marketing environment (Aaker and Day 1990). Market research helps heritage managers develop an understanding of the people who have a stake in the way heritage is managed and helps differentiate characteristics of visitors from those of non-visitors. Two classic forms of market research are community polling, which provides basic information about a cross-section of the community, and focus groups, which provide more in-depth information from a smaller sample of the community. Market research is covered in more detail in Chapter 7 (see also Case Study 6.2).

Case Study 6.2
Overcrowding in the Early Hours on Mount Fuji, Japan

Key points:

- Many visitor management issues have strong cultural dimensions.

- Visitor management must address cultural dimensions to be successful.

Every visitor to Japan wants to see Mount Fuji, and so do the Japanese. Mount Fuji has been revered for centuries as a sacred peak and is a spectacular site – almost the visual ideal of what a volcano should look like. While the Mount Fuji experience is principally marketed as distance viewing, climbing the mountain is perceived by the Japanese as a means of gaining respect and thus as a semi-religious experience. Anyone in reasonably good health can make the climb and there is no risk of getting lost. There are two approaches to the summit but both take some five hours. The official climbing season is July and August when the weather is predictable and the conditions not hazardous to inexperienced visitors. Nonetheless, as there are no restrictions on climbers, visitation takes place throughout the year.

Formerly, visitors climbed during the day. However, over the past ten years a new experience has evolved that is putting great pressure on the mountain and the quality of the visitor experience. Increasing numbers of visitors now begin climbing well after dark and continue through the night in order to experience the *goraiko* (sunrise) from the top or the flank of the mountain. In response, huts were set up at various places along the upper reaches of the trails for short overnight stays. The huts have since become crowded and run-down. A growing number of visitors are now starting the walk at midnight to avoid the use of the huts. Inaccurate marketing has made the problem worse. This marketing has led to false expectations of superb vistas when in fact the mountain is often enshrouded in mist and visibility is poor until later in the morning. Visitors then stay on for several more hours for the 'unveiling' before returning. This means that many visitors are now ascending and descending the mountain during their normal sleeping period, having not slept for up to a day. Those in a hurry to return take the 'lava slide' down a large patch of volcanic sand. Management appears at a loss to manage the increased visitation, risks to safety and environmental impact because they must deal with a culture that is determined to gain a religious experience on a fragile natural area in as short a time span as possible.

Undertaking Visitor Monitoring and Research

Monitoring and research provide the basic tools for understanding the visitor. Specifically, they can be used to:

- identify and understand the demographic, psychographic and behavioural characteristics of visitors currently experiencing heritage;
- compare the current and desired audience for a heritage experience;
- identify and understand the nature of visitor experiences;
- identify and understand visitor impacts upon the physical, social and cultural value of heritage and, to some extent, upon the visitor experience; and
- collect the information required to evaluate the performance of visitor management programmes. (McArthur and Hall 1996a)

The information and insights generated provide heritage managers with a sense of confidence that their decisions and approaches are being made with a sound understanding of the relationship between visitors and heritage. The subject of visitor monitoring and research was covered in more detail in Chapter 5.

Undertaking Promotional Marketing

In a heritage management context, marketing involves first identifying and understanding the product (heritage and visitor experience) and client (visitor), then developing and distributing images, information and ideas relating to heritage and visitor experiences. Marketing can be specifically used to:

- emphasise or omit sites or experiences, or promote one site or experience over a neighbouring one;
- present a site to focus on a particular experience;
- present experiences in a way known to attract a particular type of visitor;
- promote a certain time to visit (assisting with temporal separation);
- suggest a certain group size as the most ideal for an enjoyable experience;
- recommend that certain equipment be taken; and
- recommend certain behaviour. (Hall and McArthur 1996d)

Promotional aspects of marketing include media campaigns, advertising in the electronic and printed media, World Wide Web sites, posters, displays, brochures, presentations and familiarisation tours. Products are typically highly visual, featuring lots of photographs, occasional artwork and minimal text. Promotional marketing is one of the most proactive and cost-effective means of achieving visitor management objectives because it shapes people's expectations and behaviour before it has occurred. Heritage managers often either shirk from promotional marketing (thinking it 'too commercial' for them) or develop marketing initiatives that lack the cutting edge to be truly effective. Marketing is covered in more detail in Chapter 7 (see also Case Study 6.3).

Case Study 6.3
Managing Increasing Visitation on the Inca Trail, Peru

Key points:

- The relentless marketing of icon sites is creating unsustainable visitation.

- High visitation is often as much a result of ready access to and within a site as the uniqueness of the heritage.

- It is unwise and unsustainable to rely on a single visitor management strategy.

One example of the inability of resource management approaches to solve the paradox of heritage management is the Inca Trail in the Peruvian Andes. The trail was constructed by the Incas to access a series of remote villages and cities and ends at the famous Machu Picchu, which was not discovered until 1911 and is therefore in remarkable condition. The trail is extremely attractive to adventure tour companies, as it offers a combination of natural and cultural heritage, and a time frame and level of difficulty that are considered adventurous but not too taxing.

Machu Picchu was inscribed on to the World Heritage List in 1982 and is a major icon in all Peruvian marketing and much of the marketing undertaken for the entire continent of South America. In addition, the local villages are still occupied and the trail is therefore still used by locals, adding a living, breathing dimension to an already rich mix of experiences. During the peak season (June to August) the trail fills up with guided and independent walkers. It has been estimated that up to 400 people take to the trail each day. In response, the Peruvian government is considering imposing access limits while at the same time looking for alternative (additional) experiences. However, a recent avalanche at one of these 'alternative' sites has rendered it inaccessible. Consequently, tour companies have had to return to the original Inca Trail route, thereby swelling numbers and generating additional impacts.

Undertaking Marketing of Strategic Information

Whereas promotional marketing aims at sowing the first seed (e.g., to visit a site, book a tour, purchase a book or make a donation), marketing of strategic information presumes that the client has already made the critical decision and now needs information to implement that decision. People generating strategic information assume the visitor is already somewhat on their side and needs information to proceed. It is therefore less glitzy and more oriented to information; it essentially features the where, the how and the when. The most common techniques are brochures, displays, CD-ROMs and signs. A technique that is rapidly growing in use is the placement of material on the World Wide Web. Elements common to all of these are: maps; descriptions of what to do and where to do it; codes for difficulty, time and length; and tips on how to enhance the experience and avoid problems. Marketing strategic information is a proactive way of influencing the behaviour of visitors at the one moment in which they are truly prepared to be influenced. In this way it can be a critical player in dispersing use of heritage over space and time. Marketing is covered in more detail in Chapter 7.

Providing Interpretation Programmes and Facilities

Interpretation is a means of communicating ideas and feelings that helps people enrich their understanding and appreciation of the world, and their role within it (Interpretation Australia Association 1995). While interpretation does not reach visitors as early as marketing, it is an extremely powerful communication tool. Interpretation explores the complexity of heritage and how is managed in ways that can be thorough yet complementary to the visitor experience and the values of other stakeholders. Specifically, interpretation can be used to:

- raise awareness and understanding of the values and uses of heritage;
- raise awareness and understanding of the issues facing the management of heritage and the way in which management is dealing with them;
- influence or change visitor behaviour; and
- seek public input and involvement with various aspects of heritage and visitor management. (McArthur and Hall 1996b, 1996c)

Interpretation is typically divided into verbal and non-verbal media, but may be a combination of both. Verbal interpretation includes information duty, organised talks and discussions, organised entertainment, organised activities and theme parks. Examples of non-verbal interpretation are publications, signs, self-guided activities, visitor centres, audio-visual devices, and indoor and outdoor exhibits (see Plate 6.3). Interpretation is covered in more detail in Chapter 8.

Plate 6.3 Ecotourism operators provide an attractive alternative to mass tourism through controlled access and specialised services such as interpretation

Providing Education Programmes and Facilities

Environmental education, nature study and visitor education are more formalised versions of interpretation; they are a sanctioned system whereby participants are required to learn and demonstrate competencies. There is no such requirement for interpretation. Educational facilities can vary from a simple travelling resource kit to a comprehensive educational centre close to or within the heritage site. Educational programmes may utilise games, artwork, poetry, music, public speaking, debates, and activities that relate directly to heritage management (e.g., monitoring water quality, rehabilitating natural habitat and nursing injured wildlife). Alternatively, school-based education programmes may be based around qualified teachers employed by the heritage management organisation.

The real strength of education is the depth in which it can address a topic: no other form of communication can deal with complexity. The limitation of education is the significant long-term outlay and commitment required before significant returns can be demonstrated to those providing the financial resourcing.

Modifying the Profile of Heritage Management

Visitor awareness, attitudes and behaviour towards heritage managers can be shifted by adjusting the manner and moment in which visitors come into contact with heritage management staff.

The first dimension is the basic image generated through day-to-day products associated with heritage management, such as the nature of images on letterheads, logos, uniforms and signage. An example is the holding system used during telephone enquiries to the heritage manager. Some heritage managers have telephones with holding music provided, some use a local radio station and some play marketing information about the services they offer on site.

The second dimension is the style of management demonstrated directly to visitors, usually somewhere between *laissez faire* and a policing role. An example is the way in which heritage managers deal with complaints about the quality of their work. The reaction to complaints can suggest a management style that is traditional or innovative, reactive or proactive, authoritative or accommodating. The style of heritage management should be able to be modified according to who is being dealt with. For example, management style towards an aggressive visitor must be different from that towards a disorientated visitor.

Perhaps the most effective demonstration of management style is to schedule visitor-related works to correspond with when visitors are likely to see it being done (e.g., cleaning and repairing facilities and building new ones). This technique gives visitors the sense that heritage managers are employed for more than just looking after the heritage resource. Therefore, modifying the profile of heritage management requires the organisational culture to value visitors, and thus visitor management, as much as the heritage resource and its management. (See Case Study 6.4.)

Case Study 6.4
Safari Hunting by Tourists as a Means of Conserving Wildlife

Key point:
- Tourism need not represent the same ethics as heritage management to be a legitimate way of funding heritage management and sustaining the heritage resource.

In Africa's Zimbabwe and Tanzania some ninety-five per cent of wildlife is found outside parks and protected areas. Until 1983 locals made little attempt to stop the poaching of wildlife; they were not aware that it was causing a detrimental impact and there was no incentive to change.

It became clear to some that the best way to conserve the remaining wildlife was to give it value. This is typically done under the guise of ecotourism, whereby visitors come to view and photograph wildlife from the safety of vehicles and accommodation within natural areas. This market represents a higher yield, and thus significant value can be placed on the wildlife. However, the market is limited and does not always generate sufficient revenue to cover the substantial costs of natural area and visitor management. Another market that is smaller but represents an even higher yield is the safari hunting market. In this market individuals pay three or four times the daily yield of ecotourists, as well as high licence and service fees, for the opportunity to hunt wildlife in its natural habitat. The annual catch is relatively small and heavily monitored and regulated. For example, some 0.002 per cent of elephants in Zimbabwe are hunted by tourists each year (150 from a population of 70,000). Operators such as Safari Club International argue that, properly managed, this form of tourism is an effective agent to achieving the long-term conservation of wildlife, habitat and the cultural heritage of the host community. This is managed principally through the clear value that the animals being hunted provide, but also by the on-going supply of many more animals and their habitat. The value of wildlife in this capacity has been demonstrated to be far higher than that of agricultural use of the land. In addition, the operation requires very low numbers of tourists, generates local employment and contributes to public services. The approach has been suggested by Russell Train, former Chairman of the World Wildlife Fund, to be 'the most efficient, cost effective form of producing economic benefits for local people' (Safari Club International 1994).

Encouraging and Assisting Alternative Providers of Experiences – the Tourist Industry

Parts of the tourist industry have recognised that experiences can be created for which people are prepared to pay. The industry has utilised heritage to create three major types of ventures:

- attractions (e.g., wildlife sanctuary, zoo, museum, gallery and theme park);
- accommodation (e.g., guest house, ecolodge and tented camp); and
- guided tours (e.g., coach, off-road, walking, horse riding and diving).

In this capacity tourism operators can provide experiences, facilities and services that are either complementary to those provided by heritage managers or a complete replacement for those once offered by heritage managers. Niche-based tourism operators can also access visitor markets that are considered highly desirable by heritage managers, such as people who are:

- particularly interested in gaining personal experiences with heritage;
- particularly interested in learning about the heritage;
- prepared to behave in ways requested by the heritage manager; and
- prepared to pay for the above.

To establish tourism operations with these attributes heritage managers must develop clear and fair policies and be prepared to work in a business-like way with the operators, never forgetting that asking an operator to implement behavioural ethics is pointless if, from the operator's perspective, the ethics make the operation unviable.

Encouraging and Assisting Alternative Providers of Experiences – Volunteers

Volunteers are the other major provider of services. They can be brought into heritage management at varying levels, depending upon the interest, skill and commitment of both parties. At the base level volunteers can be utilised to provide basic manual labour, such as removal of rubbish and weeds, cleaning and other general maintenance works. At this level volunteers are usually given clothing, equipment and prescriptive instructions to help them undertake the task. At the next level are more sophisticated jobs, such as rehabilitation, restoration, visitor information and guiding. At this level specialised staff continually work with the volunteers to impart skills and allow people to build on what they have already learnt. The top level is where volunteers are given advisory roles and decision-making responsibilities at a strategic and perhaps even policy level. At this level the volunteers may have travelling and accommodation expenses reimbursed, may be given sitting fees, and are usually given considerable professional assistance.

Employing Accredited Organisations to Bring Visitors to a Site

Heritage managers look for recognised competency and relevancy when deciding whether to award licences, permits, development applications and a general degree of support and encouragement for tourism operators, organised groups and volunteers. One way of ensuring competency is by using accreditation programmes. These programmes feature a set of criteria that proponents must be able to meet in order to become accredited. For example, the Green Globe International Program, requires tourism operators to demonstrate various practices that reflect environmental sustainability (Birtles and Li-Sofield 1995). Another example is Australia's National Ecotourism Accreditation Program, which requires operators to meet criteria based on eight principles embodying ecotourism (McArthur 1997). Accreditation programmes can be used to determine authenticity, commitment, skill and experience needed to behave responsibly at a heritage site.

Assessment of Various Approaches

As indicated in the descriptions above, each approach or technique contains strengths and weaknesses. A qualitative assessment has been provided in Table 6.2 to help readers further to contrast these characteristics. The assessment in the table gives comparisons of the ability of each technique, first, to conserve heritage directly and, second, to improve the quality of the visitor experience. Strong performers in achieving both goals are marketing, interpretation, the use of volunteers and concentration on accredited organisations. The assessment suggests that marketing, interpretation, the presence of heritage management, use of volunteers and concentration on accredited organisations presents the strongest ability to create support for heritage management. There is a greater range of techniques that are perceived to be particularly proactive, including market research, visitor monitoring and research, marketing, interpretation, education, the use of tourism operators as alternative providers and favoured treatment of accredited operators. The authors do not recommend the use of any one technique at the exclusion of another. All tools have merit in particular situations; what needs to be stressed is that the greater the diversity of techniques being integrated and used together constructively, the greater the ability to address the visitor management paradox.

Despite the strong performance and general use of visitor-based approaches such as marketing and interpretation, Table 6.2 suggests that heritage managers are largely reliant on regulatory approaches and modifications to the heritage site and the way it is accessed and presented. Furthermore, many of these approaches are used in isolation. For example, the results of research may not be fed into other approaches being utilised, or marketing may fail to cover a new interpretive experience. Apart from improving overall communication, these observations suggest that managers need to integrate approaches into a broader, integrated context. One way to integrate the approaches, break the communications deadlock and provide additional insight and direction is to introduce a visitor management model.

Table 6.2 Qualitative assessment of visitor management techniques

Visitor management techniques	Ability to address heritage management paradox		Other aspects of performance		
	Conservation of heritage	Improve quality of visitor experience	Create support for heritage management	Proactiveness	Reliance by management
Regulating access	♦♦♦	♦	•	•	•
Regulating visitation	♦♦	♦♦	•	•	••
Regulating behaviour	♦♦	♦	•	•	•
Regulating equipment	♦♦	♦♦	•	••	••
Entry or user fees	♦♦	♦	•	••	•••
Modifying the site	♦♦	♦♦	••	•	•••
Market research	♦♦	♦♦	•	•••	•
Visitor monitoring and research	♦♦	♦♦♦	•	•••	•
Promotional marketing	♦♦♦	♦♦	•••	•••	•
Strategic information marketing	♦♦♦	♦♦♦	•••	••	••
Interpretation	♦♦♦	♦♦♦	•••	•••	••
Education	♦♦♦	♦♦	••	•••	•
Profile of heritage management	♦♦♦	♦♦	•••	••	•
Alternative providers - tourism industry	♦♦	♦♦♦	••	•••	•
Alternative providers - volunteers	♦♦♦	♦♦♦	•••	•••	••
Favoured treatment for accredited bodies bringing visitors to a site	♦♦♦	♦♦♦	•••	•••	•

Performance in relation to heritage management paradox:

♦ Limited
♦♦ Reasonable
♦♦♦ Good

Performance in relation to other criteria:

• Limited
•• Reasonable
••• Good

Visitor Management Models

A number of visitor management models have been generated to manage the heritage–visitor relationship. They include:

- the Carrying Capacity Model;
- the Recreation Opportunity Spectrum;
- the Visitor Impact Management Model;
- the Visitor Activity Management Program;
- the Limits of Acceptable Change; and
- the Tourism Optimisation Management Model.

The key characteristics and establishment process for each model is briefly outlined below.

Carrying Capacity

The Carrying Capacity Model attempts to determine the threshold level of activity beyond which the heritage resource-base will deteriorate (Wolters 1991). There are four major dimensions to carrying capacity: biophysical, socio-cultural, psychological and managerial. The biophysical component relates to the nature of the heritage site, such as physical space available, stability of landforms and built fabric, and scale and dynamics of biodiversity. Biophysical carrying capacity determines a level of human use that can be sustained without long-term effects on the resource base. The socio-cultural component relates to the degree that indigenous and/or local populations of people within or near the heritage can accept and happily live with visitors. Socio-cultural carrying capacity determines a level of human use that can be sustained without long-term effects on the host population. The psychological component relates to the quality of the visitor experience, such as the number and nature of encounters with other visitors and the degree to which expectations were met. Psychological carrying capacity determines a level of use that maximises the quality of the visitor experience and follow-on effects from the experience. The managerial component relates to the support services and infrastructure, such as the number and skills of heritage management staff, the size of a parking area or picnic table, and the amount of fresh water available. Managerial carrying capacity determines a level of use that reflects the ideal and sustainable type and degree of management.

Carrying capacity is typically used for planning, site design/development, and administration. Its use in planning often involves evaluating the size and character of alternative sites and pre-determining optimum levels of use for various locations. In site design and development its use involves assigning activities to areas according to natural limits, and identifying a suitable position across the activities. Administration involves the use of marketing to attract visitors to alternative destinations to those approaching capacity and the monitoring and evaluation of predicted versus actual visitation. The emphasis by many heritage managers has been on physical capacity applied to site design and development at the expense of the other dimensions and applications just mentioned (see Table 6.7 for examples).

Developing a carrying capacity for a heritage site involves at least eight steps, as listed below:

1 Specify management objectives or standards for the state of the heritage resource to be maintained or attained and the type of experience to be provided.

2 Identify current levels of use for a defined period (e.g., hour, day, week, month, year).

3 Identify indicators for the biophysical, socio-cultural, psychological and managerial components.

4 Measure the current state of each indicator.

5 Identify apparent relationships between the state of the indicator and the level of use.

6 Make value judgements about the acceptability of the various impacts.

7 Determine a carrying capacity that is more, the same or less than current visitation.

8 Implement management strategies to ensure carrying capacity is not breached.

An example of the establishment of a carrying capacity is the Angkor World Heritage Site in Cambodia. A capacity of 300 to 500 visitors at any one time has been established, with an annual capacity set at 500,000; which assumes visitors will make two visits to the site during their stay (Wager 1995).

The most defendable carrying capacity is an estimate representing a compromise between individual capacities for each component. For example, suppose there were biophysical, socio-cultural, psychological and managerial carrying capacities set at 50, 100, 80 and 90 visits per day, respectively. If each component was valued equally, an overall carrying capacity may be set at 80 visits per day. However, the typical scenario is one where the overall figure is influenced by the most sensitive or threatened factor, so in this example the capacity may be set at 50 visits per day.

Despite the concept of carrying capacity being over thirty years old, it remains, in practice, highly elusive to successful implementation:

> It is commonly recognised that there are no fixed or standard tourism carrying capacity values. Rather, carrying capacity varies, depending upon place, season and time, user behaviour, facility design, patterns and levels of management, and the dynamic character of the environments themselves. Moreover, it is not always possible in practice to separate tourism activity from other human activities. (Ceballos-Lacuarain 1996)

It is relatively easy to argue that there is no such thing as a single carrying capa-city for any given heritage site and that any capacity put forward is highly subjective and thus difficult to defend. A good example of the judgemental limitation is Green Island in far north Queensland. Concern over current crowding resulted in a carrying capacity being set at 1,900 visitors per day, or no more than 800 at any one time (Queensland Department of Environment and Heritage 1993). Green Island currently receives some 300,000 visits per year. If the maximum daily level were reached every day, Green Island would receive 693,500 visitors in a year, over twice the current level. Any visitor management model that cannot be defended is un-likely to gain or at least maintain the support of stakeholders.

The Recreation Opportunity Spectrum

The Recreation Opportunity Spectrum (ROS) is a conceptual framework to clarify the relationship between settings, activities and experiences (Clark and Stankey

1979). It is premised on the assumption that quality is best assured through the pro-vision of a diverse array of opportunities. The ROS provided a conceptual framework for thinking about how to create a diversity of recreation experiences, rather than just provide standard recreational facilities (Driver 1989).

A ROS is developed by identifying a spectrum of settings, activities and opportun-ities that a given region may contain. For example, a national park may contain a spectrum of settings that range from easily accessible, highly developed areas and facilities to remote, undeveloped areas with no facilities. A museum might have a spectrum ranging from a complex set of transcripts in a quiet corner, with detailed supporting information, to a crowded gift shop selling rubber frogs and filled with the sound of new age music. The information relating to each setting is entered into a tabular format to present the characteristics of the site, the type of activities under-taken and the opportunities available alongside each other. Comparisons can then be made across sites to determine what sort of core opportunities appear to provided and the under- or oversupply to specific activities and opportunities. The ROS can therefore be very useful at reviewing then repositioning the type of visitor experiences most appropriate to a heritage site.

Management factors to be considered when determining into which recreational class a setting should be placed include:

- access (e.g., difficulty, access system [roads and trails] and means of con-veyance);
- the non-recreational resource;
- on-site management (e.g., extent, apparentness, complexity and facilities);
- social interaction;
- acceptability of visitor impact (e.g., magnitude and prevalence); and
- regimentation.

The standard range of recreational classes established by ROS is: developed, semi-developed, semi-natural and natural.

Perhaps the key limitation to the use of the ROS is its emphasis on the setting at the expense of the type of visitor. Part of the reason is the influence of earlier cultures from the landscape planning and architectural professions that suggested visitor management could be largely addressed through site and facility design. Lipscombe (1993) suggests that although the ROS was extensively marketed in the early 1980s it was not widely adopted by heritage managers in the late 1980s and early 1990s (see Table 6.7 for examples).

The Visitor Impact Management Model

The Visitor Impact Management Model (VIMM) was developed by the United States National Parks and Conservation Association. It is a planning framework that incorp-orates visitor management principles within a process aimed at reducing or control-ling the impacts that threaten the quality of heritage and the visitor experience (Graefe 1989). The VIMM is primarily significant in its recognition of four principles:

- the relationship between the quality of the visitor experience and visitor impact is complex and influenced by more than the level of use;
- visitors and environments vary in their capability to tolerate impacts;

- visitors are not the only cause of impacts;

- effective management must go beyond carrying capacities and limits on use to involve both scientific and judgemental considerations.
(Loomis and Graefe 1992)

The VIMM framework is designed to deal with three basic issues inherent in impact management:

- the identification of problem conditions (unacceptable impacts);

- the determination of potential causal factors affecting the occurrence and severity of the unacceptable impacts; and

- the selection of potential management strategies for ameliorating the unacceptable impacts. (Graefe 1991)

To achieve this the VIMM encourages explicit statements of management objectives. It uses research and monitoring to determine heritage and social conditions and generates a range of management strategies to deal with the impacts. The VIMM process for assessing and managing visitor impacts involves some nine steps, as shown in Table 6.3. Table 6.4 is an indicative matrix that could be used to evaluate alternative visitor management strategies generated in stage eight of the VIMM process. The matrix assesses strategies under four criteria: consistency with management strategies; difficulty to implement; effects on visitor freedom; and effects on other impact indicators. Each criterion is assessed quantitatively using a score out of five and then assessed qualitatively with descriptive comment. The four scores for each strategy are averaged to suggest an overall performance.

Table 6.3 Steps to establish a Visitor Impact Management Model

Stages	Comments	Resultant outcome
1 Review and summarise what is known about the situation	• Examples of the current situation may include current policy, plans, management programmes and site conditions. • During this stage the scope of the study is refined and, if necessary, the site is broken down into sub-units.	Summary of existing situation
2 Review management objectives to ensure they define clearly the type of experience to be provided and the type of environment to conserve	• Do not avoid this step; excuses include misperceptions that focusing on particular experiences will generate inequity or that there is no need to differentiate visitors (see Chapters 2 and 7 for differentiation rationale). • Specify definitive visitor experiences and heritage resource management objectives. • Ensure objectives are consistent with legislative mandate and established policies.	Clear statement of specific area objectives, e.g. maintain natural vegetation in riparian zones
3 Identify measurable indicators to reflect the degree to which the management objectives are being met	• Select indicators most pertinent to heritage management objectives. • Selection criteria often used include: ease of measurement; relativity to objectives; sensitivity to changing use conditions, cost, complexity and amenity for management.	List of indicators and units of measurement, e.g. loss of vegetation and percentage of ground cover
4 Determine standards for each indicator	• Elements of the objectives can be recycled to become quantitatively measurable as appropriate levels or acceptable limits.	Quantitative statements of desired conditions, e.g. no more than 30% vegetation loss at specified site

continues

Table 6.3 continued

Stages	Comments	Resultant outcome
5 Undertake research or monitoring	• Research or monitoring should measure the nature of the indicators in the existing situation.	Research or monitoring programme
6 Evaluate data	• Compare data with the set standards to determine what level of difference there is between the desirable and actual situation. If there is no discrepancy, management can either continue monitoring and comparing the standards with periodic results or may choose to revise the indicators and/or standards and run the programme again. If there is a discrepancy then undertake Step 6.	Determination of consistency or discrepancy with selected standards
7 Determine probable causes of discrepancy	• Isolate the most significant causes, then examine potential relationships between indicators (typically between use and impact). • Completion of this step may require additional studies that focus on the relationships. Use the understandings just gained about the causes of the impacts.	Description of causal factors for management attention
8 Identify a range of alternative management strategies and select preferred option	• Identify direct and indirect management strategies that could reduce the probable causes of the impacts. • Generate a matrix to evaluate the alternatives against designated criteria that not only reflect the objectives but perhaps objectives of the heritage management organisation or other stakeholders. • The most appropriate strategy is usually one which covers a range of criteria.	Matrix of alternative management strategies (see Table 4.1 in Chapter 4)
9 Implement preferred management strategy(ies)	• Implement as quickly as possible. • Continue monitoring to determine the level of success and other emerging issues.	Reduced impacts

Source: adapted from Graefe (1991)

Table 6.4 Matrix to evaluate alternative visitor management strategies

Potential management strategies	Consistency with management objectives		Difficulty to implement	
	Score out of 5	Comment	Score out of 5	Comment
Indirect strategies				
Physical alterations				
Information dispersal				
Economic constraints				
Direct strategies				
Enforcement				
Zoning				
Rationing use				
Restricting activities				

Source: adapted from Graefe (1991)

The VIMM can be applied to a range of heritage settings but is particularly suited to localised sites. It has been pilot-tested in at least ten natural heritage sites in the United States and a small number in Canada and Australia (see Table 6.7 for examples).

The Visitor Activity Management Program

The Visitor Activity Management Program (VAMP) was developed by the Canadian Parks Service to help increase the level of integration of visitor management into broader heritage management planning (Payne and Graham 1984). This meant having the central planning process supported by planning systems both for the heritage resource and for visitors. At a more specific level, the VAMP was designed to integrate visitor activity demands with resource opportunities to produce specific opportunities for visitors. By integrating social science with resource management the VAMP is designed to deal with conflicts and tensions between visitors, heritage and heritage managers. The VAMP switches the heritage manager from offering experiences to anyone to deciding what people want, then developing and marketing specific experiences to match the wants (see Chapter 7 for more detail on this approach). Graham *et al.* (1988) suggests this 'represents a fundamental change in orientation in Parks from a product or supply basis to an outward-looking market-sensitive one'.

A generic version of the process generally involves:

- setting objectives for visitor activities;
- identifying and analysing visitor management issues against the objectives – e.g., current visitation characteristics, state of the setting and visitor facilities, and existing management directions and legislative frameworks;
- developing options for visitor activities and services; and
- implementing recommended options.

Theoretically, the process is flexible enough to be continually modified as feedback from monitoring and evaluation programmes are fed in. However, even Parks Canada admits that VAMP is 'a skeleton in need of further development to establish a technical capability ... there is no capability in the park management planning process

ffects on visitor freedom		Effects on other impact indicators		Average score	
core ut of 5	Comment	Score out of 5	Comment	Score out of 5	Comment

which can be called upon to express VAMP input spatially' (Graham *et al.* 1988). Lipscombe (1993) has observed that the full implementation of the VAMP in Canada and its adoption elsewhere around the world has been limited (see Table 6.7 for examples).

The Limits of Acceptable Change

The Limits of Acceptable Change (LAC) system began with the fundamentals of the Recreation Opportunity Spectrum and initial principles of carrying capacity. Its designers then shifted the focus from a relationship between levels of use and impact to identifying desirable conditions for visitor activity to occur in the first place, as well as management actions required to protect or achieve the conditions (Clarke and Stankey 1979). The LAC model implies an emphasis on establishing how much change is acceptable, then actively managing accordingly. It avoids the use/impact conundrum by focusing on the management of the impacts of use. The model tells management whether the conditions are within acceptable standards – i.e., that current levels and patterns of use are within the capacity of the host environment. When conditions reach the limits of acceptable change they have also reached the area's capacity under current management practices. Management is then equipped with a logical and defensible case to implement strategic actions before any more use can be accommodated. One action may be to limit use.

The LAC system is based on a nine-stage process:

1   Identification of area concerns and issues

2   Definition and description of opportunity classes

3   Selection of indicators for conditions

4   Inventory of resource and social conditions

5   Specification of standards for indicators

6   Allocation of alternative opportunity classes

7   Identification of management actions for each alternative

8   Evaluation and selection of the preferred option

9   Implementation of actions and monitoring of conditions

Prosser (1986a) identified a number of key strengths of the LAC system as being:

- emphasis on explicit, measurable objectives;

- promotion of a diversity of visitor experiences;

- reliance on quantitative field-based standards;

- flexibility and responsiveness to local situations;

- opportunity for public involvement;

- minimisation of regulatory approaches; and

- a framework for managing conditions.

Unfortunately, only a few LAC systems have been generated and successfully implemented, mostly in wilderness areas of North America and, to a small extent, in one or two natural areas in Australia (see Table 6.7 for examples). The most critical aspect of the development of the LAC system has been establishing stakeholder endorsement and support (Prosser 1986b). Stakeholders from the local tourist sector and community can provide valuable input into desired conditions and acceptable standards, and are usually essential in providing the economic and political support necessary to maintain monitoring programmes and implement management decisions.The failure to establish sufficient stakeholder support has occurred largely because the LAC model was created *by* managers of natural areas *for* managers of natural areas. The culture of the LAC system simply is not attuned to attracting wider stakeholder involvement. One example of this is the use of the term 'limits' within the title, which the tourist industry has interpreted as being discouraging to growth and thus business.A second example is the conventional narrow focus on the condition of the physical environment and, to some extent, the nature of the visitor experience. Other critical dimensions, such as characteristics of the visitor market, socio-cultural aspects of the local community and economic activity associated with the tourist industry, are not included.A third example is the lack of cooperative involvement of the tourist sector in identifying indicators and standards that are acceptable to the industry. Without this involvement the monitoring results become prone to conjecture, particularly if they reveal surprising or controversial implications. If the culture of the LAC system were diversified and its components broadened it may be better able to deliver the significant opportunities it was originally designed to generate.

The Tourism Optimisation Management Model (TOMM)

The Tourism Optimisation Management Model (TOMM) is one of the most recent and relatively untried models to monitor and manage visitors (McArthur 1996a).The conceptual emphasis of the TOMM is on achieving optimum performance rather than limiting activity. The TOMM positions a range of influences in the heritage–visitor relationship to focus on sustainability of the heritage, viability of the tourism industry and empowerment of stakeholders.The TOMM has borrowed the key strengths of the VIMM and LAC, then broadened their focus into fields linked with the tourist industry and the local community. Besides environmental and experiential elements, the TOMM addresses characteristics of the tourist market, economic conditions of the tourist industry and socio-cultural conditions of the local community. The expansion recognises the complex interrelationships between heritage management, the tourist industry and supporting local populations. In this respect the TOMM is more politically sensitive to the forces that shape visitation and subsequent impacts.

The TOMM contains three main components: context analysis, a monitoring programme and a management response system (Manidis Roberts 1996).The context analysis identifies the current nature of community values, the tourist product, the potential for tourism growth, market trends and opportunities, positioning and branding. This information is collected through literature reviews, face-to-face interviews with relevant expertise and a community workshop.The context analysis also identifies alternative scenarios for the future of tourism, which are used later to test the validity of the model.

The second stage of the development of a TOMM is the development of a monitoring programme.The basis for such a programme is a set of optimal conditions that tourism and visitor activity should create (rather than impacts they should avoid). In this way the model avoids setting limits, maximum levels or carrying capacities and can offer the tourist industry opportunities to develop optimal sustainable performance. The monitoring programme is essentially designed to measure how close the current situation is to the optimal conditions.The measurement yardstick is a set of indicators (one for each optimal condition). Table 6.5 provides a list of assessment criteria for selecting the most appropriate indicators for a TOMM. Each indicator has a benchmark and an acceptable range within which it may be expected to operate. Table 6.6 provides an example of the desired outcomes and their supporting indicators and acceptable ranges; in this instance they are environmentally oriented. The data generated from the monitoring programme are then plotted to determine whether the status is within the acceptable range or not. Annual performance is presented via the report charts already displaying benchmarks and via a relatively simple table that is principally designed to reflect quickly whether each indicator is within its acceptable range or not. Figure 6.1 provides an example of a report chart showing a benchmark and acceptable range for visitation. The presentation of data is designed to provide a 'quick and dirty look' that all stakeholders can utilise.

The third stage of development is a management response system. This system involves the identification of poor-performance indicators, the exploration of cause and effect relationships, the identification of results requiring a response and the development of management response options. The first part of the response system is to identify annually which indicators are not performing within their acceptable range. This involves reviewing the report charts to identify and list each indicator whose annual performance data are outside their acceptable range. It also involves identifying the degree of the discrepancy and whether the discrepancy is part of a longer-term trend. The trend is determined by reviewing previous annual data that have been entered on to the report charts. A qualitative statement is then entered under the degree of discrepancy. The second part in the response mechanism is to explore cause and effect relationships. The essential question relating to cause and effect is whether the discrepancy was induced principally by tourism activity or by other effects, such as the actions of local residents, initiatives by other industries, and regional, national or even global influences. The third part in the system simply involves nominating whether a response is required. Specific choices for the response could include a tourism-oriented response, a response from another sector, or identification that the situation is beyond anyone's control. The fourth and final part involves developing response options, dependent upon whether they:

- require a response from a non-tourist sector (which involves identifying the appropriate body responsible, providing it with the results and suggesting a response on the matter);

- were out of anyone's control (in which case no response is required); and/or

- require a response from the tourist sector (which involves generating a series of management options for consideration, such as additional research to understand the issue, modification to existing practices, site-based development, marketing and lobbying.

After the tourist-related options are developed the preferred option is tested by brainstorming how the option might influence the various indicators. This requires the re-use of the predicted performance and management response sections of the model. Once several years of data are collected the model can be transferred to a simple computer program to streamline the reporting, predicting and testing of options.

The final application of the model is to test potential options or management responses to a range of alternative scenarios. The first form of testing for application is the performance of a sample of individual indicators. The second form of testing the model's performance is against several potential future scenarios that have

Table 6.5 Assessment criteria for selecting indicators for Tourism Optimisation Management Model on Kangaroo Island, South Australia

Criteria	Explanation	Example
Degree of relationship with actual tourism activity	The indicator needs to have a clear relationship with tourism activity to be relevant to the model	The number of fur seals at Seal Bay is more relevant than the number of possums at Stokes Bay
Accuracy	The indicator needs to represent the desired condition accurately	The number of traffic accidents is more accurate than the perception of parking difficulties
Utility	The indicator is more worthwhile if it generates additional insights	Visitation (number of visitors) has greater utility than perception of crowding
Availability of data	The indicator is more worthwhile if data already exist and are accessible, rather than needing to be collected from scratch	Data on the level of expenditure is more available than operator profit
Cost to collect and analyse	The indicator is more worthwhile if it requires minimal additional human resources to collect and analyse	The level of direct tourism employment is cheaper to monitor than the number of tourism products developed by local suppliers in response to tourist demand

Source: Manidis Roberts Consultants (1996)

Table 6.6 Management objectives and potential indicators for assessing the quality of the environment at Kangaroo Island, South Australia

Optimal conditions	Indicators	Acceptable range
The majority of the number of visits to the island's natural areas occurs in visitor service zones.	• Proportion of Kangaroo Island visitors to the island's natural areas who visit areas zoned specially for managing visitors	65–100% of visitors
Ecological processes are maintained or enhanced in areas where tourism activity occurs.	• Net overall cover of native vegetation at specific sites	0–5% increase in native vegetation from base case
Major wildlife populations attracting visitors are maintained and/or enhanced in areas where tourism activity occurs.	• Number of seals at designated tourist site • Number of hooded plover at designated tourist site • Number of osprey at designated tourist site	0–5% annual increase in number sighted
The majority of tourism accommodation operations have implemented some form of energy and water conservation practice.	• Energy consumption/visitor night/visitor • Water consumption/visitor night/visitor	3–7 kilowatts 20–40 litres of water

Source: Manidis Roberts Consultants (1996)

already been developed and presented in the contextual analysis. The testing helps to ensure that the model has some degree of predictive capability.

The first TOMM was produced in late 1996 and implemented during 1997 (see Case Study 6.5). It spanned public and private land in South Australia's Kangaroo Island and was co-funded by the Federal and South Australian Tourism Departments,

Figure 6.1 Example of report chart (fictitious visitation) generated from the Kangaroo Island (South Australia) TOMM

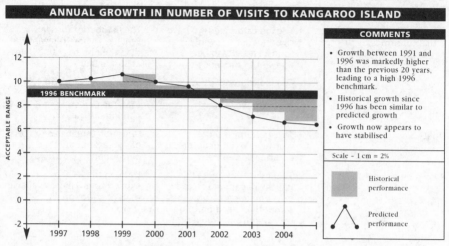

and the South Australian Department of Environment and Natural Resources. The TOMM has attracted support not only from its three public-sector funders, but from local government, the local tourist association, the tourist industry, conservation groups and members of the local community. This has been achieved because of several key characteristics, including:

- the TOMM covers a range of dimensions in the heritage–visitor relationship;

- a wide range of stakeholders collect data and therefore 'own' part of the intellectual property;

- the results of the monitoring are produced in easy-to-follow formats so that any untrained eye can pass over them and broadly deduce the health of the heritage–visitor relationship; and

- management strategies can be jointly determined through shared under-standings of the current situation and emerging trends.

Case Study 6.5
Developing a Tourism Optimisation Management Model for Kangaroo Island, South Australia

Key points:

- Impact monitoring can be oriented into a management framework that emphasises optimal rather than poor performance.

- Monitoring must be tightly integrated into the operating environment to maximise the chances of data being used to make decisions.

- Models that integrate a range of monitoring data provide greater capacity to understand relationships and cope with the complexity of heritage management.

The residents of Kangaroo Island in South Australia rely heavily upon the agriculture and tourist industries. The tourism product is largely based around a country lifestyle and isolated, yet accessible, experiences of Australian wildlife in its natural habitat. Many studies and plans have attempted to determine how the tourist industry can be made to reflect better what is distinctive about the island and its lifestyle and what is sustainable. What all of these initiatives lacked was a sound understanding of the relationship between different components of the tourism experience – namely, the market, the economy, the visitor experience, the natural environment and the socio-cultural environment.

In 1996 a system known as the Tourism Optimisation Management Model (TOMM) was specially designed to monitor tourist activity and impacts as a way of helping people to make better decisions about tourism on Kangaroo Island (Manidis Roberts 1996). The TOMM was developed by drawing on data from past studies on the Kangaroo Island, then by using a combination of face-to-face stakeholder interviews, community workshops, and a series of intensive workshops involving heritage managers, state tourism planners, local operators and marketers. Responsibility for part-time coordination was placed with the local government with guidance from a steering committee that included the South Australian Tourism Commission, the Department of Environment and Natural Resources and Tourism Kangaroo Island (the local tourism association). The TOMM integrated a range of stakeholders into its development and attracted wide interest across the tourist and heritage management sectors.

A draft report was prepared in late 1996 and presented verbally to the community via a launch and discussion session and a series of interviews with print and radio media. Professional input was developed through launching the document at an Ecotourism Conference held on the Island (McArthur 1996a). However, implementation of the TOMM was stalled for six months by a lack of local stakeholder commitment to commencing the monitoring programme. Although the programme had been designed to utilise as much existing monitoring as possible, it nonetheless required the introduction of a visitor survey and a tourism operator survey. To date stakeholders have not proven capable of pooling the resources available across the diverse set of stakeholders to implement what appeared to be a very promising method of monitoring and managing change.

Contrasting the Visitor Management Models

Each of these models reflects different visitor management emphases and different approaches, and some of the later models are evolutions of others. Examples where the various models are known to have undergone trials or implemented at some stage have been identified in Table 6.7. The table suggests that almost all known visitor management models have been created and implemented in developed countries; developing countries rarely use, let alone publish the use of, visitor management models. Table 6.8 summarises the key characteristics of each model and qualitatively contrasts them. It suggests that the ROS and carrying capacity present themselves in more simple terms than their counterpart models. The LAC system and TOMM are the most sophisticated, largely because they are on-going systems for strategic planning, monitoring and decision-making. The greatest range of stakeholders involved in the development and implementation of the models is based in the TOMM, largely because it integrates the tourist sector proactively. The authors suggest that the simpler models have been initiated to the greatest extent by more heritage managers across the world. The ROS has been applied and fully implemented more than any other model, albeit indirectly or in partial form. The next most applied model is perhaps carrying capacity, followed by the VIMM and the LAC.

Table 6.7 Applications of visitor management models

Visitor manage-ment models	Applications across the world
The Recreation Opportunity Spectrum (ROS)	• In Australia ROS has been developed for Knarben Gorge, Fraser Island National Park. • In an innovative study ROS was applied to the urban parklands around Newcastle, Australia. • ROS has been an underlying principle behind the development of management strategies for national parks in New Zealand and the United States.
Carrying Capacity Model	• Yosemite Valley, Yosemite National Park, United States – implemented by the United States Parks Service. • Boundary Waters Canoe Area, United States – investigated but not fully implemented by the United States Parks Service. • Angkor World Heritage Site, Siem Reap Province, Cambodia – the Angkor Conservation Office implemented an annual and daily capacity, as well as a capacity for any one moment in time. • Green Island, Queensland, and the Queensland Department of Environment and Natural Heritage, Australia – implemented an annual and daily capacity, as well as a capacity for any one moment in time. • In the early 1990s the New Zealand sub-Antarctic islands had a limit of 500 visits per year. • Waitomo Caves in New Zealand have a carrying capacity set at 200 persons at any one moment in time. • Bermuda in the United States has set a capacity of 120,000 cruise-ship passengers during the peak visitation period. • Lord Howe Island in the Tasman Sea has a limit of 800 visitors at any time.
Visitor Activity Management Program (VAMP)	• Cross-country (nordic) skiing in Ottawa, Canada – partially implemented by the Canadian National Parks Service. • Mingan Archipelago National Park Reserve, Canada – implemented by the Canadian National Parks Service to help establish the new park. • Point Pelee National Park, Canada – implemented by the Canadian National Parks Service with an interpretation focus. • Kejimkijik National Park, Canada – partially implemented by the Canadian National Parks Service.
Visitor Impact Management Model (VIMM)	• Florida Keys National Marine Sanctuary, Florida, United States – pilot implemented by the US Travel and Tourism Administration and the US Environmental Protection Agency. • Netherlands – pilot explored for expansion by the World Tourism Organisation. • Buck Island Reef National Monument, Virgin Islands, United States – implemented but discontinued by United States National Park Service. • Youghiogheny River, Western Maryland, United States – implemented but discontinued by Maryland Department of Natural Resources. • Prince Edward Island, Canada – pilot implemented by Parks Canada and the World Tourism Organisation. • Los Tuxtlas, Veracruz, Mexico – pilot implemented by the World Tourism Organisation. • Jenolan Caves, New South Wales, Australia – fully implemented and monitored by the Jenolan Caves Management Trust. • Villa Gesell, Buenos Aires Province, Argentina – pilot implemented by the Buenos Aires Province Tourism Authority and the World Tourism Organisation. • Peninsula Valdes, Northern Patagonia, Argentina – pilot implemented by the World Tourism Organisation.
The Limits of Acceptable Change (LAC)	• Bob Marshall Wilderness Complex, Montana, United States – tested and implemented by the United States Forest Service. • Selway-Bitteroot Wilderness, Idaho, United States – tested by the United States Forest Service. • Cranberry Wilderness Area, West Virginia, United States – tested by USDA Forest Service and West Virginia University. • The Wet Tropics World Heritage Area, Queensland – prepared for, but never fully implemented by the Wet Tropics Management Authority. • The Nymboida River, New South Wales – prepared for, but never fully implemented by the New South Wales Department of Water Resources. • Wallace Island Crown Reserve, New South Wales, Australia – developed, but never implemented by the Wallis Island Reserve Trust and New South Wales Department of Water and Land Conservation.
Tourism Optimisa-tion Management Model (TOMM)	• Kangaroo Island, South Australia, Australia – implementation in progress by the South Australian Tourism Commission, Department of Environment and Natural Resources and Tourism Kangaroo Island.

Table 6.8 Qualitative assessment of visitor management models

Visitor management models	Key characteristics of visitor management models	Level of sophistication	Range of contributing stakeholders	Actual application by heritage managers
The Recreation Opportunity Spectrum (ROS)	• Determines the threshold level of activity beyond which will result in the deterioration of the resource base • Its main dimensions are biophysical, socio-cultural, psychological and managerial • Used for planning, site design and development, and administration	√√	√√	√√√
Carrying Capacity Model	• Creates a diversity of experiences by identifying a spectrum of settings, activities and opportunities that a region may contain • Helps to review and reposition the type of visitor experiences most appropriate to a heritage site	√	√√	√√
Visitor Activity Management Program (VAMP)	• Planning system that integrates visitor needs with resources to produce specific visitor opportunities • Designed to resolve conflicts and tensions between visitors, heritage and heritage managers • Requires heritage manager to identify, provide for, and market to designated visitor groups	√√√	√√√	√
Visitor Impact Management Model (VIMM)	• Focuses on reducing or controlling the impacts that threaten the quality of heritage and visitor experience • Uses explicit statements of management objectives and research and monitoring to determine heritage and social conditions, then generates a range of management strategies to deal with the impacts	√√	√√	√√
The Limits of Acceptable Change (LAC)	• Focuses on the management of visitor impacts by identifying, first, desirable conditions for visitor activity to occur, then how much change is acceptable • A monitoring programme determines whether desirable conditions are within acceptable standards • A decision-making system determines management actions required to achieve the desired conditions	√√√√	√√√	√√
Tourism Optimisation Management Model (TOMM)	• Instead of limiting activity, it focuses on achieving optimum performance by addressing the sustainability of the heritage, viability of the tourism industry and empowerment of stakeholders • Covers environmental and experiential elements, as well as characteristics of the tourist market, economic conditions of the tourism industry and socio-cultural conditions of the local community • Contains three main parts; context analysis, a monitoring programme and management response system	√√√	√√√	√

√ Low; √√ Moderate; √√√ High; √√√√ Very high

Conclusion

Visitor management attempts to generate a symbiotic benefit between the heritage manager and visitor. It tries to provide a high-quality visitor experience without reducing the values of the heritage. It recognises that the heritage manager needs the visitor to help justify the way heritage is being managed, and the visitor needs the heritage manager to look after the heritage and provide a high-quality experience. However, it is the authors' experience that visitor management is generally not being widely practised in a confident and comprehensive manner. Most visitor management is reliant on regulations and modifying the site. These techniques are reactive, suggesting an acceptance that impact is unavoidable and a diminished visitor experience acceptable to minimise impact. This perspective can in part be explained by a number of constraints on heritage managers, including issues relating to:

- the increasing number of visits to heritage sites;
- smaller group sizes visiting heritage sites;
- visits involving shortening time frames;
- increasing pressure to respond to the needs of the tourist industry;
- increasing community expectations for simple solutions to complex problems;
- unpredictable and typically decreasing resourcing levels; and
- increasing political intervention, sometimes driven by opportunism and cronyism.
  (Bannon and Busser 1992; Craik 1992; Mercer 1994; Hall and McArthur 1996a)

These issues will probably intensify with increases in population, mobility, and interest in heritage (Hall and McArthur 1996a). This implies that visits will become shorter and more intense and that visitors will become more vocal in their demands to address the paradox of heritage management. The authors suggest that visitor management is about integrating a range of techniques, with an emphasis on planning, models and proactive approaches. There is still time to create more sophisticated approaches. The following chapters demonstrate how this can be and is being done.

CHAPTER 7

Shaping Expectations – Marketing Heritage

All too often when one visits national parks or heritage sites, one hears the complaint by visitors that 'it's not like it looks in the brochure'. Unfortunately, we've also heard heritage managers comment that they 'just don't understand' why their visitors have the expectations that they do and why they should be so disappointed. Often the managers add: 'It's not our fault; it's beyond our control. Blame the tourist industry!'

> Selling = numbers through door.
>
> Marketing aims at customer satisfaction as an end, and thus must begin with a complete understanding of the needs and expectations of these customers. (Canadian Parks Service 1988)

Marketing is a critical element in the management of heritage. However, to many people involved in heritage management, marketing is a dirty word because it is often confused with selling. For many managers, selling is typically associated with a 'bums on seats' attitude using 'hard sell' techniques that are often associated with some members of the tourist industry but that do not accord with the needs of conserving the heritage resource. The widespread misunderstanding of marketing by heritage managers has meant that, unfortunately, it has failed to be utilised as a management tool (e.g., Pearson and Sullivan 1995). Yet the shift towards providing quality service in heritage organisations is implicitly a move towards a marketing orientation. As Abell (1980) recognised, 'one imperative for service improvement is to focus on customer expectations'.

Perhaps one of the greatest difficulties for heritage managers is the language of marketing and business management in general. To some managers talking of 'customers' is anathema to their focus on the conservation resource. However, 'customers' is another way of describing the stakeholders in the management and conservation of heritage – i.e., all those who affect the managers' ability to achieve their goals and objectives. Indeed, marketing has much to contribute to the heritage manager's tasks in dealing with one of the major stakeholders in heritage – the visitor. For example, one of the problems in managing visitors is that many of them should never have come at all. Different people have different needs and no one experience can satisfy all of its visitors. Marketing aims at providing customer satisfaction as the end result of a process that is focused on understanding the wants, needs and expectations of customers and matching them with the nature of the product. In heritage management customers are stakeholders, including visitors, and the product is the heritage that we manage and the experiences it provides (Hall and McArthur 1996a; Wells 1996).

'Marketing is the process of planning and executing the conception, pricing, promotion, and distribution of ideas, goods, and services to create exchanges that satisfy individuals and organisational objectives' (American Marketing Association 1985). Therefore, marketing is essentially an applied behavioural science which attempts to understand the behaviour of buyer and seller in terms of psychological, sociological and anthropological concepts (Reed 1992).To modify Kotler and Levy's (1969) definition of marketing in heritage management terms, marketing is that function of heritage management that can keep in touch with the organisation's stakeholders, read their needs and motivations, develop products that meet these needs and build a communication programme that expresses the purpose and object-ives of heritage management. Marketing for non-profit service agencies, such as those which typically manage heritage sites, may be described as a set of voluntary activi-ties aimed at facilitating and expediting exchanges with target markets which have particular wants or which are seeking certain benefits for the purpose of achieving agency objectives (Howard and Crompton 1980). Heritage offers something of value, such as the experience of a natural environment or perceived historical authenticity, in exchange for something else of value, such as the visitor's money, time, opportun-ity costs and/or support (Weiler 1990).Therefore, marketing involves the effective management of a heritage site's resources in a manner that is of mutual benefit to both the site and the visitor. Certainly, selling and influencing will be components of heritage marketing; but, properly seen, selling follows rather than precedes manage-ment's desire to create experiences (products) that satisfy its consumers.As Drucker (1973) stated in one of the classic texts on business management:

> Marketing is not only broader than selling, it is not a specialised activity at all. It encompasses the entire business. It is the whole business seen from the point of view of its final result, that is, from the customer's point of view. Concern and responsibility for marketing must therefore permeate all areas of the enterprise.

A marketing outlook has been extremely influential in the development of the strategic heritage planning framework adopted in this book.To argue that heritage management must be oriented towards the stakeholder and towards quality is to translate contemporary business thinking about serving customers into a heritage management context. Some agencies and institutions have already adopted a cus-tomer orientation – particularly private museums or public galleries and museums that have had their government funding cut in recent years. For example, the Canadian Parks Service (1988), as part of its park service planning system, describes a customer-oriented approach in the following terms:

> At heart, park service planning is a customer-oriented process that insists that all analysis begin with a clear understanding of visitors and their needs and expectations. It aims at achieving customer satisfaction within the boundaries of the mandate and objectives of the Canadian Parks Service.
>
> Park Service planning is a management tool for making well-informed decisions about the direction and priorities of a park visitor program over a defined planning period. A park service plan translates the conceptual direction of the management plan into a more detailed offer of service to the public, with an information strategy.

Marketing as a management tool should not be regarded in isolation from other components of heritage strategies. Nevertheless, integrated heritage management is by definition geared to the demands, needs and perceptions of stakeholders (customers). Although the heritage customer is often the visitor, other forms of customer include sponsors, who wish to become allied with the heritage organisation or site, and those who wish to purchase or use a heritage organisation's research and expertise.

This chapter provides an overview of some of the key aspects of marketing heritage from a strategic perspective. The stages of the marketing planning process relate closely to the overall strategic heritage planning process. Marketing planning is the process by which an organisation matches its capabilities with the environment within which it operates. 'Marketing plans are generally developed at the SBU level, but in some cases they are developed at the total organisation or corporate level' (Reed 1992). While a marketing philosophy will hopefully permeate the entire organisation, individual units within the organisation – particularly those concerned with promotion and visitor management – will adopt marketing as a specific management tool. A successful heritage marketing plan will focus on the development of a marketing process that revolves around five stages:

1   Undertaking an internal and external situation analysis:

   • Who are the stakeholders? Who are the visitors?

   • How is the heritage site currently meeting stakeholder expectations?

2   Setting marketing goals and objectives:

   • Where would the heritage site management like to be? (scenario setting)

   • Which visitor segment do we want to serve?

   • Whom do we want to be the visitors?

   • Whom don't we want to be visitors?

3   Developing a marketing strategy

   • What can management do to get where it wants to be?

4   Establishing a marketing management framework

   • How will management achieve its objectives?

5   Evaluating marketing effectiveness

   • How will management know it has arrived at where it wanted to be?

Unfortunately, much heritage is managed without the benefit of a marketing plan or strategy. One of the reasons is that, traditionally, heritage management agencies have been product-oriented rather than customer- (i.e., visitor-) or stakeholder-oriented. Selin and Lewis (1991) noted with respect to the integration of marketing into the national recreation strategy (NRS) of the United States Forest Service:

> Many forest managers adopt a 'product' orientation towards managing the national forests. Rather than focusing on customer needs, these managers believe they know what the public wants and assume the role of the benevolent steward. A common phrase heard from these managers is, 'Give me the money and I'll give the public want they want.' This attitude among resource managers has slowed the impact of the NRS.

Nevertheless, there are numerous benefits to stakeholders (including visitors), management and the heritage resource in the development of a market orientation in heritage management (Table 7.1). However, it must be emphasised that marketing has to be integrated into the broader strategic heritage planning process (see Chapter 2) and recognised as being a tool for the achievement of heritage management aims and objectives rather than being conducted simply for its own sake.

Table 7.1 Benefits of a marketing-orientated approach in heritage management

Group	Benefits
Visitors	• Heritage management becomes customer-oriented, aimed at visitor satisfaction for selected visitor segments • Visitor travel and trip planning to heritage site is improved • Visitors are aware of the range of experiences available at a heritage site • Visitors can select a desired heritage experience • Visitors experience heritage themes in a manner consistent with their expectations, motivations and needs
Stakeholders	• Enhanced sense of ownership • Improved communication with stakeholders as to the goals of heritage management
Management	• Specifies and prioritises financial and human resource management requirements and assists in determining how resources should be allocated • Provides justification for financial resources and their allocation • Identifies specific visitor information needs • Improves marketing of heritage sites • Encourages a strategic planning approach in management • Assists the development of appropriate interpretation strategies, concepts, themes, messages and techniques.
Resource	• Limits the likelihood of inappropriate on-site visitor activities • Limits the likelihood of inappropriate facilities and infrastructure • Minimises visitor impact on heritage site • Encourages appropriate on-site behaviour

Source: after Canadian Parks Service (1988) and Hall and McArthur (1996a)

Situation Analysis: Internal Analysis and Market Segmentation

As in strategic heritage management, a situation analysis is an integral component of marketing planning. This should include not only an understanding of the resource and what the organisation is capable of providing within a marketing context – e.g., an internal analysis – but should also include an external analysis that places changes in the external environment in marketing terms, especially with respect to key stakeholder groups such as visitors. However, most heritage resource studies focus on objective data about the resource but often give little or minimal attention to human-resource issues related to the appropriate mix of opportunities, experiences, services and facilities for visitors (Payne *et al*. 1986).

One of the most commonly used tools in a situation analysis is an analysis of the internal strengths and weaknesses and the opportunities and threats that exist in the external environment (SWOT analysis). However, although SWOT is a useful tool, it is often misapplied because part of its value is to identify and rank the critical factors and influences on an organisation following, rather than preceding, the conduct of relevant research and analysis.

The purpose of the external analysis is to determine the uncontrollable factors that impact an organisation but that need to be identified and understood. The purpose of the internal analysis is to determine an organisation's capabilities and ability to respond to external threats and opportunities. The internal analysis considers a number of factors that influence the marketing abilities and approaches of an organisation. Often, these factors are described as constituting the 'internal climate' of an organisation (Reed 1992):

- management (How effective and capable are we in leadership that enables our organisation to meet our goals and objectives?);

- human resources (How appropriate are our human resources for matching our product with our market? Do we have a market or stakeholder oriented culture in our organisation?);

- process management (How effective are we in supply services to our customers?);

- research and development (Do we undertake the right research? How able are we to develop product and experiences that we can market to our stakeholders?);

- finance (What is our financial situation?); and

- marketing (How good are we? How do we compare with our competitors? How effective is our marketing and promotion?).

Visitors experiencing heritage may appear to managers to be a diverse market. No heritage can be all things to all people. Therefore, it is essential that managers incorporate an understanding of the behaviour of visitors into their marketing and promotional strategies. For example, in many cases national park or museum interpretation has a tendency to aim for the 'average' visitor. However, the result can often be bland, repetitive or superficial, fully satisfying few visitors, since different people respond in different ways to different experiences. Visitors can be remarkably diverse and so we cannot expect a standard experience necessarily to provide a highly satisfying experience. Therefore, an understanding of the market can enable managers to tie specific experiences to specific visitor groups. Heritage managers must identify those segments of the market which are in tune with the nature and resilience of a setting or, alternatively, the heritage should be developed in such a way as to meet the needs of the market (see Herbert *et al.* 1989). Therefore, heritage managers need to conduct an internal situation analysis to identify existing management objectives and market position, as well as heritage and visitor management issues. This market analysis is also a component of the environmental analysis of the strategic heritage planning process discussed in Chapter 2 and should contribute to ensuring that any marketing that is undertaken is in keeping with the overall aims and objectives of the heritage management body.

Market Segmentation: A Nested Approach

Segmentation is 'one of the most influential and fashionable concepts in marketing' – a concept that has 'permeated the thinking of managers and researchers ... more than any marketing concept since the turn of the century' (Lunn 1986). Market segmentation is a process of partitioning a market into segments of potential customers with similar characteristics who are likely to exhibit similar purchase behaviour (Reed 1992). Smith (1956) introduced segmentation to the marketing and communication fields more than forty years ago. Smith contrasted market segmentation with product differentiation. Product differentiation, perhaps akin to more traditional approaches to heritage management (see Chapter 1), attempts to bend demand to match supply (Hall and McArthur 1996c). 'Market segmentation, in contrast, works from the demand side of the market: the consumer. Segmentation bends supply to match demand by identifying ... segments of the market and developing products specifically to fit those markets' (Grunig 1989). The focus on markets and stake-holders is clearly becoming more important for heritage managers as they attempt to become more responsive to the demands and attitudes of stakeholders. As Tunbridge and Ashworth (1996) observed with respect to the development of dissonance in heritage management, 'Tensions arise through a failure to appreciate the existence of a segmented market, failure to target its diverse segments, or more usually a failure of the targeting strategies themselves to penetrate their intended markets.'

The basic idea of segmentation is simple: divide a population or visitors into groups whose members are more like one another than members of other segments (Grunig 1989). For example, a heritage market segment could be identified by grouping together all those potential visitors with similar motivations and/or propensities towards particular types of heritage or visitor experiences. However, in general, segments must be definable, mutually exclusive, measurable, accessible, relevant to an organisation's mission, reachable with communications in a cost-effective way and large enough to satisfy the organisation's heritage conservation, stakeholder and visitor objectives. However, at the most fundamental level, heritage managers should define their market segments and consumer expectations by finding answers to three questions:

- Who is being satisfied (which stakeholder/visitor/customer segments)?

- What is being satisfied (which stakeholder/visitor/customer expectations)?

- How are customer needs being satisfied (by what technologies)?

(after Abell 1980)

The marketing literature abounds with a wide range of concepts for segmenting populations. For example, segments are often identified along four main lines:

- *Geographical segmentation:* Managers should know how many people there are in the 'catchment region' of both existing and planned heritage sites and what distances people are from sites in terms of different public and private modes of transport.

- *Demographic segmentation:* Heritage markets may be segmented according to such variables as age, sex, occupation, level of income, ethnic association, religion, level of education, and class.

- *Psychographic segmentation:* Markets may be identified in terms of people's motivations and self-images.

- *Product/benefit segmentation:* Markets can be identified by the particular product characteristics they prefer, such as a particular type of heritage experience or visitor activity.

However, the behaviour of market segments can best be understood when *inferred* variables rather than *objective* variables are used (Figure 7.1). Inferred variables are measured by questioning members of a population (e.g., visitors or potential visitors) directly (see Chapters 4 and 5). These variables include motivations, expectations and attitudes. Objective variables can be measured from secondary sources and include demographic, geographic and socio-economic factors and previous travel, visitation and purchase patterns.

Although inferred variables are more effective in segmentation, marketing managers more often use objective measures because they are more readily available,

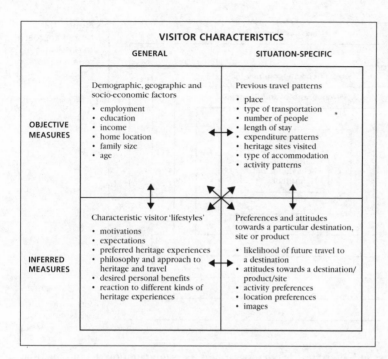

Figure 7.1
Measures and
characteristics of
visitor market
segments

less expensive to gather, and cost less in terms of media and interpersonal communication needed to reach targeted segments (Grunig 1989). As Kotler and Andreasen (1987) observed:

> field research to determine responsiveness and information source behavior is costly and time-consuming and not every organization has the funds and the patience to make the necessary investment...
>
> As a result, managers typically use surrogates for what they ideally would like to measure. Segmentation is often based on demographics, for example, because managers assume that such characteristics will be related to likely responses and reachability.

Nevertheless, a fundamental question for heritage managers is: at what point does the marginal drop in effectiveness in achieving organisational objectives equal the administrative and research costs of the more effective segmentation concepts? One of the most useful ways in which heritage managers can answer it is by adopting a 'nested approach' to classifying segmentation concepts (Bonoma and Shapiro 1983). By nested, Bonoma and Shapiro meant that 'hard-to-assess' inferred variables are located within general, more easily observed objective variables. Figure 7.2 illustrates the relationship between various segmentation concepts. 'A variable in an inner nest can pinpoint a public or a market segment precisely. A variable in an outer nest can locate the segments in an inner nest also, although it will not be able to discriminate among several segments that could be identified by variables in the inner nest' (Grunig 1989). The innermost nest contains variables that predict individual behaviours and attitudes. The second nest defines publics – individuals who behave and differ in the extent to which they construct attitudes and engage in individual and collective behaviours. The notion of publics is also closely related to the concept of stakeholders (see Chapter 3). Subsequent nests consist of communities,

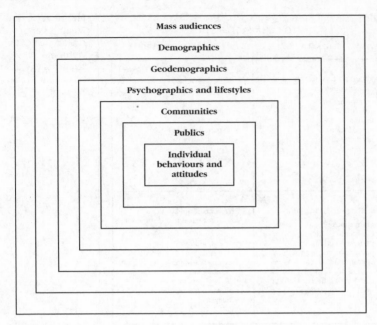

Figure 7.2
Nested approach to classifying segmentation concepts

Source: After Hall and McArthur1996d

psychographics and lifestyles, geodemographics (a segmentation technique that consists partly of lifestyle analysis and partly of geographic demographics), demographics and mass audiences. The groupings in the outer nests are less powerful in isolating the visitor behaviours, attitudes and attributes that the heritage manager is seeking in desired market segments (Hall and McArthur 1996d).

'Variables in the outer nests can serve as surrogates for the inner nests when budget constraints prohibit identification of segments in inner nests' (Grunig 1989). However, given that the variables in the inner nests are that much more effective indicators of market segments, heritage managers should begin with the inner nests (through such measures as visitor surveys) and work outwards only when resources are not available for the research and time required for adequate analysis of the inner nests. Nevertheless, whichever way the market is segmented, it should be emphasised that an attractive market for a heritage site will be one in which the market segment:

- is of sufficient size to make the site viable;

- is compatible with the nature and characteristics of the heritage site;

- has the potential for growth or maintenance of visitation levels;

- is not 'taken' or 'owned' by existing sites; and

- has a relatively unsatisfied interest or motivation that the site can satisfy.

Establishing Marketing Information Systems

Marketing planning, as with strategic planning, must be regarded as a continuous process. This means the establishment of a capacity to continue to generate information that can be used for marketing, management and planning purposes in the future rather than continuing to 'reinvent the wheel'. This can be described as establishing a marketing information system (MIS). An MIS can be defined as: 'the system of people, technology, and procedures designed to acquire and generate information from both the marketing environment and the [organisation]. Such information is integrated, analysed, and communicated to improve marketing planning, execution, and control' (Assael 1990). Information can be obtained from such sources as the internal accounting system, feedback on levels of visitor and stakeholder satisfaction and primary and secondary marketing research. Table 7.2 shows the market data identified as being relevant to the Parks Canada Visitor Activity Management Process (VAMP).

Table 7.2 Market data identified as useful for the Parks Canada Visitor Activity Management Process

Market data

- Current and anticipated trend of participation in existing activities
- Demography of existing and expected visitors
- The importance each market segment places on participating in activities and achieving benefits in their park visit
- Demands for facilities, services, access modes and locations by each segment
- Impact of national and international tourism
- Socio-economic, technological, management practice, support services and other factors that may influence visitor attractions to the activities
- Resource base:
  - areas and features best able to illustrate heritage themes
  - areas best able to accommodate potential activities
  - environmental considerations
- Regional context:
  - existing use
  - visitor activities and locations
  - support services and activities
  - existing levels of use – numbers, frequency and duration
  - analysis of existing market campaign for each activity
  - statement of socio-economic importance
- Profiles of visitor activities:
  - description (compatible/incompatible)
  - profile of activity
  - essential biological and physical elements (setting)
  - types of participation
  - levels of participation (e.g. numbers, ages and location)
  - maximum and minimum levels of service for the activity as it is, or may be provided (relates to market segment to be served)
  - public safety and security implications

Source: after Payne *et al.* (1986)

Marketing Goals and Objectives

As noted in Chapter 2, the development of appropriate goals and objectives is critical in heritage management, and planning provides the framework for the conservation of heritage and the maintenance of stakeholder satisfaction. As Pearce and Robinson (1989) recognised, 'To be effective, managers most know what they intend to accomplish.' Most fundamentally, managers must set and use goals and objectives to guide the planning, development and conservation of heritage sites and their associated values. Table 7.3 outlines the way in which marketing performance objectives can be directed (Reed 1992).

Overall marketing goals can range from raising the profile of a site or increasing awareness of a particularly sensitive site for which visitation needs to be reduced, to

Table 7.3 Direction of marketing performance objectives

Direction	Example
Market penetration Existing products in existing markets	Maintain or increase the level of visitation to a heritage site without attracting new visitors or changing the experience, by, for example, encouraging visitors to return and see the site again
New product development New products in existing markets	Encourage repeat visitation within your existing set of visitors by developing new experiences through, for example, new interpretation, tours or special events
Market development Existing products in new markets	Promote the existing range of experiences to appeal to new audiences by, for example, ensuring that promotional material is specifically prepared and targeted to your intended audience
Diversification New products in new markets	Develop and promote new interpretive experiences for a new audience by, for example, developing a children's trail on a heritage site where previously none existed

bringing income into a park or local community. For example, with respect to the development of a tourism marketing and promotion strategy for the Australian Alps, the strategy identified promotional and management goals that sought to provide a focus for tourism management across the whole of the Alps (Mackay and Virtanen 1992): 'The principal marketing goal of the national parks management is to encourage public understanding, appreciation and enjoyment of the natural and cultural heritage in ways that leave it unimpaired for future generations.' According to Mackay and Virtanen (1992) there were two principal purposes to the tourism marketing and promotion strategy: first, to identify strategies to assist park management agencies in their planning and management of tourist services, programmes and facilities; and, second, to increase public awareness of the Australian Alps National Parks as a desirable holiday and travel destination for both international and domestic markets.

Goals and objectives should be formulated through the involvement of all levels of heritage management, with due consideration of the results of the situation analysis and, where appropriate, input from relevant stakeholder groups – e.g., museum membership associations. Opportunities and issues arising from the situation analysis should be prioritised by the type of marketing action required, the decision required to implement such actions, and the long- and short-term effects of actions on the heritage resource and associated physical and human resources. This will enable managers to identify what can be achieved within an appropriate time span and the costs and benefits of specific marketing actions.

Marketing Strategy: Targeting and Positioning

Having established a set of heritage marketing objectives, it is essential to determine how these objectives can be achieved. Finding a niche in the market (through market segmentation) or developing a unique position in the market is the emphasis of many heritage organisations. This requires the determination of a set of marketing activities in a strategic plan that indicates how existing visitor services and products should be altered or maintained in order to supply the desired experiences to specific market segments.

Marketing strategies can broadly be categorised into two main types: marketing mix strategies and positioning strategies. The first type refers to strategic decisions concerned with products, prices, distribution and marketing communication. The second refers to finding ways of positioning the organisation effectively against its competitors to create and maintain a sustainable advantage (Reed 1992).

Marketing Mix Strategies

The design of an appropriate marketing mix strategy for heritage sites consists of analysing market opportunities, identifying and targeting market segments and developing an appropriate market mix for each segment. The traditional 'four Ps' of the marketing mix are outlined as follows:

- *Product*/service characteristics include the physical product, the image, the packaging and the service experience. The intangible and perishable nature of heritage services is especially important because of the emphasis it places on the centrality of the heritage experience with respect to the visitor market.

- *Promotional* decisions concerning channels and messages, also known as the promotional mix or the marketing communication mix, refer to such things as advertising, sales promotion and public relations.

- *Prices* to be charged for products/services are the value of the product or service.

- *Places* and methods of distribution of products/services concern the availability of the product and services, including their image, location and accessibility. They also include intermediaries, such as agents, wholesalers and retailers, who then sell to the consumer. When a heritage organisation uses intermediaries it needs to recognise that it has at least two levels of customer – the intermediary and the end-user (often referred to as the consumer). Heritage managers have to decide not only how long the chain of distribution will be to their market but also the extent to which they have control over distribution and their product. Managers will therefore need to choose between intensive, exclusive and selective distribution strategies. The majority of heritage managers will tend to support a selective distribution strategy because of the degree of control they are able to retain in influencing the visitor market.

In addition to the traditional four Ps of marketing, tourism analysts such as Morrison (1989) suggest another four Ps that may be held as relevant to the marketing of heritage sites: people, programming, partnership and packaging. The people dimension refers primarily to the role of staff in providing experiences and determining the quality of the heritage product. Programming refers to the variation of service or product in order to increase customer spending and/or satisfaction. For example, many gallery or museum exhibitions will include a programme of events in order to vary the nature of the experience that a visitor will have at an exhibition (see Case Study 7.1). Partnership refers to the cooperation that often develops between different heritage and/or other organisations and the mutual or shared benefits that may result. Sponsorship may be seen as a form of partnership in which the heritage organisation or site and the sponsors seek a range of benefits from the sponsorship arrangement (see below and Case Study 7.3). Strategic alliances occur when two or more organisations collaborate to achieve common objectives. For example, a gallery may engage in joint promotion with a local tourist organisation in order to draw more visitors to both the gallery and the region. Packaging is the combination of related and complementary services within a single price offering. For example, a special 'exhibition package' may include air fare, accommodation and tickets to the exhibition, all for one price.

Case Study 7.1
The Packaging and Promotion of Vincent Van Gogh in Holland

Key point:
- Marketing is critical to attracting the right number and type of people to a heritage experience.

The artistic achievements of Vincent Van Gogh were marketed strongly in Holland during 1990 – the centenary of the artist's death – as a major arts and tourist event for the Netherlands (Moulin 1990). Dutch tourist policies have long emphasised the promotion of cultural heritage and art to draw visitors (Cornelissen 1986). Approximately, 800,000 visitors were expected to attend the main retrospective exhibition of 135 paintings at the Van Gogh Museum in Amsterdam. Another 600,000 people viewed an exhibition of 250 Van Gogh drawings at the Kröller-Müller Museum in Otterlo (Turner 1990). Further exhibitions associated with Van Gogh were held at other museums and galleries in Holland and also in West Germany, Scotland (Glasgow) and France (Paris). Other special events in the Netherlands included a Van Gogh meal in the town of Sleen based on *The Potato Eaters* and, in Amsterdam, the première of an opera based on Vincent Van Gogh. 'Thus, the Van Gogh centenary functions as a cultural shorthand which leads to an eclectic assimilation of a variety of Dutch cultural objects' (Moulin 1990). The tourist marketing campaigns attracted more than a million visitors to the Netherlands in 1990. The Dutch travel industry and the museums themselves clearly benefited by packaging and promoting the international artistic reputation of Vincent Van Gogh primarily as a visitor attraction for Holland.

Target Marketing

Target marketing is the most effective form of heritage marketing. Kotler and Andreasen (1987) contrasted 'target marketing' (in which an organisation develops products for specific market segments) with 'mass marketing' (in which an organisation develops one product and attempts to get every possible person to use it) and 'product-differentiated marketing' (in which products are designed not so much for different segments but simply to offer alternatives to everyone in the market) (Grunig 1989). Target market identification typically involves three stages. First, a decision is made regarding how many market segments the heritage manager wishes to target, given management objectives and the nature of the heritage resource (e.g., which market segment(s) will bring the most benefits?). Second, a market profile is developed for each segment. Third, a marketing strategy is developed that is appropriate to the profile of the selected segments.

Heritage managers may select a 'concentrated' strategy by which they focus on a single segment. Indeed, this will be the likely strategy for many cultural heritage sites. However, some heritage attractions, such as national parks, will have a range of environments and, hence, a range of experiences available to visitors. Therefore, park managers may be able to target a number of visitor segments (a differentiated strategy), each with its own set of expectations, motivations and desired experiences and activities. For example, in the Australian Alps marketing and promotion strategy discussed above, the identified target markets (Mackay and Virtanen 1992) were:

- holiday markets;
- bushwalking and camping enthusiasts;
- specific recreation seekers;
- Australian Alps National Parks management and staff;
- tourist industry operatives and associations; and
- residents.

Positioning Strategies

Heritage does not exist in isolation. Therefore, the marketing strategy also needs to consider the *positioning* of heritage in relation to other heritage sites or alternative visitor experiences in the same target market(s). Positioning is the art of developing and communicating meaningful differences between a heritage product's offerings and those of competitors serving the same target market(s) (Kotler and Andreasen 1987). As Ries and Trout (1986) observed, 'to cope with the product explosion, people have learned to rank products and brands in the mind. Perhaps this can best be visualised by imagining a series of ladders in the mind. On each step is a brand name. And each different ladder represents a different product category'. Positioning will therefore usually mean differentiating heritage from other potential visitor options available to a target market although, increasingly, such differentiation is also occurring within the heritage sector. However, in certain cases, it may involve emphasising similarity to a competitor. For example, if a low-visitation heritage site shares similar attributes to a high-visitation heritage site, the management authorities may promote the similarities of the low-visitation site to the more favoured site in the target market in order to shift the impacts of visitation and maintain visitor satisfaction levels (Hall and McArthur 1996d).

The key to positioning is to identify the key attributes used by the target market to select a specific heritage experience among competitive offerings (Kotler and Andreasen 1987). This requires a clear understanding of the market and what it seeks from heritage experiences. A number of positioning alternatives are outlined in Table 7.4.

The relationship (i.e. position) of various heritage products can be charted on a competitive positioning map. Figure 7.3 provides an example of such a positioning map in terms of price and perceived product quality for a given market. Four museums are identified, labelled A to D. Each museum offers a particular product, or visitor experience to a market for a given price and quality. Museum A, for example, provides a quality experience that is only marginally above that of museum B. However, museum B provides its experience at a substantially lower cost. Identifying such factors may be extremely important in recognising how a heritage site competes not only with other heritage but also with other leisure activities that visitors may be able to pursue.

The goal of a marketing strategy should be to establish an integrated marketing programme, in which each of the components of the strategy helps to position heritage in the target market(s) that the heritage manager chooses to serve, or not serve, as the case may be. Thus:

Typically a good positioning strategy is achieved by a combination of management judgement and experience, trial and error, some experimentation, and sometimes field research. Finding the ideal position strategy is impossible in most situations because of the many influences that must be taken into account. Nevertheless, good strategies can be selected by following a sound analysis and evaluation process. (Cravens and Lamb 1986)

Table 7.4 Positioning alternatives for heritage products

Positioning alternative	Example
Product attribute Associate the product with an attribute or feature that may be unique	Many heritage sites will have a degree of uniqueness which often provides one of the reasons for conservation in the first place
Benefit Relate the product to a benefit, need or want of a stakeholder	Prestige for a sponsor or educational benefits for a visitor
Price/quality Value for money	Convey the impression that there will be a very high quality visitor experience at low cost to the visitor
Use or application Rarely applied to heritage products	May possibly apply to the on-going use of old industrial heritage sites
Type of user of the product Relate heritage to a particular lifestyle or part of the life cycle	Associate visiting a gallery or museum with a cosmopolitan lifestyle
Product class Relate heritage to a particular product category	International profile museums or collections
Competition Relate to a competitor, although not often used with respect to heritage	Compare a heritage site or a museum with a named well-known site or museum in order to convey a sense of prestige or significance to certain stakeholders

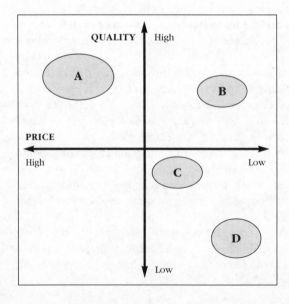

Figure 7.3 Positioning map for heritage products

Marketing Management

The development of marketing strategies with clearly identified target markets and product mix is not the end of the marketing process. Heritage managers also have to ensure that marketing strategies can be implemented and the target market reached through the development of appropriate strategies and communication strategies. Therefore, they have to ensure that human and financial resources are available for the development and promotion of marketing product, while new relationships may have to formed with stakeholder groups such as tour operators. For every major management action or responsibility that is required to give effect to the marketing strategy, plans of action should be developed which identify the communication strategy that is to be adopted. The plan of action will outline the required action, tasks, responsibilities, timeline for implementation, cost estimates and relative priority. Therefore, the plan of action becomes a valuable mechanism for not only ensuring the effectiveness of the marketing strategy but also ensuring that it is undertaken in as efficient a manner as possible (Canadian Parks Service 1988).

Promotional Techniques

One of the most important aspects of marketing management is the selection of the appropriate promotional channel by which marketing will connect the product with the customer. There are a number of marketing communication strategies, many of which will be familiar to readers, such as advertising, publicity and public relations. Table 7.5 outlines the major forms of marketing communication strategies and their various advantages and disadvantages. All of these techniques can be utilised by heritage managers in various ways.

Advertising

Advertising is one of the most commonly used strategies of heritage organisations, particularly for attractions such as galleries, museums and historic houses. However, although advertising may reach a wide audience, careful consideration may need to be given to the extent to which an advertising campaign will reach the desired market rather than many markets. There are four main decisions to be made with respect to advertising in the media (i.e., newspapers, television and radio):

- select the media mix (what combination, if any, of media do you require?);
- determine the level of target audience reach and frequency (what proportion of your target audience do you want to receive your message and how often?);
- establish timing and scheduling of the advertising campaign (how often do you want to advertise, over what period?);
- negotiate and purchase media (what is the best deal you can get in terms of the effectiveness you require?).

In addition, there are a number of criteria that can be addressed when ascertaining the appropriateness and value of any advertisement (Table 7.6).

Direct marketing

Direct marketing is a form of advertising that has become increasingly important in recent years. 'Direct marketing is an interaction system of marketing that uses one or more advertising media to effect a measurable response and/or transaction at any

Table 7.5 Marketing communication strategies

Techniques	Explanation	Strengths	Weaknesses
Advertising	Paid-for advertisements or commercials in the main media	• Low cost per person reached • Ability to create images and perceptions	• Difficult to close sale • People can easily 'switch off' • Difficult to gauge effectiveness
Direct marketing	Communication to individuals at home or at business via the mail or personal delivery – a form of advertising	• Provides quick feedback • Can target markets on a cost-efficient basis	
Personal selling	Communication to a target market via personal representation or by telephone. May also utilise the assistance of volunteers.	• Can close a sale • Easier to hold people's attention • Provides immediate feedback' • Can establish and maintain customer loyalty	• High cost per person • Images not as strong as advertising
Sales promotion	Short-term incentives to encourage purchase or sale of a product or service	• Immediate sales response • Can offer low prices for a short period of time without changing longer-term pricing strategies • Provides fast feedback on effectiveness • Low cost wastage	• Extremely short-term in regard to market development • Unless well-managed may harm image • If used too often customers may shift their purchasing behaviour to accommodate sales promotion
Event marketing	A specialised form of sales promotion	• Capacity for high profile	• Must be integrated with other strategies in order to ensure long-term effectiveness
Publicity	Product information disseminated in the main media as part of editorial or programme content (targeted and non-targeted)	• Low cost • Potentially large impact	• Lack of control
Public relations	Communication directed at 'publics' (often corporate) who may not buy or use product	• Useful for building up stakeholder support	• Long term • Difficult to measure effectiveness
Word-of-mouth	Communication to individuals from people who have experienced the product. Becomes a directed marketing communication strategy through use of volunteer network	• If positive may create substantial interest and stakeholder support • Low cost • Potentially large impact	• If negative may lead to loss of interest • Lack of control

Source: after Reed (1992)

location' (Direct Marketing Association 1987). The most common forms of direct marketing utilised by heritage organisations are direct mail (postal and non-postal), telemarketing (telephone), and newspaper and magazine inserts. An example of a commonly used form of direct marketing by heritage organisations is the promotion of a special exhibition or 'friends'' membership through an insert in a magazine relevant to the exhibition or the type of heritage attraction. Direct marketing provides an opportunity for an organisation to convey its message directly to an intended market and is therefore potentially more cost-effective than general advertising. In addition, the development of more accurate profiles of visitor markets through improved market research and the use of new technology to establish customer databases means that this strategy is likely to be increasingly used by heritage organisations in the future.

Table 7.6 Guidelines to help in the evaluation of advertisements

---

1 Does the advertisement match the positioning strategy? Is it single-minded?
2 Does the advertisement clearly address its intended target audience? Are the words appropriate?
3 Will the advertisement be strong enough to gain the attention of its target audience? Will the advertisement be distinctive?
4 Will the advertisement develop brand awareness recall – i.e. will they remember your heritage organisation or site?
5 Will the key point/positioning statement be understood (i.e. be comprehended)? (Will your intended audience understand what you are trying to convey?)
6 Is the emotional factor important? If so, will this advertisement capture the emotions? Is it likeable? Does the picture tell the story? A particularly important point for heritage managers as we are often trying to convey a 'flavour' of the experience when we advertise.
7 How credible will the advertisement be? Will it develop conviction - if this is intended?
8 Will the advertisement be persuasive and lead the target audience to action - i.e. to purchase or visit or intend to buy or visit?
9 Is the tone appropriate?

Source: after Reed (1992)

Personal selling

Personal selling is a selective form of communication, designed to be informative, persuasive or to foster a relationship, that permits the tailoring of a message to the specific needs of an individual buyer or buying influence (Reed 1992). It is one of the least used forms of marketing communication in the heritage sector, although certain elements of personal selling are to be found when heritage organisations go in search of sponsorship and when they host familiarisation tours for visiting journalists, travel writers, and tourism wholesalers. In contrast, as heritage organisations have to become more commercially oriented in order to attract financial support, sales promotion is becoming a significant component of the marketing mix.

Sales promotion

Sales promotion 'is the function in marketing of providing inducements to buy, offered for a limited time only, at the time and place the purchasing decision is made, which are supplementary to a product's normal value ... sales promotion means "Special Offers"' (Spillard 1975). Examples of sales promotion include reduced prices for certain periods of time in order to boost visitors to an exhibition, or the provision of a museum's 'friends'' membership with the entry fee for an exhibition or vice versa, again for a short period of time. By virtue of the fact that events are of limited duration, event marketing can be regarded as a special form of sales promotion. Examples of event marketing can include the hosting of festivals and fairs at a heritage site in order to boost visitation and awareness of the site to holding themed or focus weeks to highlight specific aspects of an exhibition (see Case Study 7.2).

Case Study 7.2
Expanding Audiences – *The Peopling of London* Exhibition

Key point:

- The use of several components of the promotional mix greatly enhances the meeting of marketing goals.

   We hope very much that [the exhibition] will broaden the Museum's public by attracting members of communities who rarely if ever go to the Museum, possibly because they have not seen their history represented there.
   (Nick Merrimann, Head of Department of Early London History and Collections and *The Peopling of London* Project Leader at the Museum of London, as in Selwood *et al.* 1996)

The Peopling of London project and exhibition was conceived by the University of London with the aim, amongst others, of 'broadening the Museum's public, in particular the visitors from London's ethnic minority communities' (Selwood *et al.* 1996). The project and the museum were driven by quite pragmatic concerns: 'Staff believed that people from ethnic communities were deterred from visiting the Museum partly because of its location in the City and partly because they did not see their own histories represented in the galleries' (Selwood *et al.* 1996). Previous research conducted between June and September 1993 indicated that, of its visitors, 0.5 per cent were Asian and two per cent Far Eastern, and that there were no Afro-Caribbean visitors at all. This was in spite of the fact these ethnic groups comprised twenty per cent of London's overall population (Selwood *et al.* 1996).

The museum had several target audiences for the exhibition, which ran from 16 November 1993 to 15 May 1994: existing museum visitors, non-users (especially ethnic minorities), school groups (especially from countries represented in the exhibition) and museum professionals. 'Prior to the opening of the exhibition, the marketing budget was £5,000 excluding print costs – about 5 per cent of the exhibition budget' (Selwood *et al.* 1996). Several promotional strategies were employed to reach target audiences.

- *Posters:* Two types of poster were produced for the exhibition, aimed at the existing audiences and non-users. The posters showed Chinese, Asian and Afro-Caribbean people wearing the costume of pearly kings and queens, 'the traditional "Cockneys" of popular imagination' (Selwood *et al.* 1996). These were designed to be displayed in the London Underground and in the communities featured in the posters.

- *Leaflets:* The museum published non-English leaflets for the first time. The leaflets could also be used as mini-gallery guides and as promotional material for the exhibition. They were produced in nine different languages. A total of 36,562 leaflets were mailed out and 33,438 were picked up at the museum.

- *Press coverage:* The museum generated substantial publicity through press coverage of the exhibition. Some sixty-five thousand column centimetres were generated, worth the equivalent of an estimated £244,000 of advertising, which appeared in ethnic press (30 per cent), specialist and professional publications (22 per cent), national newspapers (20 per cent), local newspapers (16 per cent), and listings magazines (5 per cent). The museum also received extensive television coverage of the exhibition.

- *Schools:* Ethnic communities were targeted through school children. One strategy was to give vouchers to school parties, which would enable children to come back free if they brought a paying parent with them.

- *Events:* The Museum ran a large number of events, such as poetry readings, theatre, and story-telling, in order to attract visitors and broaden the nature of the experience. Significantly, they also ran a series of focus weeks to encourage particular ethnic and geographical communities to participate and present themselves in the exhibition. Focus weeks included: African and Caribbean, Arab, Chinese, Cypriot, Irish, Jewish, Refugee, Soho, South Asian and Spitalfields. Information about the events were disseminated through leaflets. The museum mailed out 204,000 leaflets about the events, a further 163,000 being picked up by visitors at the museum.

According to the Museum's marketing department:

a total of 94,350 people visited the exhibition. During the six months the exhibition was open, 146,750 people visited the Museum ... 64 per cent of visitors to the Museum saw the exhibition; nearly 10 per cent said they had come specifically to see it. By comparison, 62,547 people had visited the previous Museum exhibition on the Suffragette movement, Purple, White and Green, which was shown for nine months (Selwood *et al.* 1996).

On the basis of observation it was estimated that during the exhibition the percentage of visitors from ethnic minorities rose from four per cent before the exhibition to twenty per cent during it (Selwood *et al.* 1996). However, the longer-term commitment of this audience to continue to visit the Museum is, as yet, unknown.

Publicity and public relations

Publicity and public relations are two related aspects of marketing communication that have long been a component of heritage organisations, although often their purpose within the wider strategic marketing context has not been fully appreciated. Publicity can include such things as editorial information, entertainment, events and sponsorships, personal appearances by major figures or personalities, educational efforts and the dissemination of information through controlled media – i.e., membership newsletters and magazines. Public relations is the dissemination of information to audiences that may not be potential buyers or users of the product or service at all. Public relations is therefore used to create an overall climate of support from stakeholders and decision-makers for organisational objectives, whereas publicity may create a much wider awareness.

Word-of-mouth: the role of volunteers

Whereas the early use of volunteers by heritage managers was usually as a source of cheap labour for menial tasks – e.g., track building and replanting – volunteers are now perceived as being able to offer much more. For example, many national parks, museums and art galleries around the world now use volunteers as tour guides and interpreters (Plate 7.1). One of their major attributes is that they can be used as a

Plate 7.1 Park associations often provide volunteer interpreters. Rocky Mountain National Park, Colorado, USA

Table 7.7 Stages in the corporate sponsorship process

Stage	Characteristics
1 Research	Research to identify suitable company for heritage organisation or product
2 Preparation	Preparation of sponsorship proposal which includes: (a) details of specific product for which sponsorship is sought (b) details of relationship of product to any broader themes or wider product (c) identification of potential benefits for sponsor (d) clearly identified set of legal, financial, managerial and marketing responsibilities for both the heritage organisation and the sponsoring company
3 Consideration	Consideration by potential sponsor: (a) initial contact (b) informal discussions with marketing manager/members of marketing division (c) formal presentation to marketing manager/members of marketing division (d) if large sponsorship, formal presentation to company board
4 Decision	If no, resume search; if yes, proceed to next stage
5 Agreement	Legal agreement between corporate sponsor and heritage organisation detailing responsibilities of both parties
6 Implementation	Operationalise sponsorship through promotion of product
7 Evaluation and Feedback	Feedback to company, which provides for evaluation of the success of the product and the product sponsorship, who will then decide to continue or discontinue sponsorship arrangements. Return to early stages of process

Source: after Hall (1992b)

promotional vehicle by virtue of their enthusiasm and commitment for the heritage site or organisation. Although volunteers, like visitors, need to have positive experiences in order to create favourable word-of-mouth advertising, their capacity to share their experiences with friends, colleagues and the people they meet is a powerful promotional tool.

Sponsorship

Once considered a form of philanthropy, sponsorship is now recognised as a powerful promotional and marketing tool for both private industry and heritage organisations. Indeed, such is its significance that it is worthy of discussion separately from other marketing techniques. Sponsorship is not a separate marketing communication strategy; rather, it is a specific marketing relationship that can contribute to a range of communication strategies. 'Modern sponsorship is a mutually beneficial business arrangement between sponsor and sponsored to achieve defined objectives' (Head 1981). For the corporate sponsor the primary benefit from sponsorship is 'the ability to clearly target a specific region, a specific type of person, or a specific customer or client' (Junkers 1989). Sponsorship may come in many forms – e.g., financial assistance, facilities, provision of event infrastructure, management skills and labour. Sponsors see heritage and heritage organisations as a means of raising corporate profile, promoting particular products through enhanced profile and image, obtaining lowers costs per impression than those achieved by advertising, improving sales and being seen as good corporate citizens. Nevertheless, from the perspective of the heritage organisation and the integrity of the heritage resource it is essential that the potential sponsor be appropriate to the needs and image of the event. Mismatching of product and sponsors will cause problems for both sponsor and the product. In addition, it must be recognised that some sponsors will desire to influence the nature of the heritage product, while nearly all will expect a return of some description from their investment in the form of greater product and/or corporate recognition (Hall 1992b).

Table 7.7 identifies the components of the corporate sponsorship process. Benefits from sponsorship can accrue to both sponsor and sponsored. Heritage organisations must also recognise that companies are seeking returns on their investments. Decisions about the suitability of a product for sponsorship are based on a number of criteria. Table 7.8 lists the decision criteria for sponsorship that were identified in a survey of New Zealand's top two hundred companies in the early 1990s. Regardless of the size of the sponsorship that is sought, proposals must be detailed, professionally presented, and designed to meet company philosophies and objectives (see Case Study 7.3).

Case Study 7.3
Sponsorship of a Cultural Festival in New Zealand

Key Point:
- Effective sponsorship requires a clear set of goals and strategies as well as resources to attract and hold sponsors.

Sponsorship can provide the financial input necessary to establish and organise cultural exhibitions and festivals. For example, in the case of the Te Haerenga Mai – the fourth

Commonwealth Arts Festival held in conjunction with the fourteenth Commonwealth Games in Auckland in 1990 and the 150th anniversary of the signing of the Treaty of Waitangi, sponsorship was necessary because the majority of events at the cultural festival were to have free entry. In order to attract sponsorship the Trust that ran the festival developed specific sponsorship proposals that attempted to match events being run under the auspices of the festival to specific sponsors. However, as Harland (1989) observed:

> the difficulties faced in the early stages in attracting sponsorship vital to the actual implementation of the festival may have been avoided if it had been treated as a separate entity rather than as an add-on to the main event. The lack of clearly stated goals and inadequate funding arrangements limited the ability of the proposed festival to attract sponsorship.

Therefore, it is apparent that if sponsorship is to be successful a clearly thought-out strategy of attracting and satisfying sponsors must be developed.

Table 7.8 Decision-making criteria for corporate sponsorship

Decision criteria	%	Mean
Overall value for money represented by the sponsorship	92	3.5
Extent to which the sponsorship supports the company's image	92	3.4
Relevance of the cause for the company's customers	92	3.4
Extent to which the sponsorship enhances the good citizen role	88	3.1
Relevance of the cause to the community	90	2.8
Track record of the organisation seeking sponsorship	96	2.8
Extent to which the sponsorship provides a vehicle for corporate advertising	92	2.8
Amount of free publicity that can be generated for the company	92	2.7
Location where the sponsored activity takes place	94	2.7
Professionalism with which the sponsorship request is made	90	2.6
Relevance of the cause to the employees of the company	88	2.5
Extent to which the cause has been supported in the past	90	2.0
Personal interests of the chief executive officer	53	1.7
Personal interests of the members of the board	45	1.3

The table illustrates the percentage of respondents undertaking corporate sponsorship who used each criterion. Respondents were asked to rate the importance of each criterion on a scale of 1 to 4 (*4 = very important; 3 = important; 2 = somewhat important; 1 = not particularly important*), thereby producing the mean N = 49.

Source: adapted from *New Zealand Marketing Magazine* (1991) in Hall (1992b)

Evaluating Marketing

As with the overall strategic planning process, it is crucial that heritage managers determine whether or not a marketing strategy was a success in the light of the initial marketing goals and objectives and the overall goals and objectives of any heritage site, organisation or project. Indeed, it may well be the case that some goals and objectives are met while others remained unfulfilled. The success or otherwise of a marketing strategy will only remain hearsay and conjecture unless a formal evaluation occurs.

As a component of a strategic approach to heritage planning and management, evaluation should not be regarded as an afterthought in the marketing of heritage. The costs of evaluation should be built into any marketing budget, and it should be regarded as a basic strategic management tool, which assists heritage managers to find out where they have been and, for future marketing strategies, to decide where they want to go and identify how they will get there. A detailed discussion of the role of evaluation and monitoring in the heritage planning and management is to be found in Chapters 4 and 9.

Marketing as a Heritage Management Tool

> In practice we may well be faced with the question of market differences ... Political priorities in heritage development are concerned primarily with social harmony among residents, whereas economic priorities have most to do with a tourism market which is either neutral to local heritage tensions or biased differently from residents. The challenge becomes how to project different messages to different markets, using different media, sometimes ... predominantly in different languages, without confusing or trivialising the messages, or antagonising any recipients. The sensitivity of this task, including orchestration of the numerous bodies from which heritage messages emanate, underscores the importance of the heritage marketing mechanisms. (Tunbridge and Ashworth 1996)

Individual visitor motivations, attitudes, behaviours and expectations do not remain constant. They change over the lifetime of the individual, are affected by prior experiences, and are impacted by media, word-of-mouth and other sources of information, such as those which arise from product promotions. Much market analysis focuses on the implications of these changes for target marketing and positioning and subsequent visitation to heritage. However, an understanding of the psychological changes that occur during the stages of the travel experience is also important to the effective marketing of heritage products (Hall and McArthur 1996d).

Visitation 'involves people moving from one environment through a range of other environments to a destination site and then home via a return trip ... [They] not only act in their present setting, they also plan for subsequent settings. People prepare to arrive in another setting to carry out preplanned behaviors' (Fridgen 1984). Visitation can therefore be regarded as consisting of five stages:

- decision-making and anticipation;
- travel to a heritage site;
- the on-site experience;
- return travel; and
- recollection of the experience and influence on future decision-making.

The five-stage model can be used in heritage marketing in a number of ways. For example, in New Zealand it has been used to assist in developing a marketing communication and interpretation strategy for tours (Hall *et al.* 1993), while in Australia it was used to formulate an information strategy for visitors to Tasmanian forests by the Tasmanian Forestry Commission (since renamed Forestry Tasmania). Four components of the visitor information strategy were identified: motivation, strategy, enhancement and reinforcement/extension. Existing services and products were then identified and allocated to these stages (Table 7.9).

Evaluating the effectiveness of different marketing communication strategies, such as publications and advertisements, from the visitor's perspective allowed for a

Table 7.9 Creating an information strategy based on the visitor's trip cycle

Type of visitor information

	Motivational – planting interest and ideas to experience heritage	*Strategic – assisting visitor to access and experience heritage*	*Enhancement and education – making experience more meaningful and enjoyable*	*Reinforcement and extension – providing further opportunities to discover and learn*

Techniques	• Advertising
	  – Publications e.g. travel magazines and newspapers
	  – Electronic e.g. radio and television
	• Media features
	  – Special feature articles
	  – Regular radio segments
	• Full-colour brochures
	  – Statewide covering all experiences
	  – Fliers for specific experience
	• Training programmes for travel agents and tourists
		• One-colour regional brochures that are computer-generated for regular and cheap updating
		• Recreation data base
		  – Detailed information on sites and experiences stored on computer
		• Orientation signs
		  – Routed directional
		  – Advance warning
		• Information signs
		  – Background to region
		  – Site-specific information about experience
			• Personal interpretation
			  – Guided tours by commercial tourism operators
			  – Occasional guided tours by specialists, e.g. botanists
			  – Special events, e.g. Open Days at forest sites or facilities
			• Non-personal interpretation
			  – Self-drive tours using cassettes and road signs
			  – Self-guiding walks using brochures or signs
			• Education
			  – Education camps for schools
			  – Seminars and workshops
				• One-colour notesheets on specific subjects, e.g. tree species and forest practices
				• Posters featuring images and information about experiences
				• Coffee-table books on visiting Tasmania, which include State forest experiences
				• Children's books
				• Board games
				• Cassettes, e.g. natural sounds and oral histories
				• Videos addressing management issues and responses

Funding source	• Integrated whenever possible
	  – Forestry Commission
	  – Tourism Department
	  – Parks and Wildlife Service
	  – Tourism operators
		• Typically Forestry Commission
		• Occasionally integrated with Parks and Wildlife Service
			• Typically Forestry Commission or guided tour operators
			• Sometimes integrated as partnership
				• Typically Forestry Commission
				• Occasionally external source, e.g. National Rainforest Conservation Program

Funding priority	• Generally low except for favoured experiences and training programmes	• High, particularly to keep information current	• High, particularly experiences interpreting forest management issues and approaches	• Generally low in addressing general forest values but moderate in addressing issues

Source: Forestry Commission (1992) and Hall and McArthur (1996d)

more coordinated, focused approach to meeting visitor needs. Non-representative publications relating to experiences managed by the Forestry Commission tended to confuse perceptions of the agencies' role in providing heritage experiences. Feedback from users revealed that the full-colour publications quickly fell out of date and overemphasised the motivational rather than the strategic information. By using the five-stage travel model, the Forestry Commission modified the content, design, marketing and distribution of all its pre-visit publications. It changed its national parks image to focus more on its role as a multiple-use forest manager. The changes also allowed for considerable reduction in production costs, the savings being re-distributed to other products. In addition, Forestry Tasmania and the Tasmanian Department of Tourism, Sport, and Recreation undertook a collaborative project to photograph a range of visitor experiences that could be used in tourist brochures to meet the needs of both organisations. The project involved identifying market segments, sites and a protocol for the way in which the photographs could be used. Photographs were then selected that best represented settings and the nature of the experience that visitors could expect. Rather than focusing on the most distinctive elements of the on-site visitor experience, they conveyed representative images of the setting. By undertaking a collaborative approach both organisations developed a clearer understanding of each other's needs.

Unfortunately, strategic collaborative marketing and promotion is not practised by heritage management organisations anywhere near as much as it should be. Often relationships are non-strategic in that they only serve to attract customers to a region and a site. Strategic marketing and promotion relationships are more sophisticated in that they are attempting to obtain a better product–visitor match, thereby not only increasing levels of visitor satisfaction but also helping to ensure that the qualities of the heritage resource are retained. Marketing and promotion should not be con-ducted in isolation. Heritage managers need to integrate marketing strategies within a broader strategic planning context in order to make effective use of marketing as a tool to create a better match between the product and the consumer (Plate 7.2).

Plate 7.2 Strategic market relationships between heritage organisations can often lead to substantial mutual benefits. In Victoria, British Columbia, Canada, the Heritage Victoria information booth is located outside the Royal British Columbia Museum

Conclusion

> To practise marketing, an organisation needs to develop a marketing culture.
> (Reed 1992)

Marketing has for too long been regarded as an inappropriate activity for heritage managers to engage in. However, as Moulin (1990) noted with regard to the packaging and marketing of cultural heritage resources:

> Marketing or commercialisation do not necessarily destroy the meaning of cultural products although they might change or add new meanings to old ones. [Instead,] danger lies in the marketing and promoting of cultural resources without planning for their sustainability. Visitor numbers should not be the yardstick for successful tourism.

As noted at the beginning of this chapter, marketing is not selling. Marketing is concerned with communicating effectively with stakeholders and in developing heritage products, including value-added products such as interpretation, for a specific target market. Effective heritage management requires the matching of product with audience. Marketing is the tool which achieves that goal.

CHAPTER 8

Interpretation and Education

Too often I can walk into a national park visitor centre with my eyes closed and predict where each display will be and what it will be presenting. After a sigh from my long-suffering partner, I open my eyes and yes, there before me lies a compartmentalised view of the world. We gaze at equally spaced areas designated to geology, geography, plants, wildlife and a little potted human history. Then we take a self-guiding walk in the rainforest and discover a similar level of predictability via neatly spaced, predictable stops. To relieve the boredom, one of us is blindfolded and has to guess when they have arrived at the next sign and what it might say. Each sign contains a 101-word paragraph of text and a photograph that may not be entirely relevant but nonetheless provides a 'balance to the text'. We await the recycling sign, then the parasite sign, then the recovery after disturbance sign, then the dreaded plant labels. Our most recent favourite is the guided historic walk, which is told in a relentless sequence of dates, names and anecdotes that are momentarily interesting but generally unrelated. Somehow the guide knows everything about the past, a little about the present, but next to nothing about its relevance for the future – just like our early history texts! To alleviate the tedium we start to wonder how long it will be before the guide is absorbed into the heritage, then interpreted by another guide.

Introduction

There is a vast quantity of information masquerading as interpretation or education. Much effort by individuals and organisations also goes into creating interpretation and education at the expense of planning and reviewing them. The conventional use of interpretation or education has been as a soft sell of heritage values already determined and entrenched in the heritage management organisation. Consequently, there is much duplication and predictability and not much fundamental creativity and innovation.

Are interpretation and education a soft sell about what has already been decided and what is already happening, or are they about what would, could and should be happening? In order for them to continue growing and evolving, many more stakeholders need to understand what these two approaches to heritage management mean, what they can offer and how they need to develop further. This chapter will address these questions.

Defining Interpretation and Education

There is no single definition of interpretation that has been adopted by most practitioners. Nonetheless, the definitions noted in Table 8.1 collectively reflect most of the elements that interpreters have considered when developing interpretive experiences. The most widely quoted definition has been that by Freeman Tilden (1977). However, most heritage management organisations have tailored it to serve their own needs, resulting in a plethora of similar definitions across the world. To address this issue, some interpretation-based associations have developed simpler definitions that can be recognised and utilised more easily. For example, in Australia the definition generated by the Interpretation Australia Association is quickly becoming as, if not more, popular than Tilden's definition.

Table 8.1 Definitions of interpretation

Definition	Source
An educational activity which aims to reveal meaning and relationships through the use of original objects, by first hand experience and by illustrative media, rather than simply to communicate factual information	Freeman Tilden (1977)
Interpretation is the revelation of a larger truth that lies behind any statement of fact. [The interpreter] goes beyond the apparent to the real, beyond a part to a whole, beyond a truth to a more important truth	Freeman Tilden (1977)
The communication process which aims at helping people to discover the significance of things, places, people and events... helping people change the way they perceive themselves and their world through a greater understanding of the world and themselves	Colonial Williamsburg USDA (in MacFarlane 1994).
A planned effort to create for the visitor an understanding of the history and significance of events, people, and objects with which the site is associated. Interpretation is both a program and an activity. The program establishes a set of objectives for the things we want our visitors to understand; the activity has to do with the skills and techniques by which the understanding is created	Alderson and Low (1985) for the American Association of Museums
Creating an experience or situation in which individuals are challenged to think about and possibly make decisions concerning natural resources	Vermont Department of Forests, Parks and Recreation USA (in MacFarlane 1994)
A means of communicating ideas and feelings which helps people enrich their understanding and appreciation of their world, and their role within it	Interpretation Australia Association (1995)
The process of stimulating and encouraging an appreciation of our natural and cultural heritage and of communicating nature conservation ideals and practices	Queensland National Parks and Wildlife Service (in Davie 1992).
A kind of educational enterprise where the concern is that which is interesting to the visitor, or that which can be made interesting to the visitor, not that which someone else thinks the visitor ought to know, regardless of how interesting it is	Makruski (1978)
Interpretation is how people communicate the significance of cultural and natural resources. It instils understanding and appreciation. It helps develop a strong sense of place. It presents an array of informed choices on how to experience the resources	Paskowski (1991)

Environmental education, nature study or visitor education are a more formalised form of interpretation. Education is a systematic form of instruction, training or study set up to help people to acquire knowledge, skills and awareness. Mullins (1985) suggests that

> Education is a societally approved sanctioning system in which participants are required to learn and demonstrate certain competencies. Interpretation often uses the same messages, with the same media, in similar outdoor settings; however, most organisations which sponsor interpretive services are not sanctioned by society to formally certify that learning has occurred among the participants.

Participants of education choose to make themselves a part of an organised structure that has been designed to generate certain outcomes. As a result, educators may expect more from their participants than interpreters can. For example, an educator would expect participants to engage themselves fully in all the activities established for learning to occur, whereas an interpreter would only hope that they did so. People involved in an educational programme may be required to participate, whereas people visiting a museum or taking an interpretive tour may choose to leave when it suits them. Clearly, education is in a powerful position to generate learning and self-awareness through the additional structuring of its programmes or activities and its 'semi-captured' audience. Interpretation can attract and reach greater numbers of people but must offer a greater emphasis on entertainment to attract and hold them.

Evolution of Interpretation

Tourism operators added interpretation to their product long before the terms 'interpretation' or 'ecotourism' were generated. Many guided tours had integrated interpretation as a core part of the experiences they offered without realising it. Most people called it 'guiding' rather than 'interpretation'.

Until the 1980s the most influential developments in interpretation occurred in the United States (Machlis and Field 1992). The initial flourish was largely stimulated by Ernos Mills, who worked as a nature guide in Colorado's Rocky Mountains between 1889 and 1922. Mills was a keen advocate of monitoring his visitors' behaviour and responding accordingly. He prompted guides to concentrate on inspiring visitors by communicating big ideas rather than masses of unrelated information. Mills developed principles and techniques that laid the foundation for interpretation. In the early 1970s the evolving ideas and principles were assembled into a publication specifically about interpretation. *Interpreting Our Heritage* by Freeman Tilden was the first book to define the profession of interpretation and contained two concepts central to the philosophy of interpretation: 'Interpretation is the revelation of a larger truth that lies behind any statement of fact'; and 'interpretation should capitalise on mere curiosity for the enrichment of the human mind and spirit' (Tilden 1977).

In the 1970s and 1980s interpreters working for heritage managers were encouraged to focus on developing non-verbal interpretation (McArthur 1995), which typically involved self-guiding brochures and infrastructure such as visitor centres and metal interpretation signs. These techniques tended not to be targeted to any particular market segment and lacked the continual feedback that is a natural part of verbal interpretation. Most have quickly aged and now require upgrading to remain relevant and stimulating to a discerning audience (Fox and Warnett 1992; McArthur 1996b). Thus, although the 1970s and 1980s may have seen increases in the provision and profile of interpretation, the financial and human investment failed to pay the dividends it deserved.

As visitor interest in the environment grew in the mid- to late 1980s, a small part of the market became interested in doing more than looking at natural areas; it wanted to understand more about them. In response, tourism operators and heritage managers began to realise that interpretation added value to the visitor experience and that people were willing to pay for it. Some heritage managers began charging for access to interpretive facilities and services and some heritage-based tourism operators began to elevate the role of interpretation within their products. In the case of nature-based heritage, this shift helped to create the niche-market experience known as ecotourism (Boo 1990). Ecotourism operators who utilised interpretation as a value-adding or niche-marketing exercise found that they began to access high-yield markets that improved the yield gained from each client and thus increased viability (Commonwealth Department of Tourism 1994).

The Need for Interpretation and Education

Interpretation and education can serve different functions for different stakeholders. Uzzell (1994) observed that 'good interpretation will not compensate for poor facilities, but good facilities will enhance their interpretation'. From the visitor's perspective, interpretation and education can improve the quality of an experience by giving it context and meaning and by making it more enjoyable. This creates a sense of 'value adding', which is politically important in times of high taxation and high entry and use fees. Interpretation can serve non-visitors indirectly in a similar fashion through the use of techniques delivered away from the heritage site. This implies that almost any stakeholder can benefit from exposure to some sort of inter-pretation, giving them a greater sense of place and of ownership of their heritage. This chapter covers both on- and off-site techniques.

From a heritage manager's perspective, interpretation and education can be used to:

- raise awareness and understanding of the values and uses of heritage;

- raise awareness and understanding of the issues facing the management of heritage and the way in which management is dealing with them;

- influence or change visitor behaviour; and

- seek public input and involvement with various aspects of heritage and visitor management.

At least ninety per cent of 103 county, state and federal natural area managers surveyed in the Unites States believed that interpretation aided in the management of heritage, and a similar number said they would utilise interpretation more if they had the funds (Knudson *et al.* 1995). Interpretation and education therefore repres-ent long-term investments in ensuring that the community is aware of, understands and values heritage. This value can then be transposed into a preparedness to provide political and financial support for heritage management. If this support is lost, other aspects of heritage management, such as research, planning, protection and restora-tion, become irrelevant. If these aspects of heritage management become irrelevant, so does the heritage manager.

Among the many other stakeholders who benefit from interpretation and educa-tion are tourism operators running guided tours, accommodation or complementary attractions. This sector is divided into cultural and ecotourism components. These stakeholders use interpretation and education to:

- differentiate their tourism product from more mainstream products;

- attract higher-yield clientèle;

- increase client satisfaction;

- contribute to an ethical position held by the operation;

- increase guide satisfaction; and

- gain more favourable treatment from heritage managers.

If interpretation and education are of a poor quality, eventually clients will become dissatisfied and turn to other operators or experiences. The provider must then find a new market, which is difficult and very expensive.

Conservation groups represent another key beneficiary stakeholder group. Interpretation and education can communicate ideas in a richer and more entertaining way than the media and other marketing techniques. Conservation groups occasionally take interpretive tours to 'threatened' heritage sites to reveal and demonstrate their concerns. They sometimes provide input into the development of interpretation and educational programmes and facilities run by other organisations. Interestingly, the comparative degree of emphasis that each stakeholder places on their objectives for using interpretation and education is rarely discussed or debated.

Principles of Interpretation

Interpreters often use the term 'principles' interchangeably with 'hints' or 'ideas for improvement'. Uzzell (1994) also suggests that the philosophy that underlies interpretive policy and practice needs to be recognised, articulated and questioned:

- What are we trying to achieve?
- What assumptions lie behind our actions?
- What relationships are presumed by the interpretation?

(It is too easy to head straight for the interpretive toy cupboard without considering the nature of our relationship to the past.)

- What assumptions underlie the different ways of presenting the past?
- Whose past is it?

(These questions ought to be framed normatively as well.)

- What do we want our relationship to the past to be and what should it be?
- Whose should we present?

(These are not just idle musings of purely academic interest, but fundamental to the practical implementation of any heritage project.)

In response to such questions Goodey (1994) offered the following principles for interpreters to follow:

- explore the how and why as well as the what and when of any particular piece of information;
- explore the options for an interactive and involving experience; visitors, both young and old, should be able to interact then learn from one another;
- have strong human-interest themes – the interpretation should focus on the fact that people are interested in people;
- provide interpretation at different levels to reflect the interest and comprehension abilities of different visitor groups;
- ensure interpretation is consumer-led as well as resource-led – there should be a balance between interpretation that reflects the interests and needs of the visitor and the range of messages heritage organisations seek to communicate;

- ensure that the visitor gains some new knowledge and is stimulated to know more;

- recognise that there is a limit to how much a visitor can absorb;

- recognise how unobservant people are – visitors need guidance as to what to look at and what is significant;

- build on pre-existing knowledge – this will ensure that the interpretation is relevant and meaningful; and

- provide an overall experience that stimulates all of the senses.

Planning for Performance

By utilising many of the principles just identified, people have created some very clever, innovative interpretive and educational techniques (Ham 1992). They have also been able to bind interpretation and education with other elements, such as visitor research, marketing and evaluation, by placing them all within a strategic planning framework (see Chapter 3). The structured nature of education implies a degree of inbuilt planning to create and deliver a programme, followed by evaluation to determine what participants have achieved from the programme. Unfortunately, interpretation does not have the same inbuilt safeguards and can easily emphasise the delivery technique rather than its planning and evaluation. The effectiveness of most interpretive techniques has generally been limited by poor planning (Trapp *et al.* 1991; Hall and McArthur 1993), where the interpretive plan has been 'a highly regarded yet seldom executed activity' (Goodey 1994). Without adequate planning, most interpretation programmes eventually become ineffective and, ultimately, redundant. Evidence of poor planning is easy to spot. For example, touring programmes that are not thematically linked will appear disjointed, while commentaries that are not targeted will fail to stimulate anyone in particular. Planning binds the three essential ingredients of interpretation together: the audience, the message and the technique. These three components define the three key planning stages required for successful interpretation.

The Audience

The first step in planning interpretation is to define a target audience. Every visitor is different. Each has different values, interests and mental and physical characteristics. Like any product or service, interpretation must recognise these differences and tailor itself to predicted traits. This tailoring works under the same principles as target marketing. Interpreters should attempt to identify common traits so that the interpretation can be moulded to them. Identifying a target audience ensures that the interpretation is relevant to visitors' needs.

Targeting requires the interpreter to identify the key characteristics of the visiting audience. The most typical criteria are demographic characteristics, particularly age, level of education and origin. This information is useful as an indicator of familiarity with the heritage site, likely participation in certain recreational activities and comprehension level. However, demographics alone are rarely sufficient to develop effective interpretation. For example, people access information and understanding from many other sources outside of their formal education and may not necessarily be any more familiar with a heritage site just because they live within the region. Psychographic characteristics reflect more personal traits about people, such as their motivations and expectations for undertaking an activity, or their attitude, level of interest and understanding about a topic.

Interpreters can define their own profile of a target audience or can adopt one from existing market segmentation studies. The most relevant segmentation systems for interpretation are those developed for state or national tourist organisations. Tapping into market segmentation systems already used by the tourism marketing sector permits interpreters to 'share the same language' and design programmes accordingly. This means that each part of the visitor experience, including the interpretation, can be tailored to a definable audience. An example of a target audience derived largely from psychographic characteristics is shown in Table 8.2.

Table 8.2 Examples of psychographic characteristics of a target audience for interpretation

Characteristic	Example
Group size	• Prefers small group of 10–15 clients per tour
Demographics	• Tertiary education and professional employment • Annual income of $35,000–$55,000
Experiential interests	• Be fully briefed along the way to the destination • Do a variety of related short walks of up to one hour • Sit down in a relevant area and have a detailed discussion
Content interests	• Most clients have a strong interest in: the reason why the region's native vegetation grows so slowly; the relationship between the plants and the local indigenous people; and the future use of the plants as a significant medicine
Experiential dislikes	• Being rushed or having no choice in the way they experience the area
Mental capabilities	• In comfortable conditions clients lose interest after about twenty minutes • Struggle to understand interpretation without a map
Bonuses well received	• Special guest interpreters who offer highly specialised expertise or local perspective

The Message

The second step is to determine and structure the content of the interpretation. The content of interpretation typically needs to reflect an amalgam of four components:

- the heritage being visited;
- the characteristics of the target audience;
- the expectations of the heritage manager; and
- the interests of the interpreter.

The heritage provides the baseline source of interpretive content, but typically there are limits to how much can be accessed in the time available and how much can be presented to visitors because of their varied interests and capabilities. If the visitor has no interest, the interpretation will fail to gain their attention or enjoyment. In addition, there may be a need to incorporate information and perspectives from the relevant heritage manager. The expectations of heritage managers may well include a diverse range of issues that they face in managing the site. Incorporating these expectations helps to ensure that heritage managers see merit in the operation, which is likely to result in a more favourable and constructive relationship.

The clearest way of developing and refining the content is through a structure that, at its most basic level, defines the key messages to be communicated (see Case Study 8.1). Structuring can be adjusted to accommodate different audience groups in the same venue. For example, a range of interpretive walks in a natural area may be offered in a national park. Museums have traditionally been set up in the same way by assembling exhibits thematically for visitors to choose from. Structuring can anticipate specific target audiences and cater accordingly. For example, one level of an interpretive structure could be targeted at young children with an interest in unusual animals. In this instance the interpreter may offer the children a combination of a simple story about a day in the life of an animal and the experience of physical contact with that animal. Adults accompanying the children may represent another level for the structure: instead of being expected to enjoy the same interpretation as the children, they could be offered a surrounding interactive display explaining how the animal was nearly hunted to extinction and still remains in a precarious situation owing to on-going, more subtle human impact. Structured interpretation therefore has the potential to separate content, technique and audience. Whatever the complexity of the structure, it usually works best if it has a theme, a group of messages and an overall concept to bind the content.

Case Study 8.1
Failing to Link the Past with the Present at Mexico's Anthropological Museum

---

Key points:
- Structured interpretation can help the visitor to make sense of complex information.

- Even well-structured interpretation needs imaginative interpretive techniques to be effective.

The Anthropological Museum in Mexico City is highly structured in its presentation and interpretation of Mexican culture. The exhibits have been sorted into eight themes that feature cultural heritage from the Mayan, Aztec and Toltec civilisations. Each of the themes is presented twice – on the ground floor as historical culture (the past), and on the first floor as living culture (the present). The combination of dispersing themes over space and time is a powerful one because it helps to provide a sense of structure for visitors to determine what to spend their time and attention on. However, the approach needs more work to realise its strength fully. Despite the obvious effort in separating the components spatially, the interpretation fails to link and contrast the past and the present in a meaningful way. Issues such as the loss of heritage and the impact of integration on cultures and economic systems have been ignored. The notion of past and present is of course artificial anyway, first because most cultures are an amalgam of both, and second, any exhibit on the present will quickly date and be in need of upgrading.

Further problems associated with interpretive techniques compound the structuring issue. The museum presents a huge array of artifacts from the past, using a fairly conventional approach of exhibit and labelling. The first floor uses dioramas, models and labelling to reflect on lifestyles. Both periods focus on built heritage and artifacts and so do not manage to enhance the human and spiritual dimension. Both floors could have utilised temporary exhibits, artwork and theatre to bring more life into the solid building. Without such life, it is easy to leave the museum without a clear idea of the current context of the exhibits. The world inside the museum becomes isolated from the world outside. The opportunity to build on history and make a better future is lost.

The use of a theme ensures that the interpretation is relevant to the heritage. Themes are comparatively easy to create since they reflect the characteristics of the heritage being interpreted (Hall *et al.* 1993). A theme could be rainforest, geology, convicts or indigenous culture. Themes do not on their own specify the content to be presented; this is done by a series of messages. Messages put definition and clarity into themes; they present a statement of meaning. Concepts group the messages together (like a topic sentence) to provide a framework that leads to greater visitor understanding. Examples of interpretive themes, concepts and messages are shown in Table 8.3.

Table 8.3 Examples of themes, concepts and messages

Interpretive themes	Interpretive concepts	Interpretive messages
People's homes	Peoples homes are a reflection of the resources available and what is important to them	• The people living in the suburbs of Los Angeles build large houses and create large gardens that feature front lawns • The people of the Kalahari Desert do not build permanent homes
Abandoned sawmills	The way forests are managed ultimately depends upon the nature of community values	• People have different values from forests • People's needs from forests change over time
Mixed, wet and gallery rainforests	Forests are naturally dynamic systems because they can incorporate change into their system	• Forests are complex natural systems
Mixed forests that have received natural impacts	Forests are naturally dynamic systems because they can incorporate change into their systems	• Forests have changed their diversity, structure and complexity in response to fire

The Technique

The third and final step is to select and refine the technique. Selection is typically and incorrectly undertaken before the first two stages. Many interpreters who attempt to define their audience and content usually try to make them fit their preferred technique. Most interpreters spend their planning effort on developing a technique at the expense of audience identification and content development. This is tantamount to producing a television advertisement with no notion of whom it should reach, or designing a viewing platform without visiting the site where it is to be built.

The technique must reflect stakeholder values, the philosophy and resources of the heritage management organisation and the opportunities and restraints of the heritage site being visited. Different places offer different messages. Interpretation needs to link places and messages in as logical and entertaining a fashion as possible. Therefore, a variety of ways of visiting and experiencing a site or combination of sites

Table 8.4 Interpretive planning, Southern Forests, Tasmania, Australia

Planning criteria	First experience	Second experience
Overall experience	• Two- to three-hour taste of key short experiences, heavily sewn with attractors ('hook' experiences)	• Four- to six-hour mix of short experiences and more exploratory experiences, with several optional supplementary experiences
Visitor profile: origin	• 70% domestic, 30% international	• 95% domestic (60% Tasmania, 35% interstate), 5% international
Visitor profile: market segment	• 40% socially aware, 35% traditional family, 15% visible achiever, 10% young optimist	• 50% traditional family, 20% socially aware, 20% 'something better', 10% basic needs
Visitor profile: preparation	• Minimal preparation, minimal awareness of region	• Prepared appropriate clothing, aware of region and controversy
Interpretive sites	• The Look-in Look-out† • Keogh's Creek Walk‡ • Arve River Picnic Area (short break)# • West Creek Lookout# • Demonstration Forest† • Big Tree Lookout#	• Esperance Forest and Heritage Centre† • The Look-in Look-out‡ • Keogh's Creek Walk‡ • West Creek Lookout# • The Zig Zag Walk‡ • Tahune Forest Reserve (lunch)# • Demonstration Forest† • Big Tree Lookout#
Interpretive concepts	• Forests are naturally dynamic ecosystems because they incorporate change into their systems • Forestry Tasmania acknowledges that the community considers that forests have a range of values, and therefore manages state forest for a range of uses	• Forestry Tasmania is a professional and effective public land manager • Forestry Tasmania manages forests as a renewable resource by juggling a scientific approach with changing community values • Effective conservation of our forests needs informed and active community participation

Hook experience to attract visitors; †Vital experience to engage with interpretation; ‡ Supplementary experience

Source: adapted from Forestry Tasmania (1994a, b and c)

needs to be explored. This will involve re-ordering the sequence of stops, trying out different directions, different points on which to focus and different durations to stop. Sometimes several sites can offer the same story, plus a few specific ones. Therefore, it is often possible to allocate some sites for generic messages and some for specialist ones. Table 8.4 indicates how different experiences and interpretive concepts were generated for two distinct visitor profiles. In this instance, the visitors with limited time but some interest were offered a small number of accessible, short experiences that covered the key concepts, whereas those with more time were offered several in-depth interpretive experiences that explored the concepts in more detail, as well as several supplementary experiences.

One way of integrating the key concepts with the features is to break the technique into components. This helps maximise the effect of timing and collective building of ideas and emotions. Table 8.5 outlines the purpose of four key components (staging, introduction, body and conclusion) and the likely response from the visitor.

Table 8.5 Purpose and likely client response from various parts of a guided interpretive experience

Part of tour	Purpose	Client response
Staging	• Greet and welcome clients, establish rapport • Provide strategic information about the experience to follow	• Feel accepted and more comfortable • Feel more confident that needs will be taken care of
Introduction	• Create interest in interpretive theme and introduce conceptual framework by linking the key parts of the tour with the key interpretive messages • Update the most pertinent strategic information	• Realise that the tour is coordinated and may be mentally stimulating • Feel more confident that all needs will be taken care of
Body	• Link the interpretive messages to pertinent sites and objects of interest • Open each discussion up for questions • Update the most pertinent strategic information	• Feel that each part of the tour is related and has a purpose • Feel intellectually stimulated • Feel confident and comfortable that focus can remain on enjoyment
Conclusion	• Reinforce the conceptual framework by linking the various attractions with interpretive messages • Seek feedback on the experience • Leave a follow on question(s) for further thought by clients • Thank clients for their involvement	• Feel awakened and enlightened • Feel that operator cares • Feel that ideas can be taken away and further built on • Feel that operator cares

The principles outlined in Table 8.5 can be applied to the practice described in Table 7.9.

In deciding what to say at each stop it is often helpful to begin with a sentence that focuses the group on an object, scene or idea. Asking the group a question is an excellent way of focusing attention, since visitors are usually curious about one another's behaviour and, thus, about the responses of fellow members. The main part of the interpretation can then follow, in which key features are described according to the message that is about to be delivered. Another popular idea is to determine the answer to the question by integrating a participatory activity into the discussion, such as counting the growth rings on a tree stump. The next stage is to link the description just outlined to an interpretive message, which reveals a meaning for the outline and at least part of the reason for stopping. The next stage, the transition, brings the current discussion to an end, signals the group to move on and foreshadows the next stop. It will ideally link to an earlier experience or discussion to increase clients' expectations and help them to prepare mentally, or even physically, for the next experience.

Finally, understanding one's characteristics as an interpreter is important to developing an interpretive technique. There are a number of different types of interpreters, who generate very different interpretation and, consequently, very different visitor responses. Table 8.6 categorises some of these types.

Table 8.6 Types of interpretive guides

Type of guide	Traits
Cop	• Perceives visitor activity as threatening to local environment • Tolerates audience by issuing many rules for visitor behaviour
Machine	• Regurgitates the same performance without modification • No spontaneity, personal input or adaptation to audience variation • Disapproves of client questioning or requests to change format
Know-it-all	• Focused on imparting information to suggest superiority • Cannot admit lack of knowledge; prefers to pretend
Host	• Perceives audiences as guests • Offers all clients the opportunity to speak and contribute to discussions • Happily takes questions, chats and jokes • Responds to audience needs, even if it means deviating from planned deviation

Source: adapted from Ham (1992)

Verbal Interpretation and Educational Techniques

There are countless ways in which to interpret or educate, yet in essence they all strive to utilise either verbal or non-verbal techniques, or a combination of both. Verbal techniques revolve around face-to-face communication. Verbal communication is generally considered to be far more powerful than non-verbal techniques because the interpreter or educator can respond to changing conditions, particularly the diverse needs of individual clients. For example, in a study of tourists in Kakadu National Park, Australia, Knapman (1991) observed that personal interpretation could create stronger positive feelings among visitors than even the principal heritage attraction they were visiting. The following text briefly outlines some of the more frequently used verbal interpretive and educational techniques.

Organised Talks and Discussions

Organised talks and discussions are perhaps one of the oldest and most common forms of verbal interpretation. A talk is designed to be conversational so that it sounds spontaneous and informal. Talks typically introduce an audience to a subject, often presenting basic orientation and introductory information about a site, object or experience. Discussions tend to assume a greater level of audience interest and awareness about the subject. They therefore use communication techniques that are more intellectually challenging, such as question-and-answer formats, debates and audience participation in demonstrating a relationship or process. The most frequently used settings are in amphitheatres, visitor centres, museums and around campfires. The most frequently used props used for talks and discussions are rich character within the interpreter's own rich character and enthusiasm, slides and heritage objects (the most popular being a cute small animal). Talks can be modified almost instantly to reflect the feelings of the interpreter, the characteristics of the site and, of course, the audience. The interpreter may be feeling happy, highly charged, reflective or hungover. The site may be influenced by the time of day, the weather or the presence of additional stimuli. The audience may be influenced by the group's size, age and level of interest. Therefore, one of the greatest strengths of organised talks and discussions is that they are very personal and responsive to changing circumstances.

Information Duty

Information duty is a simple means of providing 'on call' basic information and advice to inquiring visitors. At least four functions can be undertaken using this technique. The first is to welcome visitors to the heritage site, making them feel important. The second is to orient visitors around the heritage experience, indicating what can be done, where attractions and facilities are located and dispensing supporting publications. The third is to introduce visitors to the heritage values they are about to experience and, in particular, link the values with appropriate visitor behaviour. The fourth is to build on the previous discussion to explore a particular subject of visitor interest. Strictly speaking, most of these functions are not interpretation as they do not have to be entertaining so much as relevant and useful. Nonetheless, when a series of questions requires a more comprehensive account, the service delves into interpretation. The first and most typical application of information duty is to station an individual at a fixed point where visitors are known to arrive early in their heritage experience (information station). This may be at the gateway to a historic site, in the foyer of a museum or gallery, or by the enquiries counter of a visitor centre. The second method is to allow the individual(s) mobility to find the visitors. Commonly known as a roving ranger, the individual moves about the heritage site, targeting visitor groups at car parks, picnic areas, viewing platforms and other popular congregation areas. The main strength of this technique is that it is opportunistic to visitors' needs, and that it greatly increases the profile of the heritage management organisation. However, it is often difficult to find people who are prepared to undertake this work because it requires them to be highly motivated and to possess a very high standard of communication skills.

Guided Tours and Walks

Guided tours and walks are a specialised form of organised talk or discussion. The principal difference is that they are more mobile, linking various attractions together and thus maintaining a more stimulating environment for learning. Tours are typically more visual in their use of heritage (with stops to look and photograph) and usually require considerable commitment from their audience (going from stop to stop can be quite exhausting). The most popular form of tour is vehicle-based, where a group travels in a bus or four-wheel drive to series of attractions within a given region. These attractions tend to be as distinctive and accessible as is feasible. The guide introduces the attraction to visitors then runs through a generalist commentary about its significance. The next most popular guided tour is the guided walk. People choose this over a vehicle when they wish to gain a more intimate experience with the heritage. Because walkers have greater access to the guide the interpretation must be more adaptable and comprehensive. Tours can run from one hour to a week, some even for months. For this reason the character of the guide becomes more critical with tours than with talks or discussions. The majority of guided tours are commercially undertaken by tourism operators rather than heritage managers. Unfortunately for interpretation, this has largely resulted in most tours being dominated by sightseeing. The learning component has been relegated to unusual tit-bits of information rather than an interlinked experience of learning and discovery (the exception in recent years has been the emergent ecotourism industry, which has improved the quality of commentaries to the extent that some now offer genuine interpretation; see Case Study 8.2).

Case Study 8.2
Interpretation as Part of Ecotourism at Warrawang Sanctuary, South Australia

Key points:

- Interpretation is more effective when tailored to a target market.

- It is possible to make conservation issues central to interpretation.

- Interpretation is more effective when the interpreter uses emotions to convey ideas and feelings.

Warrawang Sanctuary is a privately run wildlife sanctuary in South Australia. The facility was established in response to the rapidly declining populations of Australian mammals in the foothills of Adelaide, due largely to the effects of urban sprawl, such as the clearance of native vegetation and the impact of feral cats on native wildlife. The sanctuary runs educational programmes for schools, guided tours for general visitors and tented accommodation for the ecotourism market. Interpretation is a critical component of the facility as it raises community awareness of the endangered state of the animals and raises valuable income for the upkeep of the mammals. As a result, the interpretation is based partly around general introductions to the animals and partly around the issues surrounding their future.

The interpretive experience begins with the guide providing strategic information via a short outline of the experience, such as how long it will take, what sort of walking will be involved and the fact that nobody must stray and leave the group until the experience is over. The guide then asks the audience a series of questions to determine the level of interest in merely seeing ordinary native Australian fauna as opposed to seeing and interpreting some of the more exotic species. The questions include asking whether anyone is from overseas or if anyone has not seen many Australian animals. The guide then integrates a structured story with a sense of spontaneity, created through the uncertain results of wildlife spotting. The interpretation has conservation issues woven throughout the experience in a way that is both balanced yet confronting. Each group develops a sense of feeling very special by being exposed to the guide's excitement at making an unplanned deviation from the 'normal route'. At the end of the tour clients are offered opportunities to learn more and become involved in the conservation of wildlife. Each group leaves with the impression that their experience was quite different from that of other groups.

Theatrical Performance

Theatrical performance is one of the most creative and artistic forms of learning. It may be delivered at the heritage site or it may be a travelling show, given in such places as shopping centres, libraries and local parks. If the performance is part of a broader educational initiative it is usually delivered at a school as the centrepiece to a combination of educational activities that lead up to, then build on the performance. The most frequently targeted audience is children and the most popular form of performance is the play or pantomime.

The play or pantomime may be undertaken by a drama group, school group or additional staff from the heritage management organisation. The interpreter usually writes the story line and produces sets and costumes with help from an artist. In the case of educationally oriented plays, the costumes and sets are made by the children acting in the production.

Another popular form of theatrical performance for children is the puppet show. While musical performance may not be as direct a communicator of heritage values and issues, it can transcend the age of the audience to maximise audience reach. The strength of musical performance may therefore lie in its simplicity and opportunity for each individual to shape their own interpretation.

Another form of theatrical performance is story telling. This is not the reading out of a book to a bunch of sleepy children. Instead, it is a very personal recollection of a story as told by an individual with substantial imagination and acting skill. Most theatrical performance tries to keep messages simple and positive. A narrator is often used to ensure that the events are simplified and the message communicated directly through narration as well as indirectly through the acting. Animals, plants and buildings are anthropomorphised so that children can relate to them as individuals with feelings. Performances are usually repeated many times over for new audiences and may attract interest from other stakeholders, such as organisers of special events or a restaurant or guest-house owner operating close to the heritage site. A more subtle advantage of theatrical performance is that, even though it is pitched at children, adults are also usually exposed as part of their parental role of accompanying and supporting their children.

Educational Activities

Educational activities are as broad as the imagination of the educator. At a basic level they may include games, artwork, poetry and music. Secondary students may be involved in activities such as public speaking, debates and activities directly relating to heritage management (monitoring water quality, rehabilitating natural habitat and nursing injured wildlife).

Educational Programmes

School-based educational programmes may be centred around one or more qualified teachers employed by the heritage management organisation. Before developing a comprehensive package of activities these educators undertake extensive negotiations with educational institutions to determine ways of integrating their messages into the curricula. At a minimum this determines the educational level and the time of the year at which students are most likely to be addressing subjects in common, such as geography, history, social sciences and biology. At a broader level this may involve modifications to the curricula or the preparation of a teacher's manual providing information in conceptual and detailed form, as well as activities and available resources to explore the concepts. Unfortunately, these manuals require a large human resource commitment and can date very quickly. An extension of this could be visits by educators to schools, which may involve organising the teacher and class to undertake pre- and post-visit activities so that the visit itself can be highly focused and productive.

Day-long field trips and overnight educational camps at heritage sites are a preferred alternative to educators visiting the school, because students work and interact directly with the heritage they are learning about. However, in many countries the resourcing of these facilities has diminished over the past five years because of their high demands upon teachers and because any accident involving the students can attract serious legal and financial implications for the heritage management and educational organisations.

Historic Theme Parks

Theme parks are typically an amalgam of verbal and non-verbal techniques. The verbal techniques largely involve staff or volunteers dressing up in period costume to demonstrate and contrast individual character, day-to-day behaviour and overall lifestyle. In this way the visitor observes the performance and individually interprets distinctive elements and differences from the present. The combination of what are apparently real people from a different era and background with replicas of their environment is a powerful environment for individual interpretations. The effect is enhanced when various services and products consistent with the period or setting are also offered. Products may include souvenirs, lunches and accommodation. Services may include advice, transport and the opportunity to gain hands-on experience of past customs, such as helping to cook food in a traditional way. The effect can be enhanced further by requiring the visitor to change their behaviour and thereby engage in a traditional custom, in order to access or purchase the product or service. Once a behavioural change is established, the visitor becomes far more aware of the subtleties of their experience.

There is significant variation in the quality of visitor experience and use of interpretation across theme parks. Public theme parks are more like a reconstruction and typically have a greater emphasis on engaging visitors and undertaking genuine interpretation. Private theme parks must be commercial and therefore focus on making the experience entertaining. The use of period costume illustrates the spectrum of theme parks and their use of interpretation. At one end are theme parks that dress up staff without any effort to address their behaviour. In the centre are parks that dress up staff as entertainment, at most meeting and greeting visitors. To be interpretive, this aspect of a theme park needs to engage the visitor with more actively authentic communication and behaviour. Most theme parks do not seriously consider or integrate interpretation into their product.

Theme parks are very expensive to create and maintain, and therefore have to limit the degree of variation to the day-to-day visitor experience. Interpretation is included within this repetition and is therefore limited in the degree to which it can build on a visitor's previous experience to create a greater awareness. Returning visitors may not feel entirely satisfied with such repetition and so do not return again. Therefore, theme parks typically remain viable by relying on first-time visitors and a generally unwavering experience.

Non-Verbal Interpretation Techniques

Non-verbal interpretation techniques are used far more because of their lower short-term costs and because they provide more tangible demonstration of taxpayer (or visitor) investment. The following text briefly outlines some of the more frequently used non-verbal interpretive techniques.

Indoor and Outdoor Exhibits

Exhibits are one of the most common forms of communication media, and 'the way in which artefacts are presented says something about our relationship to those artefacts' (Uzzell 1994). There is some confusion over whether the term exhibit refers to a heritage item or whether it includes an accompanying label, sign or other communication item. The first approach comes largely from the arts sector, which seeks to have the interpretation split between the heritage item and the visitor, while the second approach comes largely from the museum sector, which seeks to do more of the interpretation directly through supporting printed material. Therefore, artistic exhibits such as sculpture tend to be presented as stand-alone objects, while exhibits such as a warriors' head dress tend to be presented with an accompanying label, sign or other material.

Given that signs are covered below, we will focus here on the first form of exhibit. Indoor exhibits are typically presented hanging from walls, standing on the floor, suspended from the ceiling or sitting in cabinets, tables or benches. They may include the heritage item itself, replicas of the item, alternative interpretations if the item and models or dioramas that provide context or a simple recreation of the heritage being presented. Some exhibits have been automated so that they can present a movement or change that enhances the interpretive message. These exhibits can be as simple as a moving arm, but can also be extremely complex. For example, the London Museum contains a diorama of the City of London, which is regularly given over to a re-creation of the various stages of the infamous London fires. Most of these more complex automations are performed by computer program (see below).

Outdoor exhibits are typically presented in front of prominent features, outside the entrances of buildings, within parks and other areas where visitors may congregate. They tend to be larger, simpler and stronger than their indoor equivalents. For example, the streets and parklands of Moscow were once dominated by huge bronze sculptures of Lenin. In both cases it is the locational context and supporting design features that are critical to the success of an exhibit. Examples of inappropriate locational context could be a sculpture of Napoleon as he headed into the battle of Waterloo pointing into a McDonalds restaurant, or, an Aboriginal boomerang displayed alongside the Space Shuttle Challenger (although both were supposed to come back). Examples of inappropriate design features could be: insufficient light to distinguish any differences between two human skulls from different periods, or excessive light, generating enough heat to dry out and kill a pair of endangered cave worms.

Signs and Exhibit Labels

The communication of images and written text can be made electronically, on paper or as a sign or a label. Signs and labels are typically produced on wood, metal, plastic or glass. The first and most basic form of sign or label performs an orientation or strategic information role. Orientation information is usually based around directions, distances and names. Strategic visitor information is a broader concept that includes all basic information a visitor needs to access a heritage site and experience safely and comfortably. Strategic information may include orientation information but also background information, such as topography, weather conditions, facilities and services, charges and crowding. Orientation information is typically presented on metal signs in built or developed areas and wooden signs in natural areas. Wooden signs are usually routed with the lettering painted a different colour from the background board. These signs are relatively cheap to produce and maintain and are long-lasting. However, they have severe limits on the amount of information that can be presented and are often subjected to incremental additions that take them beyond their capacity to communicate. Exhibit labels also convey simple information. Those produced for outdoor use are usually printed on to metal. The most common of these is the plant label, which contains a basic illustration, name and sentence that depicts some sort of distinguishing characteristic. Labels for indoor use are typically produced on plastic, or on paper or card behind plastic or glass.

The development of a story and more elaborate design features can enable signs to fulfil an interpretive role. Technological advances over the past decade have provided opportunities for interpreters to be far more artistic and innovative. For example, metal and glass signs can include computer-enhanced, full-colour photographs, lift-up or slide-back flaps, and three-dimensional objects mounted on their face. Technological advances have also made signs far more resilient to visitors and weathering. Signs are now able to withstand ten or more years of ultra-violet rays and a range of hard objects traditionally used as graffiti instruments.

The major drawbacks of using interpretive signs are their lack of adaptability to different audiences, their high cost and their tendency to be ignored once installed. Exhibit labels may be cheaper, but still reflect the other drawbacks (see Case Study 8.3).

Case Study 8.3
Interpreting Heritage Management Issues in Belize

Key points:

- Interpretation is more effective when tailored to a target market.

- Structuring interpretation greatly enhances the possibility of satisfying several audience groups.

- It is possible to make conservation issues central to interpretation.

Unlike many of its Central American neighbours, the country of Belize is relatively unpopulated and less threatened by growth and development. Building on the models established in Costa Rica, Belize has embraced grass-roots ecotourism as a means of generating valuable international currency, increasing employment and community relationships in rural areas, and conserving natural areas (Maguire 1991). Ecotourism projects such as the Community Baboon Sanctuary, Gales Point Village Manatee Project and Belize Zoo have been forerunners in achieving this objective. Belize Zoo is located one hour north of the decaying city of Belize City. The zoo was started in 1983, when seventeen animals were left from the filming of a natural history documentary, and was built in late 1991 to improve conditions for the growing number of animals. Today it contains a rich collection of over one hundred animals native to Belize, some of which are endangered species. Many of the exhibits and animals are periodically moved to allow the native vegetation to renew itself and provide a more stimulating change for the animals. Profits from the operation are reinvested into the preservation of threatened habitat across Belize.

Although the zoo's revenue largely comes from tourists, its message is clearly pitched at locals whose farming and residential creep pose the greatest threat to the wildlife. The interpretation is structured and delivered at several levels. The first level is a part information, part interpretive sign. It is built from the slab of a tree and its text is painted on with a sense of randomness characteristic of the Caribbean. The text sounds as though it was written by a local resident, but from the perspective of an animal. This style is not only low-key but contains jokes and slang that make it highly amusing and perfectly placed to appeal to its target audience (see Plate 8.1). By combining the character of the animal with the pitch of a Creole a unique relationship is introduced that suggests the local animals and people share the land in a sustainable way through understanding and appreciation. Each sign nonetheless features a comment on human threats to the animal's existence. These threats are deliberately oriented around day-to-day pressures associated with urban living, rather than the

Plate 8.1 Wooden, hand-painted interpretation sign at the Belize Zoo

conventional, easy target of forestry. The second level is a larger set of two signs located at the main viewing area of each exhibit. At the top is a basic information sign designed to introduce the name, visual image and key characteristic of the animal. The text has again been written using the local Creole accent and roughly painted on to a slab of timber. Each animal is given a common name, scientific name, local name and colourful painting. Below this is a more sophisticated metal sign featuring an outline of the animal for children to draw from, a detailed line drawing and text about the distribution and characteristics of the animal. A column alongside is specifically devoted to the conservation status of the animal, identifying major threats, status and initiatives being undertaken to address the threats. The third level is the running of guided tours by local volunteers with a passion for the animals and their conservation. These tours offer deeper interpretation into the animal and its habitat. A sign towards the end of the trails seeks to remotivate and inspire and reads

> Throughout the world, tropical forests are being destroyed and animals, dependent on these forests are disappearing. Much of Belitze remains forested, and healthy populations of its wildlife live on. Belitze stand proud – as a nation, this richness of your flora and fauna will be an everlasting enhancement to your natural heritage. (Interpretation sign at Belize Zoo 1994)

The interpretation is therefore deliberately pitched at locals. Nonetheless, international visitors find the Creole characterisation equally stimulating and entertaining because it sounds so authentic. One indicator for judging the success of the Belize Zoo in reaching its local population is the way the zoo's messages have been developed into environmental education programmes. The zoo runs a series of outreach programmes that tour Belize's schools and teach children about their country's wildlife. The creation of an environmental ethic in the heart of Central America is considered quite an achievement: 'Residents of Belize City who have never been to the Cayes or the mountains speak with pride of the clear water, coral reefs, rainforests and unique animals' (Maguire 1991).

Educational Kits

Many heritage management organisations prepare simple travelling resource kits and accompanying suggested activities for teachers to select from. The resource kits often feature items to 'bring the heritage into the classroom' and stimulate activities, such as heritage objects, photographs, maps, scents and prerecorded sounds. They may also include 'fact sheets' that provide relevant background to the heritage for teachers to study and become familiar with.

Publications

Like signs, publications can play a role that is information/orientation-based, or inter-pretation-based. Most publications represent some form of printing on paper or card, though other materials, such as plastic, canvas and silk are sometimes used. The most common form of published interpretive product is the pamphlet and brochure. Typically, a pamphlet is an A4-sized sheet of paper folded into thirds to form a DL format. A brochure is a more complex production and usually contains several pages stapled or stitched together. Both products have been used extensively as the com-municating media for self-guided tours (see below). Other publications include posters, booklets, books, games, calendars and stickers. The most popular form of poster is the single photographic image with a small paragraph of descriptive text underneath (which is promotional and informative rather than interpretive). However, some interpreters have used artwork to establish a more imaginative atmosphere and layered set of messages. Booklets and books are more complex versions of brochures, with more pages, higher unit costs and thus smaller print runs. Both are predominantly used for communicating information. They may be relatively short and artistically oriented for children, or large and photographically oriented for adults. Games are most commonly based around activity resource material (see educational programmes) and game-boards, where several people face various challenges related to the management of the heritage on their way to reaching a desired destination.

Like signs, it is costly to establish a publication. A pamphlet, for example, requires researching, writing, editing, artwork, graphics, scanning, layout, printing, folding and distribution. Consequently, the updating of publications is often neglected until the situation becomes critical. This problem is compounded with more elaborate and expensive publications. To avoid this, many pamphlets are now produced by the her-itage management organisation with their own desktop publishing programs, then printed out on a laser printer and photocopied. This also allows rapid updating to take account of such changes as seasons, features, visitor patterns and infrastructure.

Audio-Visual Devices

There are perhaps three key reasons why audio-visual devices are so frequently used for interpretive purposes:

- they appeal to at least two of our senses at the same time, sound and sight;
- their programmes can respond immediately to demand and can be repeated over and over again with minimal effort or cost; and
- they can be adapted to groups of varying size.

The most common audio-visual device is the slide programme linked to pre-recorded music, sound effects and commentary. This usually involves several slide projectors working simultaneously to rapidly integrate a series of images across the screen. Visitors may see several images on the one screen or the projectors may link up to present one massive image across the entire screen. The changing shapes and overlapping nature of images provide the energy and principal entertainment. Meanwhile, the sound effects, music and comments provide the context and the narration provides the direction. The production of films is typically more expensive, but the main reason why they are avoided is because they date quickly and are more difficult to update without extensive refilming. In contrast, the slide programmes can have a few slides exchanged and modifications to the script spliced in at a reasonable cost and over a relatively short time frame. Both devices are based around a script (concept and means of interrelating the various components), a storyboard (for which images are required), photography and a soundtrack. The final component is the programming and synchronisation to pull the components together. Most slide projectors have specialist functions to respond to signals on the audio tape that indicate the need to move to the next slide, though computers are increasingly playing this role.

A simple audio programme can be just as effective as audio-visual devices. Often the heritage itself is visual enough and only needs sound to reintroduce the atmosphere of the past. For example, many historic homes, jails and fortifications play recordings of the typical conversations of past residents to try and capture the essence of how the site was used and who used it. The addition of silhouettes or mannequins of the people whom the recording is depicting can provide a focus if there is not a great deal of other supporting material. The quality of the recording and discreet positioning of the speakers are critical to creating a convincing atmosphere. Systems that are triggered by the movement of visitors are superior to those which require visitors to start them, because they create a more spontaneous and thus more realistic atmosphere.

Information Technology and Computer Programs

The simplest use of a computer has been as a data storage and retrieval system for visitor inquiries. In these cases information relating to visitors' opportunities, facilities and requirements can be entered for visitors to retrieve under a variety of approaches, depending on their interests and capabilities. The information is stored as text, photographs, illustrations, maps and audio recordings and, in some instances, may be printed out as a simple note sheet by the visitor. The system may be located in a facility housing the heritage, such as a museum or visitor centre, or it could be recorded and distributed on a disk for home computers, or it could be accessed over the World Wide Web.

As discussed above, computers are being used by some interpreters to aid the performance of audio-visual devices and exhibits. These programs are basically designed to provide continual coordination of a complex set of actions within a tight time frame. The program may be run as a continuous loop, triggered by a timer or beam through which a visitor passes, or may be manually activated by the visitor depressing a button.

The more interactive use of computers in museums, schools and some visitor centres has come about thanks to the rise of the personal computer. Building on the storage retrieval system, the more sophisticated programs present some form of challenge to the visitor. This challenge is met through the visitor making a series of decisions designed on the surface to demonstrate a degree of familiarity and expertise with the subject and, underneath, to demonstrate a principle illustrated through the pathway that leads to a successful outcome in the challenge. Computer programs can be written to monitor the choices and successes of visitors and thus provide a reliable source of information for evaluating the performance of interpretation.

The use of information technology as an interpretive or educational technique does have its limitations. First, the technology is being upgraded so frequently that it is quickly out of date. It may be impossible to design a computer program for use by all primary schools in a state or country because it would require the software to be compatible with more than ten types of hardware and another ten types of software. Furthermore, by the time the software was distributed, the schools may well have updated their systems. Second, the use of information technology and computers cannot be spread easily across many visitors without significant investment in hardware. Most visitors have experienced a seemingly eternal wait for a child to finish with a computer so that they may have a turn.

Visitor Centres, Galleries and Museums

Visitor centres, galleries and museums have the highest profiles in the interpretation sector. Their two basic ingredients are a series of exhibits and displays and a building in which to house them. Displays are covered in more detail below. The primary function of galleries and museums has traditionally been the collection and conservation of the heritage within. This can limit the way in which the heritage is presented and interpreted and thus the degree of interaction between visitor and heritage. Visitor centres tend to be more display- than exhibit-oriented. While this reduces the heritage conservation emphasis within the centre, it also reduces the relevance of the centre to the heritage. Often the visitor centre is located at the periphery of the national park or historic site and the heritage with high conservation value is located deep within. All the interpretation is contained within the centre and the heritage site has none. The result is once again a poor degree of interaction between the visitor and the heritage.

Visitor centres, galleries and museums have some fundamental visitor management problems, yet they remain a great favourite with government funding (largely because politicians relate to tangible objects that can be directly associated with their own initiatives and presented to their constituents). Often the driving force behind the development of museums, galleries and visitor centres is not the achievement of a vision, backed up by a strategic plan, but rather the fitting of displays and interpretation into an existing building. This can be contradictory to the building's function and extremely limiting on the development of interpretation because such logistics as space, light, heat and access are significantly compromised. In addition, the majority of funding is spent on the design and construction of the building rather than on the planning and production of interpretive displays. Although galleries can continually introduce major new exhibits and museums can occasionally rotate parts of their overall collection into and out of public viewing, a large part of their experience – and virtually all of the experience within visitor centres – dates quickly, is typically extremely expensive to build and moderately expensive to staff and maintain. Nonetheless, these facilities represent a very tangible demonstration of government funding and thus of government commitment to heritage management and interpretation. This makes them near irresistible to politicians eager to demonstrate their worth.

Self-Guiding Tours

A self-guiding tour is an interpretive approach for visitors who wish to pass through a heritage site on their own. A road or trail is adapted to access and feature particular attractions or experiences, linked to become a series of pre-planned sequential stops. The integration of several features is a major strength of this technique. By linking the stops, a story with a definite beginning and end can be created, allowing the interpreter to build in foreshadowing, mystery and transitions, as well as the ability to make comparisons and establish relationships. The time spent at each stop on a self-guiding tour must be short in response to the visitor being focused on continually moving to reach the end of the route. This trade-off in time is a major limitation to the self-guiding tour.

A self-guiding drive takes visitors around an hour to drive, but usually contains several stops and short walks to break up the experience and give visitors a feeling of escape and additional stimulation. The drive is usually based around an audio-cassette or a radio broadcast. The cassette is structured into sections that reflect the distance between stops. These sections are punctuated by a sound effect signalling the driver to stop the tape and get out or discuss the feature further. The radio may be a continuous broadcast loop from one transmitter or it may contain individual transmitters communicating individual, highly localised broadcasts.

A self-guiding trail usually runs over a distance of 500 to 1,600 metres and takes visitors thirty to forty minutes. The trail is punctuated by between seven and ten stops that last between half and one minute each. The features or attractions along a trail are usually interpreted using signs, but publications and audio-recordings are also used. Signs are the simplest and most popular method currently used. However, the information can only be communicated at a stop – travelling between stops is often devoid of information. Audio-recordings can provide a continuous interpretation between each stop and at the stop itself. Only issues of distribution and management of tape players prevent this technique from being used more widely.

Strengths and Weaknesses of Current Interpretation

In general, interpreters are able to transfer a strong conviction of the importance and benefit of interpretation into a source of inspiration and energy. Most interpreters have a good understanding of who visitors are and what their needs are. This understanding generates an opportunity to change the way visitors perceive and behave in their environment. It also provides a creative means of addressing general visitor and heritage management issues (such an understanding is not as well developed in other sectors of heritage management). In the spirit of providing immediate opportunities for improvements, Table 8.7 provides a list of practical suggestions for improving the day-to-day quality of interpretation.

Unfortunately, most theory about interpretation has not been produced by interpreters and is not easily accessible to interpreters outside the United States, particularly developing countries. There is a gulf between those generating theory (e.g., academics) and those generating delivery (e.g., practitioners). Without the theory, unguided passion and idealism have sometimes restricted the ability of an interpreter to be realistic and honest with their interpretation.

The profession of interpreters has been filled with optimists focusing content and technique on making people feel good, even in the face of critical heritage management issues. Recent market research by Augoustinos and Innes (1997) suggests that messages

Table 8.7 Hints for interpretation

Hint	Explanation
Expect to increase time proportionally to group size	The larger the group, the more difficult their movements and responses, so the longer they will take to get organised
Set up the theme and concept early in the experience	Interpretation and clients need warming up; an introduction using maps, figures and artifacts helps to establish realistic expectations
Carry communication helpers	Visual aids and objects help by providing additional material to explain complex ideas; they can also help to run interpretation in a vehicle or building when the weather is poor
Involve the client	Getting clients to do something makes them feel more involved and thus more useful and interested
Ensure sentences are short, positive and active	Satisfaction can easily diminish if the clients feel they are being lectured to or are hearing something that has been repeated
Avoid jargon and technical terms	Most interpretive language should able to be delivered to a reading age of eleven or twelve years
Be relevant to the heritage being interpreted	Keep as much of the on-site interpretation focused on a real object that clients can focus on and, ideally, interact with
Read the group's body language and respond accordingly	Signs of disinterest during interpretation include straying from the main group, individual conversations and playing with objects
Give equal attention to clients	Involve all clients at some stage. If something is raised in a small group discussion that could be useful for all, reintroduce it later on
Continually seek feedback	Ask people what they thought of the interpretation and the experience and keep probing until something concrete is gained which can be used to tailor the service further
Attempt to be accurate and fair to your knowledge and understanding	Some clients will ask questions that require more thorough understanding. Acknowledge your limits and buy some time to utilise additional resources, then come back to your client
Ensure neutrality and cover a range of views	Expose audiences to management issues, but avoid pushing individual value judgements. If clients request an opinion, make sure you acknowledge it as such
Continually involve clients	Interpretation needs mental and, ideally, physical involvement of the audience. Ask for contributions via client recollections, the holding of an artifact or the co-running of an activity

designed to make people feel good may not necessarily influence their judgements. People may be emotionally stirred by interpretation but not necessarily persuaded by its content. While 'colouring' the story for entertainment purposes is acceptable, it may result in presenting a single value-based view, when others clearly exist.

Avoiding a single value system implies being fair and honest to heritage, visitors and oneself. One of greatest causes for concern in interpreting values is when interpreters interpret values they do not understand. Those responsible for managing interpreters and the material they produce have also demonstrated a misunderstanding of the role of values in interpretation:

> Managers have modified, embellished, or even eliminated interpreters' messages. In the worst cases, they have told interpreters to lie to the public. At one county park, interpreters weren't allowed to discuss water quality problems in a river that was in violation of public health standards, where

the parks department operated canoe trips. Likewise, an innocent question by a student on a field trip to a national park went unanswered, as the interpreter indicated that, by answering the question, he would put his job at risk. (Knudson *et al.* 1996)

Interpreters are generally reluctant to confront and analyse the effects of the values of the heritage management organisation and the interpreter upon the interpretation being produced. Yet, often, it is the values of the organisation and the conflict between different stakeholders that have drawn the visitor to the site in the first place. One example where conflict has been confronted is the Strahan Wharf Centre in Tasmania, Australia. Plates 8.2 and 8.3 demonstrate the way in which conflict over the proposed damming of the Franklin River was interpreted. (For a discussion of the conflict, see Hall 1992a.)

Plate 8.2 Dramatic juxtaposition to interpret conflict. Strahan Wharf Centre, Tasmania

Plate 8.3 Interpretation of conflict via a protest banner. Strahan Wharf Centre, Tasmania

There is also a reluctance to target certain sectors and experiment with new ideas and techniques. There is a growing level of blandness and homogeneity in content, audience and technique. There is an overemphasis on attracting visitor attention at a general expense of communicating a given message. A great deal of interpretation attracts attention, but visitors leave half way through or complete the experience without understanding any significant idea or concept.

Perhaps the gravest professional concern facing interpretation is its limited integration into the core business of heritage management. There simply is little to no systematic approach being undertaken to develop, implement and improve interpretation. It remains a part-time or fringe activity for many heritage management organisations and guided tourism operations, and it is typically perceived as a visitor service only. Its role in delivering visitor and heritage management is generally under-acknowledged or misunderstood. Three reasons why this recognition has not occurred may be:

- a reluctance to write measurable objectives or performance criteria that could be used to evaluate and make subsequent improvements to interpretive planning and provision;
- a lack of examples to demonstrate the benefit of interpretation; and
- poor linkages with other related disciplines, such as marketing.

These reinforce the need for a more integrated and strategic approach to heritage management.

Conclusion

A direct experience of heritage can form fundamental underpinnings for the way it is valued and the way people want it managed. Interpretation offers a major opportunity towards achieving this by making a visitor's experience much more meaningful. In this manner, interpretation can form a central component of raising community awareness and support for heritage and how it should be managed. Most interpretation is greatly appreciated by visitors, more and more of whom now expect it as part of their experience, or who willingly pay sectors of the tourist industry to provide it.

The only way of achieving the multiple objectives that interpretation has proven capable of achieving is by the complete integration of interpretation into heritage management. This will require interpreters to utilise their passion and creativity to shift from day-to-day delivery of interpretation to thinking about and testing its real potential. It will also require other sectors of heritage management to be more prepared to help interpreters achieve this shift through direct and indirect support. Such a cultural shift will require greater demonstration of the way in which the objectives of interpretation are being achieved, which will in turn require more research to refine the theory and more evaluation to modify the practice. These aspects are covered in Chapters 4 and 10.

CHAPTER 9

Evaluating Heritage Management Programmes

Our team sat down with much sighing and resignation. It was budget time – the time of the year when all bets were off and where our right to do what we are supposed to would be challenged. But several of us had shifted our ground since last year, recognising that we had to do more for visitors if we wanted them to support the site and support us managing it. We had put a lot of effort into preparing a list of new projects that we thought would do a lot to improve things – not too much, but enough to make a difference. There was the extension to the car park, a boardwalk to replace the eroded track, a few interpretation signs and even a number of improvements to the maintenance programme. Excitedly, we outlined them and their proposed capital costs. But when we looked up for a sign of endorsement, the only emotion we could see on our manager's face was a questioning look: 'This organisation ran a million dollars into the red last year, and what do we have to prove it was justified? How can I authorise these new projects if I don't know whether last year's were a success or failure?'

Introduction

Evaluation is guided by the impulse to understand and to make informed judgements and choices (Kemmis 1982). There should be no need to argue the case for evaluating heritage management programmes. Any individual or organisation that does not evaluate is not committed to understanding its performance, not committed to learning from its mistakes and not committed to self-improvement. All that should have to be put forward are the consequences of not evaluating.

One consequence of not evaluating is the tendency for a plan or programme to become stale and out of touch. For example, Peregrine Expeditions run rafting tours through Tasmania's state forest. On some trips during one summer clients appeared to be slightly agitated and dissatisfied with their experience: there had been no significant change to the itinerary, the river, the equipment, the guides or the interpretation. Later in the season Forestry Tasmania evaluated the performance of the tours in meeting the needs of clients, operator and Forestry Tasmania (Forestry Tasmania 1994c). The evaluation discovered that Peregrine focused its interpretation on the natural aspects of the river and adjacent forest to the extent that guides presented the area to clients as though it was a national park. The evaluation also discovered that the rafting experience had become punctuated by occasional sounds of chainsaws and sightings of log trucks crossing bridges. The tenure of the land as state forest and the implications it had on rafting had not been integrated into the interpretation. Furthermore, the relationship between the long-scheduled logging nearby and the rafting experience had not been considered. Client satisfaction could be traced back to these oversights, as could a reduction in recommendations to undertake the rafting on the river in question.

Evaluating helps to realise the full potential of a plan or programme. For example, Philadelphia Zoo installed an exhibit on naked mole rats. Museum staff had not undertaken any preliminary market or visitor research to determine visitor interests. Instead, staff agreed on an interpretive concept based around the mole rat's social structure, believing it to be the most interesting aspect for visitors to explore. The text on the labels was established around the concept and the exhibit opened up without any evaluation being undertaken to confirm or deny the assumption made by staff. After some four years an evaluation was undertaken on the exhibition as part of a broader evaluation project. The visitor research that formed part of the evaluation identified that visitors were most interested in aspects that had not been considered or dealt with in the exhibit (i.e., were the rats blind and were they babies). In effect, the exhibit had not addressed demand for four years and thus not realised anything like its full potential (Wagner 1996). What effect this may have had on the overall experience is uncertain.

One other major consequence of not evaluating is that the culture of a heritage management organisation becomes reactive and introverted. For example, in 1996 Environment Australia undertook an evaluation of the licensing systems for tourism operators practising in Australia's protected areas (NPWS 1997). The study revealed that most of the ten or so heritage management organisations had never undertaken any significant review of their licensing systems, allowing individual systems to remain stagnant and only evolve through occasional borrowing of components from one another. The evaluation also found major inconsistencies, limitations and inequities. The implications suggested that most heritage management organisations perceived themselves as defence mechanisms rather than proactive agents of innovation. The viability and quality of the country's nature-based tourist industry may well have been greatly enhanced had that quality been demonstrated through a more efficient licensing system.

Defining Evaluation

Evaluation is the process whereby individual and public judgement processes are harnessed for reflection on action. We define evaluation as a systematic, objective assessment of the effectiveness, efficiency and/or appropriateness of a programme or part of a programme. Evaluation tends to be more focused on determining performance for outcomes such as impact assessment, justification, accountability, planning and resource allocation, improvement and continued support (after Cauley 1993).

Evaluation involves making judgements about the results of some sort of measurement against specific objectives. This is typically done by collecting and analysing information, judging the worth of something and making informed decisions for the future. There are many different legitimate and covert reasons for undertaking an evaluation. Table 9.1 provides several examples.

Evaluation is often confused with research, and the two have occasionally been blended to create the term visitor evaluation. The differences have become so blurred that many heritage managers truly believe that visitor research and evaluation are the same thing. There are even associations, newsletters and journals set up to cover visitor evaluation when in fact their focus is visitor research, largely in museums.

Visitor and market research is focused on collecting information from or about people/visitors. This is the same as visitor evaluation, which has been defined 'as an amalgam of two components ... a study and analysis of the demographic and psychological profiles of those people who come to a particular tourist site or environment [and] the visitor's appraisal of a given site, environment or display' (Pearce and Moscardo 1985). Evaluation is more broadly based around making assessments and decisions. It typically requires some form of research, which may or may not include market or visitor research. Whether evaluation uses market research, visitor

Table 9.1 Legitimate and covert purposes of using evaluation

Legitimate purposes	Explanation of legitimate purposes
Testing management assumptions	Determine whether assumptions that many visitor management approaches rely on are valid or appropriate to the heritage and organisational setting
Increasing accountability	Assess and demonstrate the degree to which a policy or programme is meeting its objectives
Improving decision-making	Access and integrate relevant information that improves the quality of decision-making in areas such as resource allocation and other policy and programme directions
Reviewing performance indicators	Consider whether the original objectives or desired outcomes remain realistic and appropriate

Covert purposes	Explanation of covert purposes
Postponing decisions	Putting off a difficult decision until the situation dies down or until the problem partially solves itself
Avoiding responsibility	Commission consultants or other staff to undertake an evaluation of the problem so that a difficult decision can be displaced to them
Manipulating public perceptions	Use positive evaluations to promote the merits of a policy or programme to stakeholders or other decision-makers, or bury or discredit negative reports. Being selective in the content and method of evaluation is also used to achieve this purpose
Meeting grant requirements	Evaluation of programme objectives may be required as part of funding programmes, especially those generated externally
Eliminating the administrator	Tie a programme evaluation to the performance of a decision-maker, then load the evaluation so that the programme appears to be failing to meet expectations, then recommend that a dismissal is the only way to change the situation

Source: adapted from Theobald (1979)

research or monitoring entirely depends upon the objectives of the evaluation and its subject matter. The difference between evaluation, monitoring and the different forms of research may well be based on the intent of the programme and the time frame in which each is used, as is illustrated in Figure 9.1.

Some of the principles of evaluation that should be kept in mind at all times are:

- what needs to be measured is determined before the measurement technique;
- the only aspects assessed are those that will provide critical information needed;
- stakeholders clearly understand the rationale and nature of the evaluation programme;
- what is to be evaluated already has some form of measurable objectives or performance criteria;
- relevant information can be collected;

- results are balanced and reliable, and recommendations are relevant, feasible and timely;

- information is presented in a way that increases the possibility of acceptance;

- the right information reaches the right people; and

- the programme is delivered to stakeholders in a way that reflects their interests and abilities – e.g., comprehension and cognitive. (See Case Study 9.1.)

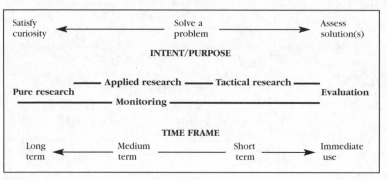

Figure 9.1 Differences between evaluation, monitoring and various forms of research

Case Study 9.1
Evaluating the Effectiveness of Three Interpretive Experiences in Tasmania's Forests

Key points:

- The use of a range of information sources, data processing methods and reporting techniques will increase the likelihood of recommendations being implemented.

- Evaluations can challenge long-held myths and generate fundamental change in management culture and decision-making.

- Evaluations require considerable objectivity, particularly when comparing alternative management approaches that may reflect different value systems.

As with many timber-producing areas in the developed world, the management of Tasmania's state forests have been plagued by conflict for many years. In the early 1990s Forestry Tasmania developed a number of interpretive walks to take visitors into areas where conflict had occurred. Across the various sites different approaches to interpretation were undertaken. Three sites depict the variation well. The first site used a mystical anthropomorphic account told by several very tall trees, the second was a light-hearted account of a family touring a demonstration forest with a forester for the first time, and the third was a layered set of media clippings depicting a diversity of opinions on forest management. Managers wanted to know what type of interpretation their precious resources should be allocated to. An evaluation programme was developed in order to:

- determine the degree to which the interpretive facilities were achieving their objectives;

- provide feedback for improved visitor management and, more specifically, interpretation planning;

- provide some insight into the effectiveness of non-personal interpretation in general; and

- develop techniques for assessing the performance of non-personal interpretive media that could be incorporated into monitoring programmes. (McArthur 1995)

The evaluation programme was targeted at managers and specialists such as interpreters, education officers, visitor managers, tour operators, marketers, visitor researchers and evaluators. A visitor research programme was designed to collect specific information relating to:

- the extent to which visitors learned from a range of non-personal interpretive experiences – e.g., knowledge and understanding gained by visitors, and changes in the perceptions and attitudes of visitors;

- the extent to which visitors modified their behaviour as a result of information and interpretation; and

- the extent to which visitors were satisfied with the experience, particularly that likely to suggest a preferences for certain techniques.

Information was collected using a combination of observations and surveys. The techniques were pilot tested over several weeks and modifications made to enhance reliability and utility. The visitor research was then carried at the three sites before and after the installation of interpretive signs.

The analysis sought to identify any change between when the interpretation was and was not present. The data from the questionnaires were entered and sorted in a database, then exported into a range of quantitative and qualitative research analysis programmes. Change was suggested via an increase or decrease in the number of responses for a given choice within the questionnaire. Observation data were entered into a spreadsheet for further manipulation. Qualitative data, such as definitions made by the respondents and comments about the walks were analysed using a grounded theory approach. Responses were physically coded, summed and converted to percentages before being compared between periods and sites because there was insufficient time for computer analysis. The degree of change for these two sources was evaluated by employing standard error (i.e., how significant the difference is if change has occurred).

A number of critical implications were quickly discovered. Some of these included:

- interpretation was more likely to perform well when it had been designed for a specific audience and when marketing had successfully attracted that audience as the main visitor group;

- simple and entertaining techniques work well with simple messages that visitors already generally endorse; and

- layered and controversial techniques are needed to communicate complex messages, but these messages are better addressed using personal interpretation than non-personal interpretation (signs).

Dissemination of the results was a critical factor in implementing change. A combination of summary printed reports and verbal presentation/discussions was developed to share the implications and seek feedback on decision-making. The key method was a series of workshops with key staff. These workshops shared results, suggested implications, then asked individuals to suggest responses. Results from other workshops were used to further stimulate contributions and commitments to implement change. The other source of pressure was external. The programme published the results widely in a number of newsletters and journals, then conducted discussions between managers and specialists at conferences and workshops. These individuals were then enlisted to apply additional direction and support for change.

Key results have been:

- the abandoning of simplistic non-personal interpretation;
- a shift in resources from non-personal to personal interpretation;
- the requirement that all interpretation be designed for clearly defined target audiences; and
- the development of a visitor monitoring and research strategy to coordinate all visitor data.

Planning an Evaluation

A typical evaluation will undergo several stages that each require different skills. The stages typically involve planning collecting information, analysing the information determining implications, making recommendations and making changes (Table 9.3).

Determine What Needs to be Known

An evaluation typically begins by identifying the element of heritage management that needs to be assessed and what it is it about that element which needs to be measured. Some of the most common elements include policies, objectives, strategies, actions, programmes/activities and resources. Some of the most commonly asked questions about these elements relate to their appropriateness, adequacy, effectiveness, efficiency and side effects. Table 9.2 provides an explanation and example of each of these questions.

Table 9.2 Commonly asked questions in evaluations

Question	Explanation	Example
Appropriateness	A value-based question that asks whether most people would agree that the plan or programme is the right thing to do	Most people agree that a policy permitting drilling for oil in coral reefs is not appropriate
Adequacy	A part qualitative, part quantitative question to determine whether the plan or programme is accomplishing what it set out to do	Whether an existing plan or programme that is capable of completely satisfying half the heritage management grievances of a local community is worth doing or not
Effectiveness	A quantitative question to contrast planned versus actual use of resources involved in implementing the plan or programme	The restoration of a rainforest using the same type of trees that were there previously. If the trees had evolved after pioneering species, the establishment of pioneer species may be more effective at providing a nurse crop for the second-order trees to grow under and, eventually, over
Efficiency	A pondering question to identify the cost of the actual implementation and investigate whether the resources could have been used in a different way to achieve the same or improved outcome	The cost of building a visitor facility from virgin timber as opposed to recycled material
Side effects	A reflective question to identify and quantify the anticipated and unanticipated side effects resulting from the implementation	Lost recreation and tourism opportunities resulting from the closure of a road to reduce environmental impact

Table 9.3 Process for undertaking visitor management programme evaluation (goal-oriented)

Stage	Explanation
Ensure visitor management programme has measurable objectives	• Clear, precise objectives are needed to help determine: what data needs to be collected; and how the data should be collected and assessed • Do not proceed with an evaluation if objectives or some sort of desired outcome can be clearly expressed and in some way measured
Define what needs to be evaluated	• Consider all stakeholder needs. The addition of their perspectives will make decision-making and changes to management much easier to accomplish • Balance what must be known with what 'would be nice to know'
Attempt to predict the results of the evaluation	• Predicting the results may help to market the need for resources for the evaluation and will guide the development of research methods
Select information-collecting techniques	• Consider available resources, skills, commitment and competition with other management obligations • Reflect on the type of information that will be generated: it needs to be easily understood and marketed to stakeholders and it needs to be compared with other programme evaluations
Run a pilot programme	• Test techniques to ensure they are appropriate. If testing on visitors, consider 5–10% of intended sample size • Briefly present to stakeholders to shore up support • Make adjustment according to the degree to which techniques reliably provide the information required within resource constraints
Pre-determine how the results should be disseminated to each stakeholder	• Consider each stakeholder's position on the programme, their available time and preferred communication technique • Ensure the presentation technique will not allow results to stagnate and lose their relevance and utility before decisions can be made
Run controlled evaluation programme	• Monitor data collection techniques to ensure consistency • Monitor the interest and commitment of stakeholders
Analyse information collected	• Make an initial browse to detect trends and identify likely success of programme before investing significant resources in further analysis or report preparation • Enter and summarise data • Re-determine trends versus predicted result • Manipulate data as required • Prepare implications and consider recommendations, considering the positions of all stakeholders
Present results and implications	• Produce in a format that reflects stakeholder needs, e.g. verbal presentations, different sized reports and posters; consider separate discussions for difficult stakeholders
Discuss implications with stakeholders	• Look for opportunities to subtly propose recommendations to stakeholders • Seek opportunities for stakeholders to arrive at recommendations
Consider alterations to programme	• Based on the data, outline what could be done to improve the programme • Implement a process for making changes to the programme
Review evaluation approach	• Determine the utility of the approach and suggest improvements

Identify Stakeholders and Involve Them in the Evaluation

Key stakeholders must be involved throughout the evaluation if it is to make real-istic and implementable decisions. Once stakeholders have been identified, their interests and preconceptions need to be determined and to be considered carefully. This information can then be used to tailor the entire evaluation approach, including the selection of techniques, presentation of results and final decision-making process (see Chapter 3 for detail on stakeholder audits). It is also useful to identify how on-going involvement will be maintained, particularly in relation to reporting back and decision-making. It may be useful to establish a reference group with protocols for decision-making and a projection of milestones for involvement.

It is also important at this stage to identify the tangible and intangible benefits of the evaluation. Ideally, a general set of benefits should be tailored to reflect each key stakeholder. These may become critical if resourcing or political support becomes stretched. Placing the emphasis on using evaluation to detect management issues and provide solutions is particularly attractive, because it typically leads to a better use of limited resources (see Table 9.4).

The use of measurable objectives and performance criteria can be of great assist-ance in integrating further the support of key stakeholders. An example of how these helped to guide and focus evaluation of an interpretation programme is provided in Table 9.5. In this instance, the performance criteria came in the form of audience characteristics and messages.

Determine What Needs to be Measured

Once stakeholders have endorsed the objectives of the evaluation, the evaluator should coordinate the identification of what needs to be measured to achieve the evaluation programme's objectives. Often it is not possible to measure exactly what is required because the situation is too complex, too politically sensitive or too

Table 9.4 Using issues and implications to market the need for evaluation

Situation	Possible result	Implication	Time and cost
Lack of management presence	Poor management identity	Impact on heritage	Unforeseen expenditure
Poorly located track	Meandering and deviation	Poor planning	Loss of productivity
Small text on interpretive signs	Visitors do not read signs	Additional demand on limited management resources	Loss of financial support
Poorly worded interpretation	Misunderstood message	Failure to meet visitor needs	Loss of stakeholder support
Untargeted interpretation	Lack of visitor interest	Failure to meet stakeholder needs	Inefficient use of resources
Unidentified audience	Unguided visitor management	Failure to support management and its objectives	Delay of future projects
Inappropriate audience	Visitors do not enjoy experience	Failure to target market effectively	Reduced staff morale
Negative impact upon resource	Loss of heritage values	Failure to meet conservation objectives	Continuation of inappropriate strategies

Table 9.5 Application of programme evaluation process to an interpretive programme

Stage	Example
Interpretive objectives	• Provide an attractive experience that can be easily marketed to convert potential to actual visitors to the site • Provide a short walk accessible to most visitors, including those with mobility disabilities • Provide an opportunity for visitors to identify plant species often found in the area • Communicate prescribed interpretive messages to the majority of independently travelling visitors to the region
What needs to be evaluated	• Comparison of desired versus actual visitor profile • Define visitor motivations and satisfaction • Determine behavioural reactions to plant species signs • Contrast understanding of prescribed messages before and after interpretive experience
Predict results	• Experience is predominantly attracting target audience • Target audience understands key messages of interpretation • Target audience distinguishes experience as enjoyable
Select techniques	• Vehicle counter before turnoff; track counter • Observations of visitor behaviour (pre- and post-interpretive experience) conducted by a trained field evaluator • Interviews (pre- and post-interpretive experience) conducted by a trained field evaluator
Pilot-test techniques	• Test methods on site • Meet with interpreters, rangers and guided tour operators to discuss results and confirm support • Adjust time that observations and interviews are conducted • Adjust interview questions (simplified)
Disseminate results	• Propose a presentation to rangers and interpreters, with a follow-up report supplied upon request • Propose a separate meeting for guided tourism operators
Run programme	• Train and monitor field evaluator • Arrange key stakeholders to visit field evaluator and, ideally, conduct some observations and interviews
Analyse information	• Trends identified and most of predicted results confirmed • Data entered into simple database, with trends summarised on paper • One technique confirmed as unsuccessful, resulting in no further analysis of information collected from this technique • Three sets of implications re-worked according to three stakeholders' perspectives
Present results and implications	• Separate verbal presentations to rangers and guided tour operators • Written report to interpreters, followed by a general discussion
Programme adjustments	• Additional meeting with all three stakeholders to decide on changes
Review evaluation methods	• Recommend longer period to collect data and additional field evaluator

Source: after McArthur and Gardner (1993) and McArthur and Hall (1993, 1996d)

resource-hungry. In these cases it may be useful to select and work with indicators that provide a reasonably good suggestion of the condition of the specific measure.

Determine the Evaluation Technique(s) and Measurement Method

The evaluation objectives and information needed are used as a guide for the identification, development and refinement of some form of evaluation technique and measurement method. When selecting the measurement method it is critical to have a thorough understanding of the difference between monitoring and the various forms of research (see Chapter 5). It is also critical to determine whether existing data can be used directly or indirectly, or whether totally raw data must be collected. Furthermore, it is sometimes useful to develop performance criteria to determine the merits of alternative methods.

One of the simplest forms of evaluation may be a staff member reviewing existing data, such as monitored statistics, financial statements, minutes of meetings, newspaper articles and letters of support or complaint. Alternatively, staff or peers may be brought together to undertake clinical examinations, generate ratings or participate in some form of group discussion or workshop. A more elaborate approach may be to collect and analyse raw data via interviews, questionnaires or observations, or to undertake tests and modelling to establish projective forecasts (see previous section for a selection of evaluation methods and Chapter 5 for a selection of monitoring and research techniques).

Test the Measurement Method and Evaluation Technique(s)

It is always useful to consider how and by whom the data should be collected, and when and by whom the analysis should be done. Testing the proposed measurement method and evaluation technique is a wise course of action to ensure accuracy, reliability and cost-effectiveness and acceptability to stakeholders. Pilot testing is particularly relevant if the evaluation is substantial, complex or politically sensitive. Once pilot testing has been completed, an evaluation of the results should result in refinements that improve performance. At this point it may be extremely useful to bring the key stakeholders (or reference group) together to endorse the methods and perhaps market the programme further to other stakeholders.

Collect and Analyse the Information

The analysis is typically oriented towards determining relationships and performance, and so statistical testing may be required to confirm apparent trends. The collection and analysis of data must be done under the evaluation principles identified earlier.

Determine Issues, Implications and Recommendations

Interpreting findings, developing implications, then converting them into recommendations for decision-makers is a delicate and sometimes highly politicised task (Hall and Jenkins 1995). This is one of the most critical periods for key stakeholders or steering group to be intimately involved in. The most likely way to get recommendations endorsed and acted on is to get the stakeholders themselves to arrive at them. The use of an interactive workshop provides an excellent forum for discussion, synthesis and agreement on critical issues and responses. The discussion should also look at prioritising the recommendations according to the seriousness of the implications driving them and the available resources to implement them. The reference group should be considering such questions as:

- What do the findings mean in terms of the plan or programme objectives?

- How can the findings be utilised to bring about change?

- What implications would the implementation of findings have for the overall plan or programme?

- What follow-on steps are necessary, such as new evaluation efforts, implementation of change, or movement to new stages of programme development?

Make and Implement Decisions

Recommendations and decisions must relate to the plan or programme's original objectives and the evaluation brief. Some of the ways in which a positive response to decisions can be achieved include:

- concentrating on refining the policy recommendations rather than making an extensive list of specific actions;
- sorting recommendations into common groups based on similar fields, stakeholders or issues;
- sorting recommendations according to the organisational scale in which they are being pitched (e.g. policy recommendations should be listed before specific actions);
- presenting a set of recommendations that reflect alternative courses of action; and
- making recommendations succinct in words that reflect the position and character of those being expected to endorse and implement them.

When attempting to implement critical decisions arising from the evaluation among stakeholders it is sometimes useful to adopt the following initiatives:

- be non-defensive about the information and treat it as an indication of success or possible trouble rather than gospel;
- ensure the stakeholder has the information required to understand the rationale for the decision and no other information likely to cloud it;
- present useful comparisons between the results covered and other similar situations;
- use existing channels of communication and decision-making within the organisation;
- build in incentives and rewards for using the results and implementing the recommendations; and
- prepare a brief dialogue between yourself and the stakeholder(s) to anticipate their and your responses, and give feedback in a way that will encourage the other person to change their behaviour.

Disseminate Relevant Information to Other Stakeholders

Evaluations that present a written report that includes results, implications and recommendations as a *fait accompli* reduce the opportunity for other stakeholders to be a part of the process. This situation is totally unacceptable if the recommendations need to be either supported or implemented by the stakeholders themselves. Briefings, workshops and informal discussions are excellent ways of gaining additional stakeholder input and support (see Chapter 4 for more detail).

Written reports should only be considered as a back-up to verbal communication and information sheets. It is critical to present information within the reports in a clear and concise way. The use of bullet points to cover critical information and tables to back it up ensures the reader can quickly get the picture. The best way to present the evaluation is the reverse of the format of a standard scientific report –

i.e., recommendations/decisions, key implications and results driving the decisions, then other supporting data. Raw data and supporting details must be placed well behind key results, implications and decisions. (See Case Study 9.2.)

Case Study 9.2
Collective Evaluation of Three Environmental Education Programmes in Central and South America

---

Key points:

- It is possible to develop relatively simple evaluations to determine whether objectives are being met.

- Recommendations of an evaluation are more likely to be implemented when the programme has a reputable control to compare against.

- Recommendations of an evaluation are more likely to be implemented when critical decision-makers and implementers of decisions are involved in the evaluation from the outset.

Three environmental education programmes in Central and South America were evaluated by the Latin American Studies Center and the Program for Studies in Tropical Conservation. The first programme was run at the Mayan site known as Uxmal, on Mexico's Yucatan Peninsula (Fisher and Koran 1995). The second was run in a state park in Brazil (Gutierrez de White and Jacobson 1994). The third was run at a Colombian Zoo (Padua and Jacobson 1993). The evaluations were generated to determine whether to use them again or reject them.

The Uxmal evaluation attempted to evaluate the effectiveness of interpretive material by:

- recording general information about visitors;

- testing visitor knowledge of the Maya;

- comparing knowledge gained between male and female visitors, and between Spanish- and English-speaking visitors; and

- assessing visitor satisfaction.

The visitor research confirmed that the interpretation had generated a significant increase in visitor knowledge of the Maya. It confirmed differences in knowledge between Spanish- and English-speaking visitors. It also identified that the more time visitors spent experiencing the interpretation and site in general, the more information they retained and the more their curiosity was satisfied. The principal results of the evaluation were a conclusion that the educational programme was meeting its cognitive and affective outcome objectives and a collection of suggestions to improve performance. However, the education programme was not modified and the improvements were not implemented. The evaluation lost credibility because it did not have a control against which to compare results (such as a similar site without a programme). Furthermore, insufficient effort was made to convert the Yucatan Tourist Board's general awareness and interest in the evaluation into support for change. While the evaluation provided a valuable contribution to the research base, it generated a sense of security in the performance of the programme that resulted in consolidating a conservative management culture.

The environmental education programme in Brazil focused on the development of an instructional experience designed to generate greater awareness and preservation of endemic and rare birds and mammals, particularly the black lion tamarin. The part of the programme that was specifically evaluated was a slide show and guided visit to the Brazilian Morro do

Diable State Park. The evaluation began with the specification of goals and objectives, a needs assessment and an assessment of available resources and planning support. A major part of the evaluation programme was visitor research, comprising of pre-, post- and retention testing to compare how one group exposed to the programme differed from another that was not exposed (control). Some 144 ten- to thirteen-year-old schoolchildren were randomly assigned to both groups. The evaluation then determined outcomes, modified the programme and disseminated information. Results suggested increases in awareness and knowledge, indicating that the programme's objectives were being met.

A Colombian zoo was offering two training methods aimed at raising awareness of its animals and changing attitudes towards the conservation of Colombia's wildlife. One training method was a slide show and a visit to the zoo, the other added a workshop about wildlife conservation to the slide show and visit to the zoo. A visit to the zoo without slide show or workshop was used as a control. Visitor research involved students from twenty-six randomly selected schools in Cali participating in one of the two programmes or the control experience. Results suggested that there was minimal change in knowledge or attitude from those in the control or the slide show. However, those involved in the workshop were found to improve their knowledge and change their attitude significantly. The programme recommended making the workshop a core part of environmental education across Colombia. The recommendations began to be implemented because the evaluation had a reputable control and sample and because the individuals involved in environmental education were involved in the evaluation itself.

Evaluate the Evaluation

If the evaluation has been correctly conceived, it will have measurable objects from which to assess its own performance. Objectives need not just relate directly to the information required and decisions made. Evaluation may be based completely around these objectives, and therefore may be a straightforward assessment of whether the correct data was collected, appropriate implications generated and relevant recommendations or decisions implemented. Goal-free evaluation has the capability of generating significant insights that could not have been predicted or would have been missed in the sea of data and analysis. Therefore, it is wise to insert a generalist, yet measurable, objective to cover some sort of broader understanding of the plan, programme, or heritage management organisation. Marketing the success of the evaluation in terms of the key stakeholder benefits is critical to ensuring that a culture of evaluation is maintained and enhanced.

Different Types of Evaluation

Evaluation can be approached from many dimensions. One approach is from the product being evaluated – e.g., policies, plans, programmes and projects. Another is from the timing of the evaluation relevant to the timing of the plan or programme being evaluated – e.g., before, during and after the life of a policy or programme (Hall and Jenkins 1995).

Policy, Plan and Programme Evaluation

Policy and plan evaluation are largely oriented around assessing effectiveness and efficiency, and more specifically, to determine whether:

- goals, objectives and strategies are appropriate to stakeholder needs and the organisation's vision;
- objectives and strategies are being achieved;
- resources are optimally allocated to achieving objectives and strategies; and
- resources are optimally used across objectives and strategies.

There have been few published evaluations of heritage management policies and plans (Knudson *et al.* 1995; Ceballos-Lacuarain 1996).

Programme evaluation is largely orientated around assessing effectiveness and efficiency, and more specifically, to determine whether a programme's objectives are being achieved, whether its outcomes are appropriate to its objectives and stakeholder needs and whether its resources are optimally allocated across programmes and optimally used within each programme. A programme evaluation and review must include a re-assessment of the need for the programme, a review and revision of the programme's objectives to ensure appropriateness, a review of the effectiveness, social justice and quality of service delivery, and an assessment of the efficiency and cost-effectiveness of service delivery (Rose-Miller 1993). Table 9.6 provides an indication of some of the different models used in programme evaluation.

Table 9.6 Models of programme evaluation

Model	Emphasis
Goal-oriented	• Assessing progress towards goals • Assessing the effectiveness of innovations
Decision oriented	• Assisting decision-makers to make intelligent judgements
Responsive	• Depicting programme processes and the value perspectives of stakeholders
Evaluation research	• Focusing on explaining effects, identifying causes of effects • Generating generalisations about programme effectiveness
Goal-free	• Assessing the effects of a programme using criteria not represented in the programme's own conceptual framework
Advocacy–adversary	• Assessing contrasting points of view
Utilisation-oriented	• Increasing the utility of findings for specific stakeholders and users

Source: adapted from Ince (1993)

Formative, Process and Summative Evaluation

Formative (or front-end) evaluation assesses a policy, plan or programme before it is operational. This typically involves some form of test via a trial delivery, time period or a mock-up. Process evaluation is carried through the entire life of a plan or programme. Summative evaluation is undertaken after the designated life of the plan or programme has ended. Formative evaluation is becoming more and more important in seeking approval and funding for management programmes. For example, the widespread use of Environmental Impact Assessments and (to a lesser extent) Social Impact Assessments are mandatory for many proposed land uses within or alongside heritage sites. These assessments attempt to determine the impact of policies, strategic decisions and potential developments on physical and social systems by focusing on predicted resultant changes. Both are extremely time-consuming and costly, but can generate profoundly useful insights – though they are often challenged because there is no consensus on acceptable criteria against which to evaluate them. The strength of formative, and to some extent process, evaluation is that they offer an opportunity for change and improvement while the plan or programme is still in operation. In this context, they both require an organisational culture that is familiar and proactive to change. (See Case Study 9.3.)

Case Study 9.3
Optus Community Consultation Programme, South Australia

Key points:

- Formative evaluation provides a much greater opportunity to implement immediate change than summative evaluation.

- Evaluation can reveal where heritage values are positioned within a broader political environment.

- Evaluation can generate lessons about organisational culture and relationships that are far more profound than the day-to-day discipline-based lessons.

In the early 1990s the Australian government sought to increase competition in the telecommunications industry. The Telecommunications Code (1995) was established to introduce a second telecommunications carrier, Optus. Optus developed a revolutionary fibre optic cable that could deliver local telephone calls, pay-television and interactive services all at once. Most of Australia's electricity and telephone services are delivered above ground via wooden or concrete poles. The Code required Optus to use existing infrastructure. Given that underground services were sporadic or too small to accommodate additional cable, this implied installing the cable just below the existing above-ground cables. The installation in Sydney and Melbourne reduced visual amenity in the streets and generated substantial displeasure from the community, and, in some sectors, outrage. The federal government then adjusted the Code to require Optus to undertake consultation of the community before installing more cable.

At first glance, the consultation seemed positioned for considerable success. First, it was an ideal opportunity to clarify the reasons why the cable had to go underground (it would cost Optus too much time and money to go underground on its own). The federal government and Optus were confident that the explanation would dispel public unrest. Second, the consultation could open up opportunities to switch the emphasis to getting both telecommunications carriers and the electricity suppliers to combine forces and all go underground. The next city to receive cable was Adelaide.

Optus engaged Manidis Roberts Consultants to coordinate the consultation and facilitate community meetings. The consultation involved advertising, posters, a staffed Information Centre and community meetings in most local government areas. Before starting the project, Manidis Roberts Consultants identified sets of objectives from the perspectives of client, consultancy, team members and community. The company then undertook formative and summative evaluation of the consultation programme. The formative evaluation was undertaken half-way through the project by the entire project team. The first task was to have each member provide a score out of five for each objective and a qualitative comment next to each score. All the team members' scores and comments were then listed on a white board for the group to view and discuss. Four key areas were identified for team members to explore further. The follow-on discussion revealed that many of the surprise poor results had come about because of unanticipated events, such as the client changing the meeting programme from consultation to information exchange. To evaluate the management of these unforeseen events more realistically, team members undertook a goal-free evaluation to further explore positive and negative outcomes. All of this material was then used to reflect on how the final report should be undertaken. This generated several fundamental shifts in emphasis and presentation that would not otherwise have been made.

At the end of the project (with the final report submitted), a summative evaluation was undertaken. This involved a second objective and goal-free evaluation being undertaken for comparison with the first. Differences were then used to generate a set of lessons for application on similar high-profile consultations. The evaluation process and the lessons learnt were then presented to the rest of the Manidis Roberts Practice for discussion and suggestions for integration into existing and future projects.

Cost-Effectiveness Assessments

Assessments of cost-effectiveness provide useful input to the overall allocation of resources. Gauging the cost to set up a programme can be done but only adds one component of the larger need of measuring overall cost-effectiveness. Assessing the 'cost per contact' of some programmes is a quick method of contrasting costs per visitor. The technique can come unstuck without other dimensions. For example, while personal services may cost twice as much per contact as non-personal, they may be twice as effective at communicating their message (twice as many concepts; understanding held for twice as long; and twice as many proactive reactions to experience). Few attempts have been made to assess the cost-effectiveness of different visitor management approaches (e.g., interpretive programmes) because of the obvious difficulty of comparing intangible outcomes with the more tangible cost outlays (Beckmann 1988).

Benchmarking

Benchmarking seeks to improve performance by comparing how other organisations conduct similar programmes. It has been defined as 'a systematic and continuous process of measuring and comparing your organisation's business processes against leaders, anywhere in the world, to gain information which will help drive continuous improvement' (Andersen 1993, in Sharp 1994). The key steps in benchmarking involve some pre-planning, research, decision-making, implementation and review, and are illustrated in Figure 9.2.

Cost–Benefit Analysis (CBA)

The Cost–Benefit Analysis (CBA) involves evaluating the merits of two or more approaches to a problem or objective by measuring and comparing the tangible and intangible costs and benefits of a policy or programme against their monetary costs (Compagnoni 1986). It is a method of recording individual preferences and preparedness to pay for alternatives. Along with political and administrative considerations, cost-benefit analysis seeks to contribute to discussions and decisions on social choice. Its aim is either to minimise the cost or conversely to maximise the benefits for a given cost; the process assumes that a project is acceptable if the total benefits outweigh the costs. The three stages in a cost–benefit analysis are: identification of

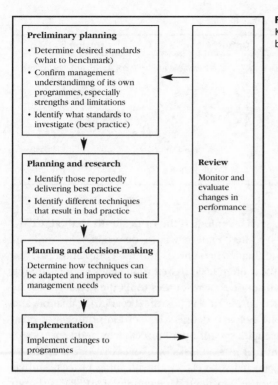

Figure 9.2
Key steps in benchmarking

Preliminary planning

- Determine desired standards (what to benchmark)
- Confirm management understandimng of its own programmes, especially strengths and limitations
- Identify what standards to investigate (best practice)

Planning and research

- Identify those reportedly delivering best practice
- Identify different techniques that result in bad practice

Planning and decision-making

Determine how techniques can be adapted and improved to suit management needs

Implementation

Implement changes to programmes

Review

Monitor and evaluate changes in performance

all relevant changes in the physical and biological inputs and outputs resulting from a proposal; valuation of all inputs and outputs in a common unit; and the computation of differences between costs and benefits at points over the life of a project expressed in value terms (Ulph and Reynolds 1980).

The major limitation with CBA is that many benefits and costs cannot be given monetary values and therefore cannot be considered. Intrinsic values and some use values of heritage are therefore left out of the system.

Goals Achievement Matrix (GAM)

Like the CBA, the Goals Achievement Matrix (GAM) involves evaluating the merits of two or more approaches to a problem or objective. The GAM provides an assessment of alternative approaches that reduces (but does not necessarily eliminate) personal or political bias (Compagnoni 1986). Developing a GAM involves listing and weighting the relative importance of clearly defined project criteria. The proposal(s) is scored first for its direct ability to satisfy the criteria (out of 3 or 5), and then, to determine a final score, this figure is multiplied by the value of each criterion weighting. Scores for different proposals/techniques can then be compared and ranked (Table 9.7).

The Critical Path Method (CPM) and Program Evaluation and Review Technique (PERT)

Often after a plan is generated the heritage manager faces an almost overwhelming list of actions to be undertaken. Prioritising and organising the actions into something that is manageable for resourcing and implementing can be made easier by

Table 9.7 Example of Goals Achievement Matrix

		Option A		Option B	
Objective or desired outcome	*Weighting (out of five)*	*Initial score by weighting*	*Score multiplied (out of five)*	*Initial score by weighting*	*Score multiplied*
First objective	5	3	15	4	20
Second objective	3	4	12	3	9
Third objective	2	2	4	3	6
Total score			31		35
Ranking			Second choice		First choice

using a scheduling technique. One such technique is the Critical Path Method (CPM). The CPM can build on previous related experience to determine the trade-off between the amount of human and financial resources and the completion date for large programmes and projects. CPM is often used to determine gaps in the planning process and the need for additional services or resources to fill the gaps.

One of the most frequently used forms of CPM is the Program Evaluation and Review Technique (PERT). The PERT helps to define, then scrutinise, a plan or planning process in order to rationalise all levels of operation (Kelcey and Gray 1985). It develops a map or flow diagram that lists all tasks or events that occur *en route* to implementing a plan. The diagram helps to clarify the planning process so that gaps can be identified and resource use enhanced. An example of a PERT is shown in Table 9.8 and Figure 9.3. A PERT network is established by defining and listing

Table 9.8 Example of time performance in the PERT network

No.	Events	Predecessor events	Sussessor events	Time estimate (weeks)
1	Goals and objectives	0	1	0
2	Supply analysis	1	2	9
3	Population analysis	2	3	4
4	Demand analysis	2	4	4
5	Standard analysis	2	5	4
6	Agency action plan	3, 4, 5	6	3
7	Expenditure analysis	6	7	4
8	Action plan	7	8	4

Source: Kelcey and Gray (1985)

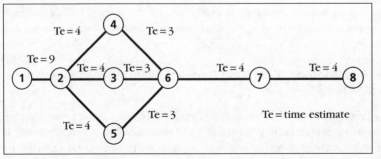

Figure 9.3 Example of a PERT

Source: adapted from Kelcey and Gray (1985)

separately events (milestones), activities (broadly how the event will be achieved) and tasks (specific types of work that make up an activity). Each event is given a number and each activity is given a letter. Simple PERT networks are then drawn on to a flow diagram whereas more complex ones become maps. A flow diagram is generated by writing the numbers and letters on to a page and connecting them up with lines. Each activity lies between two events, the first number representing the first event to be initiated. An activity cannot be completed until its initiating event has taken place, and an event is not considered to have taken place until all activities leading to it have been accomplished. After the flow diagram has been generated, time estimates are made for each activity and/or event. These estimates can be made in hours, days, weeks or months and qualified as optimistic time, most likely time or pessimistic time. The estimates then generate the overall time to complete a project, after which the flow diagram shows the actual times expected to reach each event and, ultimately, implement the entire planning process.

The diagram can also generate a critical path analysis that shows which events are critical to completing the overall plan and, thus, which events must receive the most management attention. The PERT and various versions of the CPM are widely available on computer, implying that all the user must do is list the activities and times then modify them to evaluate and modify the critical path.

Importance–Performance Analysis

Importance–performance analysis (IPA) bases evaluation on a consumer's rating of a particular product or service (Guadagnolo 1985). In heritage management, IPA typically involves seven stages.

1 Compile a list of attributes that heritage managers need to evaluate.

2 Develop a questionnaire that asks visitors to rank the importance of each attribute from 1 to 5 (known as Likert scaling) and rank the performance of the same attribute from 1 to 5.

3 Calculate the average perceived importance and performance for each attribute from the total sample.

4 Create an 'action grid', labelling the vertical grid as importance and the horizontal grid as performance, and mark the 'cross-hair lines' according to where the average values range between (somewhere between 1 and 5, typically between 2.5 and 5).

5 Plot the average values importance and performance on the action grid.

6 Determine where each attribute sits on the action grid. The top-left quadrant is the most important one for alerting the need for more management attention, since it implies importance is high but performance levels are fairly low (called 'Concentrate here'). The top-right quadrant is a pat on the back, as it implies high importance and high performance (called 'Keep up the good work'). The bottom-right corner provides opportunities for management cut-backs, as it implies low importance but high performance (called 'Possible overkill'). The bottom-left quadrant is a signal to maintain minimal management effort, as it implies low importance and low performance (called 'Low priority').

7 Identify management responses accordingly.
(Adapted from Henderson and Bialeschki 1995)

IPA is most often used by visitor managers to assess relative performance of recreational and interpretive facilities. For example, managers in the Great Smoky Mountains National Park in the United States assessed the performance of the Sugarlands Visitor Center (Mengak *et al.* 1986). Their study revealed an over-emphasis on the building and natural values, and not enough emphasis on service and cultural values. IPA has also been used by heritage managers to determine the performance of tourism operators providing visitor experiences at heritage sites. For example, Forestry Tasmania undertook an extensive assessment of guided nature-based tourism in Tasmania's state forests (Australia) and discovered that operators had substantially different perceptions from those of their clients and that it was unwise for heritage managers to rely upon operator surveys (McArthur 1994). Part of the results resulting from the use of IPA by Forestry Tasmania can be seen in Figure 9.4.

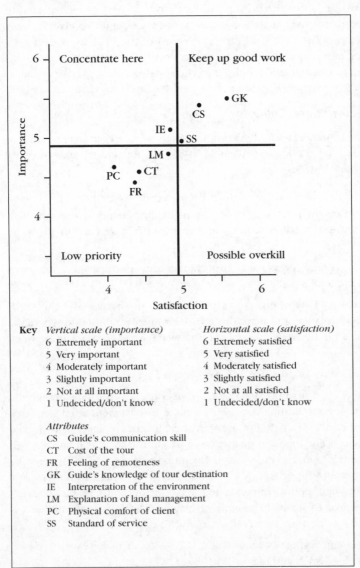

Figure 9.4 An 'action grid' – part of the application of importance – performance analysis via client satisfaction ratings of various aspects of guided nature-based tourism

Key *Vertical scale (importance)*   *Horizontal scale (satisfaction)*
    6 Extremely important   6 Extremely satisfied
    5 Very important   5 Very satisfied
    4 Moderately important   4 Moderately satisfied
    3 Slightly important   3 Slightly satisfied
    2 Not at all important   2 Not at all satisfied
    1 Undecided/don't know   1 Undecided/don't know

Attributes
    CS   Guide's communication skill
    CT   Cost of the tour
    FR   Feeling of remoteness
    GK   Guide's knowledge of tour destination
    IE   Interpretation of the environment
    LM   Explanation of land management
    PC   Physical comfort of client
    SS   Standard of service

Source: McArthur (1994)

Self- and Peer Evaluation

An evaluation need not have to be undertaken by an individual or organisation external to the policy, plan or programme. Self- and peer evaluation are legitimate and cost-effective forms of evaluation that can produce substantial insights, provided the evaluation is balanced and thorough. To do this they assess professional standards of quality with respect to various performance criteria. Some of the criteria that are often assessed include:

* cost – both initial and operating;
* simplicity;
* ease of implementation;
* reliability;
* relationship to other visitor experiences and facilities;
* flexibility – particularly adaptability to change; and
* durability.

Given the significant personal involvement in heritage management, peer evaluation can be a threatening and self-destructive process if not managed carefully and sensitively. Peers need to be both detached and experienced in the discipline to assess the degree to which a plan or programme meets the same criteria.

Goal-Free Evaluation

Plans and programmes operate outside their objectives; they generate outcomes that are outside the scope of planned objectives. It is therefore useful to evaluate plans and programmes in a broader, more flexible manner to add in the reality that heritage management never ends up being delivered in the way it was planned. In goal-free evaluation the evaluator operates in a freer environment, where any feedback can be considered as potentially useful. The evaluator must work hard to remain removed from any objectives that may have been guiding the plan or programme. Unintended outcomes can often be traced back to objectives or, alternatively, suggest that the objectives themselves need to be modified to better meet fundamental needs (Scriven 1972; Scriven and Roth 1977).

One framework within which to operate a goal-free evaluation is to review the effects of a plan or programme against a collection of effects that can be demonstrated to have occurred as a result of the plan or programme. The evaluation begins by focusing progressively on what is important and capable of being evaluated, by asking questions and investigating the concerns, claims and issues of stakeholders. The initial investigation is then narrowed to a more detailed examination of key areas, typically by interviews and workshops, but also by open-ended questions in questionnaires, self-reporting and diary records. The evaluator should add to the feedback their own reflective observations and speculations. This tends to stimulate critical thinking rather than just acting as a recording instrument. Initial analysis may be done loosely through simple remarks on the margins of the data or may move straight into a more detailed approach that involves looking for relationships across the data. These relationships can help place the data into categories that help generate new ideas and theories. There are now a number of sophisticated computer programs to sort qualitative data into these relationships and build theories about how they operate (Cauley 1994). The software includes names such as The Ethnograph, Hyper-RESEARCH, AQUAD, QUALOG and NUD•IST.

Evaluation in the Political Arena

The Intervention of Politics

Patton (1978) said that to be innocent of politics in evaluation is to become a pawn. Evaluation cannot escape politics. Results typically support or refute the views of stakeholders, generating criticism of processes and outcomes. At any rate, people are involved throughout an evaluation: in the determination of objectives and approach, in the collection and analysis of data, and in the subsequent decision-making process. Henderson and Bialeschki (1995) suggest that:

> by their nature, evaluations are political when the information is used to 'manipulate' other people even though the manipulation may be postive ... [and] even non-use [of evaluations] may make a political statement ... If we acknowledge that evaluations are often political, then these politics can be used to our advantage by not resisting or ignoring them.

In order to accept and work with the political dimension of evaluation, one must understand that there are ethical and moral issues to deal with. Ethics are publicly accepted notions of what is right and wrong, whereas morals are more personalised versions of ethics that typically relate to unintentional biases and mistakes. Table 9.9 explains critical ethics and morals such as realism, privacy, non-coercion, avoidance of harm upon others, avoidance of preconceived perceptions, objective procedure, avoidance of positional influence, truthful information, fairness in reporting and timeliness of the dissemination of information. Posavac and Carey (1992) suggest that the personal traits needed to deal with ethical and moral issues are humility, patience, practicality, and self-reflection of one's own work.

The Lack of Evaluation Undertaken

Heritage managers have never really been particularly active evaluators (McArthur 1995). Most interest is centred on responding to immediate problems rather than evaluating why the problem exists and assessing the merit of alternative strategies. Remaining interest sporadically generates new initiatives before existing ones have been examined. The only proactive evaluative trend has been an overall increase in the number of individuals and organisations interested in conducting market research that provides feedback for simple and practical improvements.

The lack of evaluation is denying managers solid evidence with which to make critical management decisions on policy, planning and resource allocation, and forcing senior officials and politicians to argue for the value of effective and efficient programmes. The longstanding reliance on 'gut feelings' is being stretched to its limit and cannot be seen as reliable in such a dynamic world. The cost of not evaluating will also limit the effectiveness of any new programme. A programme running below its capacity represents poor investment and severely damages the performance of other programmes, as well as the general reputation of management.

There are a number of reasons why overall commitment to evaluation remains poor, including:

- a lack of financial resources and expertise;
- misunderstanding of the nature and benefits of evaluation;
- poor planning, leading to a near policy vacuum; and
- the absence of an evaluation culture.

Beckmann (1988) identified a perception by Australian park managers that 'although almost all organisations providing interpretive services do see a need for detailed and formalised evaluation, they believe that such approaches are necessarily complex and expensive, and that existing resources are better channelled into

Table 9.9 Ethical and moral issues of evaluation

Issue	Explanation
Realism	Being realistic about the limitations and potential outcomes of an evaluation helps stakeholders to adjust their expectations and input to the evaluation process
Privacy	Privacy implies assuring anonymity and confidentiality if it is required. Anonymity implies that none of the data gathering will pick up names, positions and contacts, whereas confidentiality implies that the evaluator may know them but not make them available to others
Non-coercion	People should never be forced to take part in an evaluation unless involvement is a necessary prerequisite that is understood and accepted by the participant. In some instances, such as when involving children, written consent may be needed
Avoidance of harm upon others	An evaluation should not pose physical or psychological harm to an individual
Avoidance of preconceived perceptions	The evaluator will usually have an idea of what the likely outcome may be before starting the evaluation. While this can be extremely useful in streamlining the approach, it should not influence the evaluator to centre the evaluation on proving the preconceptions through the avoidance or addition of procedures
Objective procedure	An objective procedure requires evaluations objectives to be clearly communicated, the methods to reflect the objectives, the data samples to be representative and the analysis to be accurate
Avoidance of positional influence	The evaluator must not abuse the strength of their position to influence the entire evaluation and must also avoid influences from other people with position, such as employers, stakeholders, colleagues or friends
Truthful information	Sometimes evaluations reveal what managers do not want to here, and even what evaluators do not want to hear. It is vital to present all results as objectively as possible. It is also important to outline the approach used so that stakeholders understand the context of the evaluation
Fairness in reporting information	It is critical to ensure that all stakeholders have access to the results of an evaluation, not just those sympathetic to the organisation or the results generated. The way in which an evaluation is communicated will influence who has genuine access to it – e.g. language, length, complexity, written or verbal presentation and timing
Timeliness in the dissemination of information	An evaluation can be rendered nearly useless if it is not made available when needed, or at least when it was promised. Public heritage managers are notorious for late reports, but private heritage managers are notorious for never doing evaluations in the first place

Source: adapted from Henderson and Bialeschki (1995)

new interpretive services rather than into evaluation of existing ones.' This perception is deeply rooted among the constraints noted above, particularly a misunderstanding of the nature and benefits of evaluation. Most heritage management organisations spend less than one per cent on evaluation, yet programmes and projects should adopt a figure between five and ten times this. In a survey of the major Australian park management agencies, respondents stated that evaluation was a low priority. The cost of evaluation programmes was ranked as the major reason why they had not been adopted more readily (Beckmann 1988).The cost is in human resources, since evaluation is dependent on skills and can be very labour-intensive.

The lack of commitment to evaluation may begin within planning systems that are highly influenced by the values of an organisation or some of its individuals (see Chapter 3 for more explanation on this influence). Often these organisations and individuals cope with the world as it is by relying on adaptive learning, which involves simply building on existing information and experience. In contrast, those utilising generative learning allow problems to facilitate a creative tension that generates new ways of viewing things and leads to strategically important opportunities. Heritage management organisations may avoid the use of evaluation in order to remain totally flexible in their politically volatile climates. Alternatively, they may be experiencing a policy vacuum that has been allowed to occur because the organisational culture has been unconsciously created from individual staff values. A vacuum may be caused by the absence of:

- an organised constituency of policy makers to whom the research is directed;

- agreement among significant constituents on clear policy issues and identifiable research questions to be addressed;

- a consistent policy over a given area, and hence clear-cut policy options to be decided;

- coordination among the independent agencies responsible for developing policies; or

- concrete on-going operational programmes targeted to use the research findings. (Hamilton-Smith and Mercer 1991)

The lack of commitment to evaluation is also the result of an under-developed or absent evaluation culture (Amies 1994) (see Case Study 9.4). Evaluation is often perceived as a third person entering the inner sanctum of an organisation to spot all the faults, identify the guilty persons and leave them to face the music. The very personal commitment of some heritage managers can highlight this perception when individuals become too personally committed to, and thus defensive over, a particular policy or programme. Some heritage managers may perceive evaluation as failing to incorporate the daily pressures and political influences that may have influenced the design and delivery of a policy or programme. An evaluation culture may require:

- individuals and groups (including programme staff) to become genuinely interested;

- critical debate about a programme, including debate by programme staff;

- reflection in action by programme staff; and

- the impulse of programme staff and others to understand and make informed judgements and choices about the programme. (Cauley 1993)

Case Study 9.4
Using Evaluation to Change an Organisation's Culture: The Desert Botanical Garden, Phoenix, Arizona, USA

Key points:
- Evaluation can be used to enhance the sophistication of a heritage management organisation's culture.
- Evaluation can free up staff and volunteers to generate rational yet creative ideas.
- Evaluation can help demonstrate a clear mandate for resourcing.

The Desert Botanical Garden in the heart of metropolitan Phoenix was designed to undertake research and share information about the importance of desert plants and environments. During the mid-1980s the establishment was restructured to generate a greater emphasis on visitor education. Following the development of an interpretive plan, management received a significant grant to link and coordinate the extensive plantings and trails. Formative evaluation was undertaken during the redevelopment to determine visitors' impressions. One of the key findings was the need to gain greater long-term acceptance of visitor-centred management approaches from staff and volunteers. The evaluation resulted in increased involvement by the two sectors in the developments and in on-going evaluations. Four critical steps were then developed and implemented to bring about cultural change (Socolofsky 1996).

The first step was to create an institutional vision for the importance of visitors. Staff discussions emphasised the importance of visitors as the primary audience for fulfilling the educational mission of the institution and as its primary source of support (financial, political and organisational). The second step was to promote an understanding of the importance of visitor research and evaluation. Several individuals with recognised expertise in this field were brought face to face with the organisation's key decision-makers to discuss the merits and strategic advantages of adopting the cultural change. The third step was to use the expertise to train staff and volunteers in basic visitor research techniques, such as observations and interviews. The training included field practice that provided immediate feedback to participants, increasing their interest and commitment to a cultural change. The fourth step was to use evaluation to guide the development of the exhibits. Mock-ups were tested with visitors, staff and volunteers to demonstrate further the value of evaluation in improving performance and job satisfaction. Decisions were shifted from being based on personal feelings to being based on the results of evaluation that everyone could accept.

Three major outcomes were achieved from the approach just outlined. First, staff and volunteers developed a more visitor-centred perspective, which influenced decision making favourably in every area of the organisation. Second, staff and volunteers became more supportive of develop new ideas. Lastly, staff and volunteers have been able to secure more funding for interpretation because they are better able to articulate a rationale and strategic advantages.

The Quality of Evaluation Undertaken

Most evaluations within the heritage management have not delivered significant change, perhaps because in order to meet the budgetary pressures on performance, most of have tended to focus on outcomes rather than process (Knudson *et al.* 1995). The situation in heritage management shares many similarities with other fields of government. For example, Cauley (1993) noted:

> In general most government program evaluation ... serves upper level managers and not line managers. Upper level managers and their Parliamentary audience tend to want to know about outcomes and not processes. Line managers are not well served by evaluation since evaluation does not look at the whys of the outcome, that is, process. Process and outcomes need to be the concern of the line manager if evaluation is to make a difference.

Therefore, many evaluations do not deliver change because they are not targeted at those who can best implement change. This issue begins with the lack of integration of existing monitoring and research information into periodic major reviews conducted across entire heritage management organisations (Cauley 1993). The problem is more prevalent in the later stages of an evaluation when recommendations are made but not allocated to the appropriate stakeholders for implementation. For example, in Australia, a major review of the Tasmanian Forestry Commission in 1993 commented:

> over the past decade, the FCT [Forestry Commission of Tasmania] has been subjected to sustained criticisms – not just from conservation groups but at times from the industry, from other government departments and from Members of Parliament. These criticisms have not always been well informed. Indeed, the recent Curran Report observed that 'the forestry debate has possibly been perceived by the public at an excessively emotional level, and ... were the public to be better informed ... the issue could be more properly debated.' This observation, which the consultants strongly endorse, implies a continued public education role for the FCT.
> (ACIL Economics and Policy 1993)

The evaluation subsequently recommended that 'the Corporation should continue to contribute actively to public education on forestry issues, reflecting the Curran Report's view that the present debate [was] both excessively emotional and not well informed' (ACIL Economics and Policy 1993). However, at the time that these observations were being made, efforts by the Commission's Education and Visitor Services Branch to integrate issues relating to forest management, public ignorance and emotionalism into interpretive planning frameworks and programmes (Forestry Commission 1992) were being frustrated by a culture that was resistant to change (McArthur and Gardner 1992). In this instance, a major review identified a desired direction but did not identify existing stakeholders, integrate and build upon their efforts, or directly present the desired direction to them.

The quality and utility of an evaluation can also be affected by the interests and priorities of those driving it: 'evaluation results will have a far greater impact on decision-making when administrators and other policy makers insist less on findings that are acceptable to them, and more on understanding those elements that determine program effectiveness' (Theobald 1979). This problem can be critical in instances where those evaluating the policy or programme are the same people as those who created it.

Why So Little Evaluation is Published

Unfortunately, the results of most evaluations of heritage and visitor management plans and programmes have not been published and have therefore generally not been available for others considering their own evaluation.

> One of the major inhibiting factors to increasing the body of knowledge in recreation and parks is the lack of available information on such research as programme evaluation ... Often, the sponsoring agency, as a condition of conducting the evaluation will swear the evaluator to absolute secrecy in regard to the study results. At other times, the design or procedures are so poorly conceived or carried out that the study fails to live up to the standards of good scholarship. (Theobald 1979: 167)

The lack of published material is probably a reflection of practical restraints and the resistance to be 'judged'. It is difficult enough to secure sufficient human and financial resources to undertake an evaluation, let alone write it up in a manner that can be understood and considered by others in similar situations. Given the general resistance to programme evaluation, resistance to have an evaluation informally evaluated is to be expected. The result could be uncomfortable questioning of the issues raised in the evaluation, criticism of the methods and results, or even vastly different conclusions and recommendations being suggested (McArthur 1995). The end result of a lack of available material is that many efforts to develop and run evaluation programmes are dampened by the prospect of reinventing the wheel, and typically revert to being based around conducting research rather than considering problems and solutions.

Conclusion

Evaluation involves collecting information and developing insights that improve the quality of decision-making. Evaluation differs from pure research in its emphasis on assessment and its close integration with the decision-making process. Informal evaluation, such as general observations and discussions by specialists and managers, is widely practised and provides valuable input that contributes small but frequent improvements to the quality of heritage management. In contrast, formalised evaluations have the capacity to make major contributions, but are either poorly practised or avoided altogether. Restrictions on time and human and financial resources often lead heritage managers to respond immediately to a problem by attempting to alter or implement an alternative policy or programme. In many instances these responses rely on limited information about the problem and involve the application of paradigms created in different physical and organisational contexts. This approach prevents the development of an organisational culture that is professionally effective and accountable. A lack of evaluation often suggests a lack of strategic planning and a tendency for heritage management to be reactive rather than proactive and to be heavily influenced by the values of individuals supporting it, often without an awareness of the impacts of those values on the management and ownership of heritage.

CHAPTER 10

Conclusion: Values, Principles and Practice – A Strategic Approach to Heritage Management

One of our most remarkable encounters with heritage occurred in Lava Beds National Monument in northern California. We visited 'Captain Jack's Stronghold', a natural fortress made up of walls and trenches of solidified lava. The Stronghold had been the site of a remarkable stand by the Modoc Indians against the invasion of their lands by European settlers in 1872 and 1873. However, like so many other tribes, they lost their fight, for, although they won every battle in their war against the US Army, they ran out of food and had to give themselves up. Many Modocs were exiled to Oklahoma, though some were allowed to stay on the Klamath Reservation in neighbouring Oregon. These were not their lands, but the traditions of the ancestors were maintained. In 1990 the Modoc from both Oregon and Oklahoma returned to the Stronghold and raised their medicine flag (Plate 10.1). Many Modoc would like to re-establish the Modoc tribe in Oregon and California. However, for the present, the Modoc, in partnership with the US National Park Service are revisiting their past in order to find strength for the future in the celebration, remembrance and recovery of the Modoc heritage.

Plate 10.1 Modoc medicine flag. Lava Beds National Park, California, USA

The Modoc gathering at the Stronghold has occurred a number of times since. We happened to walk the Stronghold just after such a gathering – analysing the interpretation and the visitor management strategies, thinking about the representation. Without expecting to, we came across the medicine pole. No feeling of heritage, or of belonging or ownership, could have been greater. Interpretation was unnecessary. This was their place.

There is no perfect system or approach to the management of heritage. Heritage management is something that adapts and changes to the economic, political, social and physical environment in which it operates. New techniques emerge to solve new problems. However, the heritage manager needs to be able to place them within some overall framework that helps to evaluate their effectiveness and utility. Therefore, perhaps more importantly, heritage managers require a set of values and principles that help to determine proactive management responses.

Recognising Values, Developing Principles, Implementing Practice

This book, and the various approaches and strategies it espouses, are based on a set of principles that we believe should underlie all heritage management: namely, that heritage managers need to make the values on which their work is based explicit in the management system. Questions of ownership of heritage (see Chapter 1) underlie all that we do. And when we ask questions of whose heritage is it we are managing, we are therefore in the realm of the interests and values of the various stakeholders and communities who are concerned with their heritage. Heritage does not exist in and of itself; it only exists because of the values that people attach to it. The person who states that 'heritage would be easy to conserve and manage if it wasn't for people' is actually half right, but often fails to recognise that if it were not for people valuing heritage then it would not be heritage and they would not have to manage it! The underlying philosophy of this book therefore is that we have to recognise values. We need to identify them, understand them and learn how to work with them in a constructive fashion so as to ensure that people's ownership of their heritage is as rich an experience as we can possibly make it, and conserve such heritage so that it can continue to be valued.

One of the outcomes of recognising the importance of values is that they also provide a better understanding of the way in which notions of quality are formed. As noted in Chapter 1, quality is increasingly becoming an issue for heritage managers. However, the standard setting processes and the resultant standards that are established are themselves the result of the values and interest of various sets of stakeholders. Therefore, the application of quality approaches to heritage management means that managers need to identify the role of stakeholders in standard setting. It is not only the quality of the heritage resource that has to be monitored and evaluated but also the quality of the management process. This means that heritage managers have to encourage the develoment of a learning organisation that is concerned with:

- the 'who' of quality (stakeholders and their values and interests);
- the 'how' of quality (the goals, objectives, strategies, actions and systems that lead to the achievement of quality); and
- the 'what' of quality (the standard setting, evaluation and monitoring of the first two areas).

Each of the chapters in this book has addressed the above elements of a learning organisation to various degrees. An express concern has clearly been the extent to which heritage managers recognise stakeholders and their associated values and interests and are able to communicate effectively with them the 'whys' and 'hows' of management. Such communication often leads to the involvement of stakeholders in heritage management in a way that meets the needs and interests of many of the parties involved. Such a collaborative approach is becoming increasingly recognised as a means of meeting the wide range of political, cultural and economic pressures that are being placed on managers and heritage organisations. As Taylor (1994) recognised with respect to the conservation of the natural environment in the British context, 'Whether developing a site explicitly for conservation or promoting greater awareness of the need of conservation of the wider countryside, few practitioners can operate in isolation.' Such a collaborative approach, based as it is on notions of quality and the role that stakeholders have in setting quality standards for heritage managers and organisations, can be very threatening to those who take the view that 'the manager is expert, knows best and would prefer not to talk to anyone else'. However, such an attitude is not equipped to deal with the changes and pressures that affect contemporary heritage management.

As in many other areas of life, change has become one of the seeming constants of heritage management. Organisations and individuals need to be both proactive and reactive with respect to change. One of the starting-points of appropriate response is that of individual reflection on heritage and the way in which we value it, want to see it conserved and managed, and deal with others' values, attitudes and behaviours. As Tunbridge and Ashworth (1996) have put it, 'We, of course, are inheritors of our own individual selective pasts, for better or worse, and would not pretend otherwise, and perhaps our most valuable benefit is that self-knowledge of the contexts of our own uses of the past.' It is that reflection which was the starting-point for the authors with respect to their own perspectives on heritage, which are conveyed in this book. But this individual perspective has been mediated through involvement with, and observation of, various organisations and how they are seeking to understand and adapt to their changing business environment. Therefore, reflection and recognition of change and how it may be implemented need to be done at an organisational as well as at an individual level, and it is to this that we will now turn.

Organisational Cultural Change

Values play a major role within and between organisations. The term 'organisational culture' refers, in part, to a shared set of values, norms and procedures that operate within organisations. Two organisations may be responsible for similar resources, yet their management and planning approaches to those resources may be fundamentally different because of their organisation's objectives and associated organisational cultures (Hall and Jenkins 1995). For example, national park management organisations have traditionally had most of their objectives loosely based around preservation of natural values. Their organisational culture therefore is typically a defensive one, centred on minimising change and reacting to events that threaten natural values. In contrast, forest management organisations have traditionally had most of their objectives largely based around economic values through the production of timber. Their organisational culture therefore is often a proactive one, centred on maximising productivity (yield) through experimentation and review.

As pointed out in Chapter 3, various heritage management organisations have developed particular cultures by virtue of their employment of specialist individuals, who often have scientific backgrounds and a traditional focus on the conservation of heritage rather than the various values and interests associated with such heritage. However, recognising current values and cultures is one thing, changing them is another.

In one sense this book, and the fact that you are reading it, is a part of organisational change. Unfortunately though, it is often the case of talking to the converted. It is also the case that many individuals are tired of restructuring. Inappropriate restructuring may even lead to a loss of much needed expertise from organisations and the unintended reinforcement of previous management approaches. However, restructuring is not necessarily organisational change. Indeed, much restructuring seems to revolve around political and managerial fadism rather than being led by a concrete focus on what needs to be done, how it will be done and how success will be recognised. These are basic principles which should underlie the culture of heritage management organisations.

Evidence suggests that one of the key aspects of successful organisational change is to focus on process (e.g., Hammer 1990; Cortada 1993). Hence, in part, process is one of the main thrusts of this book. Breaking away from outmoded practices and long-standing assumptions is crucial in any attempt to improve the effectiveness of a heritage organisation fundamentally. However, this can only happen if the underlying strategy of transformation focuses on reorganising people's roles, responsibilities and relationships so that they concentrate on solving specific problems. The most effective transformations begin with vision at the top of an organisation or division; they succeed because they reach and are owned at all levels of the organisation. Initially, this will happen through informal discussions and meetings to solve specific problems. Later, management can institutionalise these efforts for greater impact. Yet such changes are not easy. As Cortada (1993) put it within a wider business context: 'After the wild enthusiasm of the first year discovering quality is over, after the Deming videotapes have been misplaced, and after the realization that changing your culture is an uncomfortable job, comes years of hard work.' The issue is therefore one of 'constancy of purpose', to paraphrase Deming (in Cortada 1993). There needs to be both a personal and practical commitment to the value base of quality, strategy and stakeholder orientations in heritage management. The level of personal commitment we leave to the reader, but there are a number of practical observations that can be made with respect to appropriate organisational change.

One of the most substantial problems that individuals face is a lack of commitment to principles of quality at the top of the organisation. This is often a case of managing the manager. Several suggestions can be made with respect to encouraging managerial change:

- *Training on quality:* Have individuals attend seminars on the topics of quality and consultation, which may be part of annual meetings or conventions or which may be separate events. These may be a valuable start to the process.

- *Peer group meetings:* Encourage the hosting of peer group meetings which include individuals who have already begun the process of appropriate organisational change. This further exposes managers to ideas and solutions to present management problems in a way that is not as threatening as something that comes from immediately below them.

- *Benchmarking:* Provide managers with working papers and documents that detail the work being done with respect to strategic approaches to heritage management in other organisations or even within other divisions of your organisation. This attention to the successes of the 'opposition' may become especially useful if it points out the bottom-line efficiencies and effectiveness of such a process.

It is noticeable that a combination of the above methods have been utilised with respect to the diffusion of the 'ecosystem management' idea within US federal natural resource agencies (see Chapter 3), a process that is still very much in train, but that is also having a practical affect on government heritage initiatives – e.g., the American Heritage Rivers Initiative.

Another important point with respect to changing organisational culture is that, somewhat paradoxically, managers are typically better off focusing on the work in hand rather than abstract concepts such as cultural change. From a study of organisational change, Beer *et al.* (1990) concluded that senior management typically incorrectly believed that programmes led to change and that employees changed their attitudes and behaviour when management simply modified formal structures or systems. Education is not enough. Individuals do different things because of the organisational roles they are asked to play. To make people change, they need to be put into new organisational contexts. To do that requires coordination, commitment and competencies all handled in an integrated manner towards a specified vision and objectives (Cortada 1993). Organisations that achieved success in changing their culture took several actions:

- they found specific problems and engaged those affected by them to diagnose issues, thereby gaining ownership and commitment to organisational change;

- they developed a shared vision regarding organisation (structures and positions), management (roles and responsibilities), systems and measurements of success;

- management assisted in the fostering of consensus on a vision that emerged through focusing on how to solve specific problems – e.g., through the use of various communication strategies and, sometimes where there was no alternative, staff replacement;

- management sought to extend horizontal and vertical change across the organisation, while avoiding an explicit top-down approach (techniques included the establishment of cross-functional teams that were problem-based);

- as the cultural change of the organisation advanced, changes became institutionalised through policies, structures and systems – e.g., new problem-specific teams become formally recognised in the organisational structure for a period of time in relation to their goals, objectives and measures of success; and

- the whole process was monitored and evaluated, and then, if necessary, adjusted, to ensure that the process was appropriate from one stage of change to another.

The purpose of change is to create a learning heritage organisation that is capable of adjusting and meeting the demands of a changing environment, not change for change's sake.

Advantages of a Strategic Approach: Integration and Dissonance

A strategic approach to heritage management presents critical advantages in improving planning systems, consolidating resources and enhancing stakeholder satisfaction. Table 10.1 provides a number of examples to demonstrate this.

Table 10.1 Examples of the value of a strategic approach to heritage management

Values	Examples
Better planning systems	• Better selection of strategies and techniques with which to achieve management goals and objectives • Improved monitoring and evaluation of heritage management processes and strategies with corresponding benchmarking of programme success • Improved formulation of goals, objectives and strategies
Better resourcing	• More effective and innovative use of scarce resources at times of less government financial involvement in heritage conservation and management
Greater stakeholder satisfaction	• Expanded ability to meet stakeholder interests • Greater ability to establish collaborative relationships and partnerships with stakeholders • Better matching between the heritage resource and the use demands of stakeholders, particularly visitors • Increased levels of visitor satisfaction

One word that could be used to describe most of the above is 'integration'. A strategic approach to heritage management suggests the need to create a sense of the whole in what heritage organisations and individual managers are trying to achieve. As noted in Chapter 1, the discussion of heritage has often occurred in two different streams, with little contact between the two. One has commented on the more conceptual problems of authenticity, ownership and the need to provide an avenue for other voices to be heard. The other has focused on more empirical issues of identification, recording and physical conservation. The space between them has had only limited attention (e.g., Harrison 1994; Hall and McArthur 1996b), interpretation being one of the few areas where the two discourses meet (e.g., Hewison 1989; Uzzell 1989; Hooper-Greenhill 1992; Tunbridge and Ashworth 1996). However, the notion of a strategic approach to heritage management, which is focused on the role of stakeholders and ideas of quality, perhaps provides a framework that can help to integrate such concerns.

Heritage management is extremely complex. It is surrounded by differing legitimate claims for heritage ownership, which, themselves, can occur over a number of scales – e.g., individual, local, regional, national and international. As with many other areas of management, particularly resource management, no single organisation has absolute control over all the factors affecting the heritage resource. Such multidimensional levels of communication between stakeholders mean that heritage organisations and managers are often faced with substantial problems in trying to resolve issues of heritage dissonance. In the case of the Ottawa–Hull region of Canada, and the consequent difficulties in projecting national images as well as local and provincial identities, Tunbridge and Ashworth (1996) came up with three major approaches towards resolution:

- *inclusivist,* which is the incorporation of all perspectives into a 'patchwork quilt' of national heritage;

- *minimalist,* an approach that seeks to avoid dissonance by developing only those heritage themes which are common to all inhabitants, 'thereby evading the possible objection of one or another group to particular patches in the "inclusivist" quilt'; and

- *localisation,* which is 'the promotion or tacit acceptance of different heritage messages emanating from different locations, and different scales in the spatial hierarchy', requiring local agreement on what constitutes heritage.

In the face of global pressures for cultural and, perhaps, environmental convergence, the idea of localisation has much that appeals. Yet, as Tunbridge and Ashworth (1996) recognise, '"Localisation" may therefore prove an interim line of least resistance to dissonance, but as a long-term solution it runs the risk that consequent overall centrifugality will outweigh the value of local self-expression.' Nevertheless, it is also important to recognise that in many countries appropriate recognition of regional differences is an important component of the long-term stability of the state as a whole.

Dissonance, the different and conflicting values over the ownership, representation and appropriate use of heritage, is here to stay. 'The inescapable reality ... is that proliferating facets of dissonance continue to emerge with the apparently inexorable growth of heritage itself, as both a phenomenon and an industry' (Tunbridge and Ashworth 1996). However, dissonance is not inherently negative. Instead, dissonance should be seen as a sign of life. Rather than be stuck in time, dissonance implies that cultures, attitudes and values are alive and well and that people are actively creating their own futures from their past. As Corner and Harvey (1991b) have stated, 'In any period of human history a culture and society are partly sustained by the tension between that which is thought to be of value, inherited from the past, and that which is the product of energetic, dynamic, and deliberate innovation.'

Tunbridge and Ashworth (1996) argued for what they described as:

> active dissonance management [which involves the development of a coherent framework that anticipates the problem of dissonance]; where possible, defuses it before confrontations develop; and simultaneously draws attention to the diversity of the potential heritage resource, as a basis for determining the particular broader or narrower strategy for its exploitation which might be deemed appropriate to particular circumstances.

The framework adopted by this book, in part, meets some of the criteria of dissonance management. With its emphasis on value recognition in heritage management there is much common ground between our approach and that of Tunbridge and Ashworth. Most significantly, this book has also illustrated a series of principles and practice that provide a basis by which dissonance can be managed creatively.

This book will not solve every problem that faces a heritage manager or organisation (and at any rate we do not recommend a problem-centred approach). Rather, it provides a basis by which appropriate problem solving can be developed. Most significantly, it suggests that rather than paste over competing claims and visions of the past, we need to provide a framework by which dissonance becomes a functional and accepted component of management. Heritage is dynamic and changing. If it is removed from its value context, it dies. Our management, planning and organisational structures, processes and actions must be able to reflect this. Heritage management should therefore be seeking to satisfy the fundamental reason why heritage is conserved – because it is valued.

References

Aaker, D.A. and Day, D.S. (1990) *Marketing Research,* 4th edn, John Wiley & Sons, Brisbane.

Abell, D.F. (1980) *Defining the Business: The Starting Point of Strategic Planning,* Prentice-Hall, Upper Saddle River.

ACIL Economics and Policy Pty Ltd: Price Waterhouse; Economic Forestry Associates (1993) *Costs of Production, Constraints, Valuation and Future Organisation of the Forestry Commission of Tasmania, Report to the Forests and Forest Industry Council,* ACIL Economics and Policy Pty Ltd, Canberra.

Alderson, W.T. and Low, S.P. (1985) *Interpretation of Historic Sites,* 2nd edn, American Association for State and Local History, Nashville.

American Marketing Association (1985) AMA Board approves new marketing definition, *Marketing News,* 19 (5): 1.

Amies, M. (1994) Program evaluation: A Commonwealth perspective – Where are we now?, *Evaluation Journal of Australasia,* 6 (1): 31–42.

Assael, H. (1990) *Marketing Principles and Strategy,* Dryden Press, Chicago.

Augoustinos, M. and Innes, J.M. (1997) Affect and evaluation in nationalistic advertising, *Australian Journal of Social Research,* 3 (1): 3–16.

Aukerman, R. and Thomson, M. (1991) Estimating the economic value of park facilities and service, in A.J. Veal, P. Johnson and G. Cushman (eds) *Leisure and Tourism: Social and Environmental Change, Papers from the World Leisure and Recreation Association Congress, Sydney,* University for Technology, Sydney, 46–50.

Bannon, J.J. and Busser, J.A. (1992) *Problem Solving in Recreation and Parks,* 3rd edn, Sagamore, Illinois.

Beckmann, E. (1988) Interpretation in Australia – current status and future prospects, *Australian Parks and Recreation,* 23 (6): 6–14.

Beer, M., Eisenstat, R.A. and Spector, B. (1990) Why change programs don't produce change, *Harvard Business Review,* November–December: 158–66.

Birckhead, J., De Lacy, T. and Smith, L. (eds) (1993) *Aboriginal Involvement in Parks and Protected Areas,* Aboriginal Studies Press, Canberra.

Birtles, A. and Li-Sofield, T. (1995) Green Globe – A Worldwide environmental program for the tourist industry, in H. Richens (ed.) *Ecotourism and Nature-based Tourism – Taking the Next Steps,* The Ecotourism Association of Australia.

Bjorklund, E. and Philbrick, A. (1972) Spatial configurations of mental processes, in M. Belanger and D. Jenelle (eds) *Building Regions for the Future,* Department of Geography, Laval University, Quebec.

Boniface, P. (1995) *Managing Quality Cultural Tourism,* Routledge, London and New York.

Bonoma, T.V. and Clark, B.H. (1988) *Marketing Performance Assessment*, Harvard Business School Press, Boston.

Bonoma, T.V. and Shapiro, B.P. (1983) *Segmenting the Industrial Market*, Lexington Books, Lexington.

Boo, E. (1990) *Ecotourism: The Potentials and Pitfalls*, The World Wildlife Fund, Washington, D.C.

Braithwaite, R.W., Reynolds, P.C. and Pongracz, G.B. (1996) *Wildlife Tourism at Yellow Waters: An Analysis of the Environmental, Social and Economic Compromise Options for Sustainable Operation of a Tour Boat Venture in Kakadu National Park*, Commonwealth Department of Tourism, Australian Nature Conservation Agency and Gagudju Association Inc., Canberra.

Buckley, R. (1991) *Perspectives in Environmental Management*, Springer-Verlag, New York.

Bureau of Land Management (1997) *BLM Vision*, Bureau of Land Management, Washington D.C., http://www.blm.gov/nhp/facts/vision.htm

Byars, L.L. (1984) *Strategic Management: Planning and Implementation*, Harper & Row, New York.

Canadian Parks Service (1988) *Getting Started: A Guide to Park Service Planning*, Canadian Parks Service, Ottawa.

Cauley, D.N. (1993) Evaluation: does it make a difference?, *Evaluation Journal of Australasia*, 5 (2): 3-15.

Cauley, D.N. (1994) Qualitative methodology – qualitative data analysis in program evaluation, *Evaluation News and Comment*, 3 (2): 68-73.

Ceballos-Lacuarain, H. (1996) *Tourism, Ecotourism and Protected Areas: The State of Nature Based Tourism Around the World and Guidelines for its Development*, IUCN, Gland.

Chaffee, E.E. (1985) Three models of strategy, *Academy of Management Review*, 10 (1): 89-96.

Chester, G. and Roberts, G. (1992) The Wet Tropics of Queensland World Heritage Area: the planning challenge, in *Heritage Management: Parks, Heritage and Tourism, Conference Proceedings*, Royal Australian Institute of Parks and Recreation, Hobart, 177-84.

Cifuentes, M. (1992) Capacidad de Carga Turistica en Areas Protegidas, Paper presented at the Fourth World Congress on National Parks and Protected Areas, IUCN, Gland.

Clark, R.N. and Stankey, G.H. (1979) *The Recreation Opportunity Spectrum: A Framework for Planning, Management and Research*, USDA Forest Service, General Technical Report PNW-98, Seattle.

Collins, J.C. and Porras, J.I. (1996) Building your company's vision, *Harvard Business Review*, September-October: 65-77.

Commonwealth Department of Tourism (1994) *National Ecotourism Strategy*, Australian Government Publishing Service, Canberra.

Commonwealth Government (1989) *Fraser Island Environmental Inquiry: Final Report of the Commission of Inquiry*, Commonwealth Government, Canberra.

Compagnoni, P.T. (1986) *The Goals-Achievement Matrix in Plan Evaluation and Land Evaluation*, CSIRO Divisional Report 86/3, CSIRO, Canberra.

Cornelissen, J.A.T. (1986) Dutch tourism; a big industry in a small country, *Tourism Management*, 7 (4): 294-7.

Cornelius, H. and Faire, S. (1994) *Everyone Can Win: How to Resolve Conflict*, Simon and Schuster, Sydney.

Corner, J. and Harvey, S. (eds) (1991a) *Enterprise and Heritage: Crosscurrents of National Culture*, Routledge, London and New York.

Corner, J. and Harvey, S. (1991b) Introduction: Great Britain Limited, in J. Corner and S. Harvey (eds) *Enterprise and Heritage: Crosscurrents of National Culture*, Routledge, London and New York, 1-20.

Cortada, J.W. (1993) *TQM for Sales and Marketing Management*, McGraw-Hill, New York.

Craik, J. (1992) *Resorting to Tourism: Cultural Policies for Tourist Development in Australia*, Allen & Unwin, North Sydney.

Cravens, D.W. and Lamb, C.W. (1986) *Strategic Marketing: Cases and Applications*, 2nd edn, Richard D. Irwin, Homewood.

Daniels, S.E., Lawrence, R.L. and Alig, R.J. (1996) Decision making and ecosystem based management: applying the Vroom-Yetton Model to public participation strategy, *Environmental Impact Assessment Review*, 16 (1): 13-30.

Davie, F. (1992) Regional interpretive planning: from chaos to creative connective, in *Open to Interpretation 1993, Proceedings from 1993 National Conference of the Interpretation Australia Association*, University of Newcastle, Newcastle, NSW, 76-83.

De Sario, J. (1987) *Citizen Participation in Public Decision Making*, Policy Studies Organisation, New York.

Dennis, S. and Magill, A.W. (1991) Professional disposition of wildland-urban interface recreation managers in Southern California: Policy implications for the USDA Forest Service, *Journal of Parks and Recreation Administration*, 9 (4).

Department of Parks, Wildlife and Heritage (1991) *Tasmanian Wilderness World Heritage Area 1991 Draft Management Plan*, Department of Parks, Wildlife and Heritage, Hobart.

Ding, P. and Pigram, J. (1995) Environmental audits: an emerging concept in sustainable tourism development, *Journal of Tourism Studies*, 6 (2): 2-10.

Direct Marketing Association (1987) *Fact Book on Direct Marketing*, Direct Marketing Association, New York.

Driver, B.L. (1989) Recreation Opportunity Spectrum: A framework for planning, management and research, in *Proceedings of a North American Workshop on Visitor Management in Parks and Protected Areas*, Tourism Research and Education Centre, University of Waterloo and Environment, Canada Park Service, 127-58.

Drucker, P. (1973) *The Practice of Management*, Pan Books, London.

Drucker, P. (1974) *Management: Tasks, Responsibilities, Practices*, Harper & Row, New York.

English Tourist Board/Department of Employment (1991) *Tourism and the Environment: Maintaining the Balance*, English Tourist Board, London.

Environment Protection Agency (1996) *Environmental Impact Assessment Training Resource Manual*, United Nations Environment Programme, Nairobi.

Fisher, S. and Koran, J.J. Jr. (1995) Epistemic curiosity and knowledge in males, females, Spanish speaking and non-Spanish speaking visitors to the Maya site of Uxmal: A summative evaluation, *Visitor Behaviour*, 10 (1): 4.

Forest Service (1996) *Toward a Scientific and Social Framework for Ecologically Based Stewardship of Federal Lands and Waters, December 4-14, 1995, A Private-Public Partnership to Develop a Common Reference For Ecological Stewardship, Interim Report* (Draft 2/15/96 Rev. H), http://www.fs.fed.us/eco/interim1.htm

Forestry Commission (1992) Communication Strategy for the Education and Visitor Service Branch, unpublished report, Forestry Commission, Hobart.

Forestry Tasmania (1994a) *Assessment Criteria for Assessing Submissions for Tourism in State Forest*, Internal Discussion Paper, Forestry Tasmania, Hobart.

Forestry Tasmania (1994b) *Arve Road Visitor Management Strategy, Working Draft*, Forestry Tasmania, Hobart.

Forestry Tasmania (1994c) *Tourism in Tasmania's Forests: A Discussion Paper*, Forestry Tasmania, Hobart.

Forestry Tasmania (1995) *Tourism Policy for Tasmania's State Forests*, Forestry Tasmania, Hobart.

Fox, A. and Warnett, M. (1992) An interpretive haven in the desert: Yulara Interpretive Centre, *Australian Parks and Recreation*, 28 (2): 19-20.

Fridgen, J.D. (1984) Environmental psychology and tourism, *Annals of Tourism Research*, 11 (1): 19-40.

Friend, G.R. (1987) Monitoring of management practices, in D. A. Saunders, G. Arnold, A. Burbridge and A. Hopkins (eds) *Nature Conservation: The Role of Remnants of Native Vegetation*, Surrey Beatty and Sons, Chipping Norton, 369-71.

Fuller, S. and Hussain, M. (1996) Co-management on the rooftop of the world, in *World Conservation*, International Union for the Conservation of Nature, Gland, 10-11.

Garratt, B. (1987) *The Learning Organisation*, Fontana, London.

George Washington University (1996) *Green University Strategic Plan, Revised Working Draft July 12, 1996*, George Washington University, Washington D.C., http://gwis.circ.gwu.edu/~greenu/signed.htm

Glasson, J., Godfrey, K. and Goodey, B., with Absalom, H. and Van Der Borg, J. (1995) *Towards Visitor Impact Management: Visitor Impacts, Carrying Capacity and Management Responses in Europe's Historic Towns and Cities*, Avebury, Aldershot.

Gluck, F.W., Kaufman, S.P. and Walleck, A.S. (1980) Strategic management for competitive advantage, *Harvard Business Review*, July-August: 154-61.

Goldsmith, B. (1991) Monitoring overseas: Prespa National Parks, Greece, in F.B. Goldsmith (ed.) *Monitoring for Conservation and Ecology*, Chapman & Hall, London, 213–24.

Goodey, B. (1994) Interpretative planning, in R. Harrison (ed.) *Manual of Heritage Management*, Butterworth-Heinemann, Oxford, 302–15.

Graefe, A.R. (1989) Visitor management in Canada's national parks, in *Towards Serving Visitors and Managing Our Resources, Proceedings of A North American Workshop on Visitor Management in Parks and Protected Areas*, Tourism Research and Education Centre, University of Waterloo and Canada Parks Service.

Graefe, A.R. (1991) Visitor impact management: an integrated approach to assessing the impacts of tourism in national parks and protected areas, in A.J. Veal, P. Jonson and G. Cushman (eds) *Leisure and Tourism: Social and Environmental Change, Papers from the World Leisure and Recreation Association Congress, Sydney*, University of Technology, Sydney, 74–83.

Graham, R., Nilsen, P. and Payne, R.J. (1988) Visitor management in Canadian national parks, *Tourism Management*, 21: 44–62.

Gray, B. (1989) *Collaboration: Finding Common Ground for Multiparty Problems*, Jossey-Bass, San Francisco.

Griffin, J. (1994) Strategic linkages and networks, in R. Harrison (ed.) *Manual of Heritage Management*, Butterworth-Heinemann, Oxford.

Griffiths, B. (1994) Financial management, in R. Harrison (ed.) *Manual of Heritage Management*, Butterworth-Heinemann, Oxford.

Grunig, J.E. (1989) Publics, audiences and market segments: segmentation principles for campaigns, in C.T. Salmon (ed.) *Information Campaigns: Balancing Social Values and Social Change*, Sage Annual Reviews of Communication Research Vol. 18, Sage, Newbury Park, 199–228.

Guadagnolo, F. (1985) The importance-performance analysis: an evaluation and marketing tool, *Journal of Park and Recreation Administration*, 3 (2): 13–22.

Gutierrez de White, T. and Jacobson, S.K. (1994) Evaluating conservation education programs at a South American Zoo, *Journal of Environmental Education*, 255 (4): 18–22.

Hall, C.M. (1992a) *Wasteland to World Heritage: Preserving Australia's Wilderness*, Melbourne University Press, Carlton.

Hall, C.M. (1992b) *Hallmark Tourist Events: Impacts, Management and Planning*, Belhaven Press, London.

Hall, C.M. (1994) *Tourism and Politics: Policy, Power and Place*, John Wiley & Sons, Chichester.

Hall, C.M. (1995) *Introduction to Tourism in Australia: Impacts, Planning and Development*, 2nd edn, Longman Australia, South Melbourne.

Hall, C.M. and Jenkins, J. (1995) *Tourism and Public Policy*, Routledge, London.

Hall, C.M. and McArthur, S. (eds) (1993) *Heritage Management in New Zealand and Australia*, Oxford University Press, Auckland.

Hall, C.M. and McArthur, S. (eds) (1996a) *Heritage Management in Australia and New Zealand: The Human Dimension*, Oxford University Press, Melbourne.

Hall, C.M. and McArthur, S. (1996b) Introduction: the human dimension of heritage management: different values, different interests... different issues, in C.M. Hall and S. McArthur (eds) *Heritage Management in Australia and New Zealand: The Human Dimension*, Oxford University Press, Melbourne, 2–21.

Hall, C.M. and McArthur, S. (1996c) Strategic planning: integrating people and places through participation, in C.M. Hall and S. McArthur (eds) *Heritage Management in Australia and New Zealand: The Human Dimension*, Oxford University Press, Melbourne, 22–36.

Hall, C.M. and McArthur, S. (1996d) The marketing of heritage, in C.M. Hall and S. McArthur (eds) *Heritage Management in Australia and New Zealand: The Human Dimension*, Oxford University Press, Melbourne, 74–87.

Hall, C.M., Springett, D. and Springett, B. (1993) The development of an environmental education tourist product: a case study of the New Zealand Natural Heritage Foundation's Nature of New Zealand Program, *Journal of Sustainable Tourism*, 1 (2): 130–6.

Ham, S. (1992) *Interpretation for People with Big Ideas and Small Budgets*. North Colorado Press, Colorado.

Hamilton-Smith, E. and Mercer, D. (1991) *Urban Parks and Their Visitors*, Board of Works, Melbourne.

Hammer, M. (1990) Reengineering work: don't automate, obliterate, *Harvard Business Review*, July–August: 104–12.

Harland, J. (1989) Festival and event sponsorship case studies from New Zealand, in Travel and Tourism Recreation Association, *Travel Research: Globalization, the Pacific Rim and Beyond*, Graduate School of Business, University of Utah, Salt Lake City, 309–18.

Harrison, R. (ed.) (1994) *Manual of Heritage Management*, Butterworth-Heinemann, Oxford.

Haywood, K.M. (1997) Creating value for visitors to urban destinations, in P. Murphy (ed.) *Quality Management in Urban Tourism*, John Wiley, Chichester, 169–82.

Head, V. (1981) *Sponsorship: The Newest Marketing Skill*, Woodhead-Faulkner, London.

Heath, E. and Wall, G. (1992) *Marketing Tourism Destinations: A Strategic Planning Approach*, John Wiley & Sons, New York.

Henderson, B. (1989) The origin of strategy, *Harvard Business Review*, November–December: 139–43.

Henderson, K.A. and Bialeschki, M.D. (1995) *Evaluating Leisure Services: Making Enlightened Decisions*, Venture Publishing, Philadelphia.

Herbert, D.T., Prentice, R.C. and Thomas, C.J. (1989) *Heritage Sites: Strategies for Marketing and Development*, Avebury, Aldershot.

Hewison, R. (1989) Heritage: an interpretation., in D. Uzzell (ed.) *Heritage Interpretation*, Vol. 1, *The Natural and Built Environment*, Belhaven Press, London, 15–23.

Hewison, R. (1991) Commerce and culture, in J. Corner and S. Harvey (eds) 1991, *Enterprise and Heritage: Crosscurrents of National Culture*, Routledge, London and New York, 162–77.

Hinds, W.T. (1984) Towards monitoring of long term trends in terrestrial ecosystems, *Environmental Conservation*, 11 (1): 11–18.

Hooper-Greenhill, E. (1992) *Museums and the Shaping of Knowledge*, Routledge, London.

Howard, D.R. and Crompton, J.L. (1980) *Financing, Managing and Marketing Recreation and Park Resources*, William C. Brown, Dubuque.

Hudson, K. (1987) *Museums of Influence*, Cambridge University Press, Cambridge.

Hunsaker, C.T. and Carpenter, D.E. (1990) *Environmental Monitoring and Assessment Programme: Ecological Indicators*, EPA 60/3-90/060, US Environment and Protection Agency, Office of Research and Development, Research Triangle Park.

Ince, R. (1993) What is the state of play in state public sector evaluation in Australia today?, *Evaluation News and Comment*, 2: 6–9.

International Union for the Conservation of Nature and Natural Resources (IUCN) (1995) *Proceedings of the Karakoram Workshop*, IUCN Pakistan Programme.

Interpretation Australia Association (1995) *Welcome to the IAA* (brochure), Interpretation Australia Association, Collingwood.

James, B. (1991) Public participation in Department of Conservation management planning. *New Zealand Geographer*, 47 (2): 51–9.

James, D. and Boer, B. (1988) *Application of Economic Techniques in Environmental Impact Assessment*, Australian Environment Council, Sydney.

Johnson, G. and Scholes, K. (1988) *Exploring Corporate Strategy*, Prentice-Hall, Hemel Hempstead.

Jonas, W. (1991) *Consultation with Aboriginal People About Aboriginal People*, Australian Heritage Commission, Canberra.

Junkers, J. (1989) Experience with major corporate sponsorship, in Travel and Tourism Recreation Association, *Travel Research: Globalization, the Pacific Rim and Beyond*, Graduate School of Business, University of Utah, Salt Lake City, 319–21.

Kearsley, G.W. (1995) Managing the consequences of over-use by tourists of New Zealand's conservation estate, paper presented at the International Geographical Union Study Group on the Geography of Sustainable Tourism Regional Symposium, University of Canberra, Canberra.

Kelcey, C. and Gray, H. (1985) *Master Plan Process for Parks and Recreation*, American Alliance for Health, Physical Education, Recreation and Dance, Reston.

Kemmis, S. (1982) A guide to evaluation design, in L. Bartlett, S. Kemmis, and G. Gillard (eds) *Case Study Methods*, Vol. 6, 2nd edn, Deakin University Press, Geelong, 1–10.

Kennedy, R. (1993a) *Better Service Through Consultation: Approaches to Consultation for Government Agencies*, Best Practice Paper 1, Office on Social Policy, Sydney.

Kennedy, R. (1993b) *Resourcing Consultation: A Manual to Assist Consultation by Government Agencies*, Best Practice Paper 2, Office on Social Policy, Sydney.

Knapman, B. (1991) *Tourists in Kakadu National Park: Results from a 1990 Visitor Survey*, University of Technology, Sydney.

Knudson, D.M., Cable, T.T. and Beck, L. (1995) *Interpretation of Cultural and Natural Resources*, Venture Publishing, Philadelphia.

Kotler, P. (1982) *Marketing for Nonprofit Organizations*, 2nd edn, Prentice-Hall, Upper Saddle River.

Kotler, P. (1991) *Marketing Management: Analysis, Planning, Implementation and Control*, 7th edn, Prentice-Hall, Upper Saddle River.

Kotler, P. and Andreasen, A.R. (1987) *Strategic Marketing for Non-Profit Organisations*, 3rd edn (5th edn, 1996, pp 155–6) Prentice-Hall, Upper Saddle River.

Kotler, P. and Fox, F.A. (1985) *Strategic Marketing for Educational Institutions*, Prentice-Hall, Upper Saddle River.

Kotler, P. and Levy, S.J. (1969) Broadening the concept of marketing, *Journal of Marketing*, 33: 10–15.

Lipscombe, N. (1992) Communication or confusion: the terminology of planners, *Australian Parks and Recreation*, 28 (3): 29–35.

Lipscombe, N. (1993) Recreation planning: Where have all the frameworks gone?, in *Track to the Future, Managing Change in Parks and Recreation*, Royal Australian Institute of Parks and Recreation, Cairns.

Long, P.E. (1997) Researching tourism partnership organizations: from practice to theory to methodology, in P. Murphy (ed.) *Quality Management in Urban Tourism*, John Wiley, Chichester, 235–51.

Loomis, L. and Graefe, A.R. (1992), Overview of NPCA's visitor impact management process, Paper presented to the World Congress on National Parks and Protected Areas, International Union for the Conservation of Nature, Gland.

Lunn, T. (1986) Segmenting and constructing markets, in R.M. Worcester and J. Downham (eds) *Consumer Market Research Handbook*, 3rd edn, North Holland, Amsterdam, 387–423.

MacFarlane, J. (1994) Some definitions of interpretation, *HII News*, July.

Machlis, G. and Field, D. (eds) (1992) *On Interpretation: Sociology for Interpreters of Natural and Cultural History*, Oregon State University Press, Eugene.

Mackay, J. and Virtanen, S. (1992) Tourism and the Australian Alps, in *Heritage Management: Parks, Heritage and Tourism, Conference Proceedings*, Royal Australian Institute of Parks and Recreation, Hobart, 159–65.

Mackinac State Historic Parks, Mackinac Island State Park Commission (1995) *Management Plan, Fiscal Year 1995–96*, Mackinac State Historic Parks, Mackinac Island State Park Commission, Michigan.

Macquarie University (1991) *Macquarie Dictionary*, 2nd edn, Macquarie Library Pty Ltd, Sydney.

Magill, A.W. (1988) Natural resource professionals: the reluctant public servants. *The Environmental Professional*, 10 (4): 314–16.

Magill,A.W. (1991) Barriers to effective public interaction, *Journal of Forestry*, 89 (72)

Magill,A.W. (1992) Outdoor recreation careers: a need for socially sensitive people and training in the social science. *Journal of Environmental Education*, 23 (3): 4-8.

Maguire, P.A. (1991) Ecotourism development policy in Belitze, in A.J.Veal, P. Jonson and G. Cushman (eds) *Leisure and Tourism: Social and Environmental Change, Papers from the World Leisure and Recreation Association Congress, Sydney*, University of Technology, Sydney, 624-30.

Makruski, E. (1978) A conceptual analysis of environmental interpretation, PhD dissertation, Ohio State University. University Microfilms, Ann Arbor.

Malpai Borderlands Group (1995) *The Malpai Borderlands Group: A Partnership for Sustainable Resource Management*, .ftp://keck.tamu.edu/pub/bene/bene_texts/Malpai_Borderlands_Group_2_071 295.txt, Contributed to BENE 07.12.95 by Steve Young

Manidis Roberts (1996) *Sustaining the Willandra*, Department of the Environment, Sport and Territories, Canberra.

Manidis Roberts Consultants (1996) *Tourism Optimisation Management Model for Kangaroo Island*, Working Draft, South Australian Tourism Commission, Adelaide.

Mathieson, A. and Wall, G. (1982) *Tourism, Economic, Physical and Social Impacts*, Longman, New York.

McArthur, S. (1994) Guided nature-based tourism; separating fact from fiction, *Australian Parks and Recreation*, 30 (4).

McArthur, S. (1995) Evaluating interpretation – what's been done and where to from here, in *Interpretation Attached to Heritage, Papers Presented at Third Annual Conference of Interpretation Australia Association*, Interpretation Australia Association, Collingwood, 116-25.

McArthur, S. (1996a) Beyond the limits of acceptable change – developing a model to monitor and manage tourism in remote areas, in *Tourism Down Under: 1996 Tourism Conference Proceedings*, Centre for Tourism, University of Otago, Dunedin.

McArthur, S. (1996b) Interpretation, is it running on borrowed time?, *Australian Parks and Recreation*, 32 (2): 33-6.

McArthur, S. (1997) Introducing The National Ecotourism Accreditation Program, *Australian Parks and Recreation*, 34 (2).

McArthur, S. and Gardner, T. (1992) *Forestry Commission Visitor Manual*, Forestry Commission Tasmania, Hobart.

McArthur, S. and Gardner, T. (1993) Evaluating visitor services in Tasmania's forests, *Evaluation Journal of Australasia*, 5 (2): 55-66.

McArthur, S. and Hall, C.M. (1993) Evaluation of visitor management services, in C.M. Hall and S. McArthur (eds) *Heritage Management in New Zealand and Australia: Visitor Management, Interpretation and Marketing*, Oxford University Press, Melbourne, 107-25.

McArthur, S. and Hall, C.M. (1996a) Visitor research and monitoring, in C.M. Hall and S. McArthur (eds) *Heritage Management in Australia and New Zealand: The Human Dimension*, Oxford University Press, Melbourne, 52–73.

McArthur, S. and Hall, C.M. (1996b) Visitor management principles and practice, in C.M. Hall and S. McArthur (eds) *Heritage Management in Australia and New Zealand: The Human Dimension*, Oxford University Press, Melbourne, 37–51.

McArthur, S. and Hall, C.M. (1996c) Interpretation: principles and practice, in C.M. Hall and S. McArthur (eds) *Heritage Management in Australia and New Zealand: The Human Dimension*, Oxford University Press, Melbourne, 88–106.

McArthur, S. and Hall, C.M. (1996d) Evaluation, in C.M. Hall and S. McArthur (eds) *Heritage Management in Australia and New Zealand: The Human Dimension*, Oxford University Press, Melbourne, 107–25.

McLoughlin, J.B. (1969) *Urban and Regional Planning: A Systems Approach*, Faber and Faber, London.

McNeely, J.A., Harrison, J. and Dingwall, P. (eds) (1994) *Protecting Nature: Regional Reviews of Protected Areas*, IUCN, Gland.

Meiss, S. (1983) Strategic and tactical lessons for effective evaluation, in *Natural and Cultural Heritage Interpretation Evaluation, Conference Proceedings*, Interpretation Canada, Ottawa, 37–48.

Mengak, K., Dottavio, F.D. and O'Leary, J.T. (1986) Use of importance-performance analysis to evaluate a visitor centre, *Journal of Interpretation*, 11 (2): 1–13.

Mercer, D. (ed.) (1994) *New Viewpoints in Australian Outdoor Recreation Research and Planning*, Hepper, Marriot and Associates Publishers, Melbourne.

Middleton, P. (1994) Measuring performance and contingency planning, in R. Harrison (ed.) *Manual of Heritage Management*, Butterworth-Heinemann, Oxford, 34–6.

Middleton, V. (1994) Vision, strategy and corporate planning: an overview, in R. Harrison (ed.) *Manual of Heritage Management*, Butterworth-Heinemann Ltd, Oxford.

Mitchell, B. (1979) *Geography and Resource Analysis*, Longman, New York.

Mitchell, B. (1989) *Geography and Resource Analysis*, 2nd edn, Longman, New York.

Morgan, J. (1997) Jetboat racers, Maori agree. *The Dominion*, 15 April: 3.

Morrison, A.M. (1989) *Hospitality and Travel Marketing*, Delmar Publishers, Albany.

Moulin, C. (1990) Packaging and marketing cultural heritage resources, *Historic Environment*, 7 (3/4): 82–5.

Mullins, G.W. (1985) The changing role of the interpreter, *Journal of Environmental Education*: 1–5.

Mulvaney, J. (1989) Aboriginal Australia: custodianship or ownership; a reflection on the National Estate, *Heritage News*, 11 (4): 11–12.

Museum of New Zealand (1997) Promotional video for the Museum of New Zealand shown at the Wellington Regional Tourism Conference, April 18.

Museums Australia (Victoria) (1997) *Strategic Planning*, museaust@VICNET.NET.AU, bit.listserv.museum-1, 4 February 1997

Natal Parks Board (undated) *Natal Parks Board Neighbour Relations Policy* (brochure), KwaZululu-Natal Nature Conservation Service (formerly the Natal Parks Board and Department of Nature Conservation), Natal.

National Park Service (1994) *Ecosystem Management in the National Park Service, Discussion Draft, Vail Agenda: Resource Stewardship Team Ecosystem Management Working Group*, September, National Park Service, U.S. Department of the Interior

National Parks and Wildlife Service (NPWS) (1997) *Draft Public Access Strategy, A Discussion Paper*, New South Wales National Parks and Wildlife Service, Sydney.

New Zealand Marketing Magazine (1991) Sponsors demand tangible returns. *New Zealand Marketing Magazine*, 10 (7): 33–4, 36.

Norkunas, M.K. (1993) *The Politics of Memory: Tourism, History, and Ethnicity in Monterey, California*, State University of New York Press, Albany

Ohmae, K. (1983) *The Mind of the Strategist*, Penguin Books, New York.

Organization of World Heritage Cities (1996a) *The Management Guide. C. A Case Study Guide to Planning Issues in Historic Towns, D.3.1 Charters and Principles, Bath, United Kingdom, The Manifesto of Bath*, Organization of World Heritage Cities, http://www.ovpm.org/ovpm/english/guide/cas/gec-bath.html

Organization of World Heritage Cities (1996b) *The Management Guide. C. A Case Study Guide to Planning Issues in Historic Towns, C.2.1 Housing, The Medina of Tunis, Tunisia, Integrated Approach to the renewal of the Hafnia quarter*, Organization of World Heritage Cities, http://www.ovpm.org/ovpm/english/guide/cas/gec-tuni.html

Padua, C.V. and Jacobson, A. (1993) A comprehensive appraisal of an environmental education program in Brazil, *Journal of Environmental Education*, 24 (4): 29–36.

Parks and Wildlife Service (1994) World Heritage Significance and Values: A Survey of the Knowledge of the Tasmanian Community, unpublished report, Parks and Wildlife Service, Tasmania.

Parks Canada (1996) *Guiding Principles and Operations*, Parks Canada, Ottawa.

Paskowski, M. (ed.) (1991) *Santa Fe National Historic Trail: Interpretive Prospectus.* U.S. National Park Service, Harpers Ferry.

Patton, M.Q. (1978) *Utilization-focused Evaluation*, Sage Publications, Newbury Park.

Payne, R.J. and Graham, R. (1984) Towards an integrated approach to inventory, planning and management of parks and protected areas, *Park News*, 20 (4): 20–32.

Payne, R.J., Graham, R., and Nilsen, P. (1986) *Preliminary Assessment of the Visitor Activity Management Process (VAMP). A Technical Report prepared for Environment Canada, Parks*, Interpretation Visitor Services, Environment Canada, Parks, National Parks Research, Ottawa.

Pearce, J.A. and Robinson, R.B. Jr. (1989) *Management*, McGraw-Hill, New York.

Pearce, P. and Moscardo, G. (1985) Visitor evaluation: an appraisal of goals and techniques, *Evaluation Review*, 9 (3): 281–306.

Pearson, M. and Sullivan, S. (1995) *Looking After Heritage Places: The Basics of Heritage Planning for Managers, Landowners and Administrators*, Melbourne University Press, Carlton.

Pizam, A. (1991) The management of quality tourism destinations, in Association Internationale d'Experts Scientifiques du Tourisme, *Quality Tourism: Concept of a Sustainable Tourism Development, Harmonising Economical, Social and Ecological Interests*, Association Internationale d'Experts Scientifiques du Tourisme, St. Gallen, 79–88.

Porter, M. (1980) *Competitive Strategy: Techniques for Analyzing Industries and Competitors*, The Free Press, New York.

Porter, M. (1987) Corporate strategy: the state of strategical thinking, *The Economist*, 23 May: 19–22.

Posavac, E.J. and Carey, R.G. (1992) *Program Evaluation: Methods and Case Studies*, Prentice-Hall, Upper Saddle River.

Primozic, K, Primozic, E. and Leben, R. (1991) *Strategic Choices: Supremacy, Survival, or Sayonara*, McGraw-Hill, New York.

Prince, D.R. and Higgins-McLoughlin, R.H. (1987) *Museums UK: the Findings of the Museum Database Project*, Museums Association and Butterworths, London.

Prosser, G. (1986a) The Limits of Acceptable Change: an introduction to a framework for natural area planning, *Australian Parks and Recreation*, Autumn, 5–10.

Prosser, G. (1986b) Beyond carrying capacity: establishing limits of acceptable change for park planning, in *Developing Communities into the 21st Century: Proceedings from the 59th National Conference of the Royal Australian Institute of Parks and Recreation*, Royal Australian Institute of Parks and Recreation, 223–33.

Queensland Department of Environment and Heritage (1993) *Green Island and Reef Management Plan*, Department of Environment and Heritage, Cairns.

Reed, P. (1992) *Marketing Planning and Strategy*, Harcourt Brace Jovanovich, Sydney.

Richardson, B. and Richardson, R. (1989) *Business Planning: An Approach to Strategic Management*, Pitman, London.

Ries, A. and Trout, J. (1986) *Positioning: The Battle for Your Mind*, McGraw-Hill, New York.

Roberts, N.C. and King, P.J. (1989) The stakeholder audit goes public, *Organizational Dynamics*, 17 (3): 63–79.

Rose-Miller, M. (1993) Evaluation in the Queensland public sector, *Evaluation News and Comment*, 2 (1): 9–13.

Rubenstein, R. (1991) Focus groups and front-end evaluation, in S. Bitgood, A. Benefield and D. Patterson (eds) *Visitor Studies: Theory, Research, and Practice*, Vol. 3, Centre for Social Design, Jacksonville, 87–93.

Safari Club International (1994) Tourist safari hunting, a low impact, high result conservation tool, in *1994 World Congress on Adventure Travel and Ecotourism*, Adventure Travel and Ecotourism Society, Englewood.

Saleem, S. (1992) Monitoring and evaluation of area based tourism initiatives, *Tourism Management*, March, 71-7.

Scherl, L. (1994) Understanding the outdoor recreation experience: applications for environmental planning and policy, in D. Mercer (ed.) *New Viewpoints in Australian Outdoor Recreation Research and Planning*, Hepper, Marriot and Associates Publishers, Melbourne.

Scriven, M. (1972) Objectivity and subjectivity in educational research, in L.G. Thomas (ed.) *Philosophical Redirection of Educational Research*, University of Chicago Press, Chicago.

Scriven, M. and Roth, J. (1977) Special feature: needs assessment, *Evaluation News*, 2: 25-8.

Seber, G.A.F. (1977) *Linear Regression Analysis*, John Wiley & Sons, New York.

Selin, S. and Lewis, F. (1991) Marketing tourism in the Ozark–St. Francis National Forest: Implementing the National Recreation Strategy, paper presented at Leisure & Tourism: Social and Environmental Change, World Congress, Sydney, 16–19 July.

Selman, P.H. (1992) *Environment Planning: The Conservation and Development of Biophysical Resources*, Paul Chapman Publishing, London.

Selwood, S., Schwarz, B. and Merriman, N. (1996) *The Peopling of London: Fifteen Thousand Years of Settlement from Overseas, An Evaluation of the Exhibition*, Museum of London, London.

Sewell, W.R.D. and Phillips, S.D. (1979) Models for the evaluation of public participation programmes, *Natural Resources Journal*, 19 (2): 338-57.

Sharp, C. (1994) Industry best-practice benchmarking in the evaluation context, *Evaluation News and Comment:*, 3: 27-33.

Simpson, C. (1975) *This is Japan*, Angus and Robertson, Sydney.

Smith, W.R. (1956) Product differentiation and market segmentation as alternative marketing strategies, in C.G. Walters and D.P. Robin (eds) *Classics in Marketing*, Goodyear, Santa Monica, 433-39.

Socolofsky, K. (1996) Institutional acceptance of visitor evaluation, *Visitor Behaviour*, 11 (2): 14.

Spillard, P. (1975) *Sales Promotion*, Business Book, London.

Sullivan, H. (ed.) (1984) *Visitors to Aboriginal Sites: Access, Control and Management*, Australian National Parks & Wildlife Service, Canberra.

Tabata, R.S., Yamashiro, J. and Cherem, G. (1992) *Joining Hands for Quality Tourism: Interpretation, Preservation and the Travel Industry, Proceedings of the Heritage Interpretation International Third Global Congress, 3-8 November, 1991*, Honolulu, Hawaii. University of Hawaii, Sea Grant Extension, Honolulu.

Taylor, G. (1994) Working with other interests: the natural heritage, in R. Harrison (ed.) *Manual of Heritage Management*, Butterworth-Heinemann, Oxford.

Templeton, J.F. (1987) *Focus Groups: A Guide for Marketing and Advertising Professionals*, Probus Publishing, Chicago.

The Centre for Livable Communities (1995) Using the visual preference survey to redesign the city of Sumner, in J. Corbett and S. Sprowls (eds) *Participation Tools for Better Land-use Planning: Techniques and Case Studies*, Local Government Commission, Sacramento, California, 2–38.

Theobald, W.F. (1979) *Evaluation of Recreation and Park Programs*, John Wiley & Sons, New York.

Thomas, I. (1996) *Environmental Impact Assessment in Australia: Theory and Practice*, The Federation Press, Sydney.

Tilden, F. (1977) *Interpreting Our Heritage*, 3rd edn, University of North Carolina Press, Chapel Hill.

Trapp, S., Gross, M. and Zimmerman, R. (1991) *Signs, Trails and Wayside Exhibitions: Connecting People and Places*, UW-SP Foundation Press, University of Wisconsin, Stephens Point.

Tunbridge, J.E. and Ashworth, G.J. (1996) *Dissonant Heritage: The Management of the Past as a Resource in Conflict*, John Wiley & Sons, Chichester.

Turner, J. (1990) The merchants of Vincent, *ARTnews*, 89 (3): 155.

Tweed, D.M., and Hall, C.M. (1991) The management of quality in the service sector: an end in itself or a means to an end? In Australian and New Zealand Association of Management Educators Conference Proceedings, Bond University, Queensland.

Ulph, A.L. and Reynolds, K. (1980) *An Economic Evaluation of National Parks*, CRES, Canberra.

Unger, D.G. (1994) The USDA Forest Service Perspective on Ecosystem Management, Symposium on Ecosystem Management and Northeastern Area Association of State Foresters Meeting, Burlington, Vermont, July 18.

United Nations Educational, Scientific and Cultural Organisation (UNESCO) (1993) *Report of the Expert Meeting on 'Approaches to the monitoring of World Heritage Properties: Exploring Ways and Means, Cambridge, UK'*, Convention concerning the Protection of the World Cultural and Natural Heritage, 17th Session, Cartagonia, Columbia, UNESCO, Paris.

University of New England – Northern Rivers (1993) Monitoring the efficiency and effectiveness of the Wet Tropics Management Plan, unpublished report for the Wet Tropics Management Authority, Cairns.

Uzzell, D. (ed.) (1989) *Heritage Interpretation*, Vol. 1, *The Natural and Built Environment*, Belhaven Press, London.

Uzzell, D. (1994) Heritage interpretation in Britain four decades after Tilden, in R. Harrison (ed.) *Manual of Heritage Management*, Butterworth-Heinemann, Oxford, 293–302.

Waddock, S.A. (1991) A typology of social partnership organizations. *Administration and Society*, 22 (4): 480–515.

Wager, J. (1995) Developing a strategy for the Angkor World Heritage site, *Tourism Management*, 16 (7): 515–23.

Wagner, K.F. (1996) Acceptance or excuses?: The institutionalisation of evaluation, *Visitor Behaviour*, 11 (2).

Wearing, S. and New, J. (1996) Managers of Parks: What are their attitudes to tourists?, mimeograph, School of Leisure and Tourism Studies, University of Technology Sydney, Lindfield.

Weiler, B. (1990) The international tourist and the coastal destination: matchmaking through marketing, in *Environmental Management of Tourism in Coastal Areas* (eds) I. Dutton and P. Saenger, University of New England - Northern Rivers, Lismore, 72-83.

Wellington City Art Gallery (1991) *Inheritance: Art, Heritage and the Past*, Wellington City Art Gallery, Wellington.

Wells, J. (1996) Marketing indigenous heritage: a case study of Uluru National Park, in C.M. Hall and S. McArthur (eds) *Heritage Management in Australia and New Zealand: The Human Dimension*, Oxford University Press, Melbourne, 222-30.

Wet Tropics Management Authority (1992) *Wet Tropics Plan: Strategic Directions*, Wet Tropics Management Authority, Cairns.

Wet Tropics Management Authority (1995) *Draft Wet Tropics Plan, Protection Through Partnerships*, Wet Tropics Management Authority, Cairns.

Wholley, J.S. (1994) Evaluability assessment, *Evaluation News and Comment*, 3 (2): 2-13.

Wiersma, G.B., Otis, M.D. and White, G.J. (1991) Application of simple models to the design of environmental monitoring systems: a remote site test case, *Journal of Environmental Management*, 32: 81-92.

Wisconsin Department of Tourism (1996) *Missions and Programs - Heritage Tourism*, Wisconsin Department of Tourism, Madison.

Wolters, T.M. (1991) *Tourism Carrying Capacity*, WTO/UNEP, Paris.

World Heritage Centre, UNESCO (1994) *The World Heritage Newsletter 4*, March.

World Heritage Committee (1984) *Operational Guidelines for the Implementation of the World Heritage Convention*, WHC/2 Revised, UNESCO, World Heritage Committee (UNESCO, Intergovernmental Committee for the Protection of the World Cultural and Natural Heritage), Paris.

Zeppel, H. and Hall, C.M. (1992) Arts and heritage tourism, in B. Weiler and C.M. and Hall (eds) *Special Interest Tourism*, Belhaven Press, London, 47-68.

Index

Index by Anne Hayward